THE ART OF RHETORIC IN ALEXANDRIA
ITS THEORY AND PRACTICE IN THE ANCIENT WORLD

THE ART OF RHETORIC
IN ALEXANDRIA

ITS THEORY AND PRACTICE
IN THE ANCIENT WORLD

by

ROBERT W. SMITH

Alma College

MARTINUS NIJHOFF - THE HAGUE - 1974

ISBN 90 247 5173 X

PRINTED IN BELGIUM

TABLE OF CONTENTS

Goethe's great love for the ancient classics once prompted him to write ("Gespräche mit Eckerman," April 1, 1827), "Man studiere nicht die Mitgeborenen und Mitstrebenden, sondern grosse Menschen der Vorzeit, deren Werke seit Jahrhunderten gleichen Wert und gleiches Ansehen behalten haben ... Man studiere Molière, man studiere Shakespeare, aber vor allen Dingen die alten Griechen und immer die alten Griechen." Anyone examining the history of Western ideas has found this statement to prove eminently true: one *must* study above all others the ancient Greeks.

This book, by its study of the Greeks and others, seeks to fill in a small way the large gap which has obtained in the history of rhetoric in the Eastern Mediterranean area: the rhetoric (formal spoken discourse) of the courtroom, street corner, classroom, and legislative hall. Scholars have long investigated, and with considerable success, the figures and movements in Rome and Athens until Constantine, or even later, but for some reason they have neglected the role and impact of oratory in most Asian and North African centers (Antioch excepted). If this monograph can provide outlines of its activity in Greco-Roman Alexandria to approximately A.D. 400 and encourage further scholarship in Pergamum, Tarsus, and elsewhere, it will have fulfilled its purpose. At the same time, it is not intended as a history of the city, nor an economic, political, or religious account of its life. It seeks to focus on the rhetorical training and practice for some seven hundred years in the Delta city which was renowned for its literary accomplishments, and to subordinate other matters to this one end.

In fulfilling this goal, my investigation has cut across a number of fields common to rhetoric: library science, sociology, preaching, law, education, and political speaking. In each case, however, I have

sought to restrict the discussion rather severely so as not to impede
the general thrust dealing with the spoken word, nor unduly extend
myself into areas where I lacked the necessary background. The
literature dealing with these many facets of the one topic of Alexandrian rhetoric is vast and scattered in numerous directions in journals,
papyri, and ostraca and printed in a half-dozen or more modern
languages. I have attempted to bring together those matters bearing
on the subject, and only when necessary touch on items in Egypt
at large.

Value judgements appear from time to time, not because my
personal opinion carries any particular weight, but because a writer
who has examined the facts is placed under some kind of obligation
not simply to narrate and profile the story, but to notice satisfactory
performance, or to suggest ways—albeit with hindsight—by which
the picture might have been drawn differently and perhaps better.
For the most part, however, I have contented myself with describing
the scene as either contemporaries or later scholars perceive it, or
as the papyri now suggest.

If one often observes qualifying statements such as "it appears,"
"it now seems," or "the papyrus suggests," he does so because
this is often as far as objectivity will permit us to go. Unlike the
European scene where the evidence for the teaching and practice
of rhetoric is much more complete, Alexandria with its ancient site
now below the water table simply will not permit the sweep of the
brush we should often like to give it. Perhaps, however, a century
from now the dimly-lit picture will be cast in brighter shadows.

By way of overview, one can note that Chapter I sets forth the
establishment of the city with its ethnic, economic, and educational
beginnings. In turn, the human diversity led to deep jealousy and
ultimately to turmoil and pogroms of the worst sort (Chapter II)
involving all elements of the city. Out of these conditions secular
and religious spokesmen emerged in a variety of public speaking
situations (Chapters III & IV), but often, in view of the Alexandrian
temperament, with uncertainty as to their outcome. Chapter V characterizes the rhetorical instruction in the schools, examines speech
models and rhetorical fragments pertaining thereto, and concludes
with a profile of the status of teachers of the spoken word. A concluding chapter (VI) draws the parts together, offers some judgments
in retrospect, and indicates the causes of the eclipse of rhetoric as a
significant discipline within and without the classroom.

Only a brash author would attempt to publish a work without the help of others who with their expertise make his job easier and more trustworthy. Frederick W. Haberman's stimulating seminars at the University of Wisconsin provided me with my first serious introduction to the ancient theory of the spoken word. He taught us to read the ancient authors themselves, rather than content ourselves with commentaries about them. Years later Ernest T. Thompson, now Professor Emeritus, of Union Theological Seminary (Richmond, Virginia) gave graciously of his time in trying to unravel baffling problems in ancient preaching in Egypt. Samuel R. Cornelius, formerly Dean of Alma College, encouraged me in countless ways to bring the work to light. Then, Professor Erwin Seidl of the Institut für römisches Recht, University of Cologne, graciously sent me his copy of the hard-to-obtain doctoral dissertation of Herward Schmidt cited elsewhere. Two helpful classicists, Messrs. Eric G. Turner, Professor of Papyrology, University College, London, and John J. Bateman, Department of Classics, University of Illinois at Urbana, read the manuscript in its entirety and provided numerous suggestions to prevent my wandering into erroneous pathways. If I failed to follow their advice where proferred, it was done only after due reflection and great respect for their learning. The Old Dominion Fund, University of Virginia, saw merit in this project and launched me on the exciting excursion into ancient Alexandrian literature. Finally, to the members of my family—Barbara and Kelvin who continuously with their questions encouraged me to push on, and to my wife, Margaret, whose keen eye spotted numerous grammatical oddities and who sought to create ideal writing conditions in our home during a pleasant sabbatical leave—to these I express my deepest thanks and appreciation. If this volume on ancient rhetoric succeeds in its original purpose, it will have been in large measure due to others who made it a pleasant task.

R.W.S.

ABBREVIATIONS

The works cited below are repeatedly quoted in the following study, hence are abbreviated to expedite their citation. All papyri are cited by number in a particular collection. Expanded the works read as follows:

Archiv	*Archiv für Papyrusforschung und Verwandte Gebiete* (by volume, year, and page)
AJP	*American Journal of Philology*
BGU	*Aegyptische Urkunden aus den Königlichen (Staatlichen) Museen zu Berlin: Griechische Urkunden* (Berlin, 1895ff) (by number)
BSA	*Bulletin de la Société Archéologique d'Alexandrie*
Ch. d'Eg.	*Chronique d'Égypte*
CPJ	*Corpus Papyrorum Judaicarum* (Cambridge, Mass., 1957ff)
CQ	*Classical Quarterly*
JEA	*Journal of Egyptian Archeology*
JHS	*Journal of Hellenic Studies*
JJP	*Journal of Juristic Papyrology*
JRS	*Journal of Roman Studies*
Mnem.	*Mnemosyne*
P. Ant	Colin H. Roberts, J[ohn] W.B. Barns, and H[endrik] Zilliacus, *Antinoöpolis Papyri*, Pts. 1 & 2 (London, 1950 and 1960)
P. Athen	G[eorgios] A. Petropulos, *Papyri Societatis Archaeologicae Atheniensis* (Athens, 1939)
P. Berl	*Papyri der Staatlichen Museen Berlin ...* (Berlin, 1899ff)
P. Brit Mus	H.J.M. Milne, *Catalogue of the Literary Papyri in the British Museum* (London, 1927)
P. Erl	W[ilhelm] Schubart, *Papyri der Universitätsbibliothek Erlangen* (Leipzig, 1942)
P. Giss	O. Eger, Ernest Kornemann, and Paul M. Mayer, *Griechische Papyri im Museum des Oberhessischen Geschichtsvereins zu Giessen* (Leipzig and Berlin, 1910-12)

P. Hamb   (No editor), *Griechische Papyri der Hamburger Staats-und Universitäts-Bibliothek* ... (Hamburg, 1954)

P. Harr   J. E[noch] Powell, *Rendel Harris Papyri of Woodbrooke College, Birmingham* (Cambridge, 1936)

P. Hib   B[ernard] P. Grenfell and A[rthur] S. Hunt, *Hibeh Papyri* (London, 1906), Pt. 1

P. Lond   F[rederic] G. Kenyon and H. I[dris] Bell, *Greek Papyri in the British Museum* (London, 1893-1917)

P. Mich   (Various editors), *Papyri in the University of Michigan Collection* (Ann Arbor, 1931 and later)

P. Milan   A[chille] Vogliano, *Papiri della Regia Università di Milano* (Milan, 1937), Vol. I; I[gnazio] Cazzaniga, *et. al., Papiri della Università degli Studi di Milano* (Milan, 1961), Vol. II

P. Oxy   (Various editors), *Oxyrhynchus Papyri* (London, 1898ff)

P. Vindob (*Boswinkel*)   E[rnst] Boswinkel, *Einige Wiener Papyri* (Leiden, 1942)

PSI   (Various editors), *Pubblicazioni della Società Italina: Papiri Greci e Latini* (Florence, 1912 and later)

PW   Pauly-Wissowa, *Real-Encyclopädie der classichen Altertumswissenschaft* (Stuttgart, 1894ff) (Citation by article)

SHA   *Scriptores Historiae Augustae* (Loeb)

TAPA   *Transactions of the American Philological Association* (by volume)

CHAPTER I

THE CROSS ROADS OF THE EAST

Egypt had served as a trade-center for variant cultures and businesses for millenia before Alexander the Great founded the city of Alexandria in 330 B.C. Not only was the political history of Egypt over three thousand years old—the First Dynasty was established about 3400 B.C.—but Jews had traveled in and out at least since Joseph was sold into slavery by his brothers in the middle of the second millenium B.C. With the establishing of the city, Jewish merchants found both it and the country ideal for commercial purposes. Large numbers of Jews settled throughout Egypt, so that by the time of Jesus of Nazareth over 100,000 Israelites lived in Alexandria and perhaps a million in the country at large—nearly one-seventh of the country's population.[1] They would presently be found in all strata of society from the lowest to nearly the highest. Despite the early presence of Jewish merchants and settlers, however, the Greeks never credited the Jews with playing any role in founding the city, and seemed to admit the Jews were an important part of the city only when they felt the latter did not fully enter into urban life.

Greeks too had settled in Egypt hundreds of years before Ptolemaic times. Naucratis, founded in the late seventh century B.C., soon became an important eastern settlement of Greeks. As polytheists, they had more contact with the local Egyptians than did the monotheistic Jews, but despite this the Greeks were generally ignorant of the country, largely lived apart from the indigenous element, and understood neither the latter's institutions nor culture.[2]

---

[1] S[imon] Davis, *Race Relations in Ancient Egypt* (London, 1953), pp. 90 and 96-98 and Pierre Jouguet, "Vie Municipale Dans L'Égypte Romaine," *Bibliothèque des Écoles Françaises d'Athènes et de Rome*, CIV (Paris, 1911), p. 483.

[2] Davis, *Race Relations*, pp. 25, 32 f.

A GREEK OUTPOST

After the Greeks conquered Egypt in 332 B.C. and spawned the city shortly afterwards, the victor with his illustrious literary and cultural past assumed the superior role over the vanquished. When the jealousy thus created combined with the enmity of more than a thousand years between Jew and Egyptian (Genesis xliii. 32), the country seethed with suspicion, accusations, hatred—and later riots and pogroms.

Culture followed the flag so that Alexander's conquest brought a desire to Hellenize Egypt, thus teasing Greeks to emigrate to the area. Foreign service, cheap land, mercenary soldiering, the lure of the East all combined to bring the Greek to Egypt.[3] For hardship and financial reasons, many could not bring women with them, so numerous soldiers took Egyptian wives and settled down.[4] Such an arrangement could have resolved cultural differences, and undoubtedly did in many instances after a time, but not sufficiently to resolve deep-seated hatreds which grew out of political and economic discrimination. Moreover, the Ptolemies were not so bent on Grecianizing the Egyptians as they were on providing an outpost of Hellenic culture and education for the immigrating Greeks. True, the first Ptolemy, Soter, had wished to assimilate the Egyptians into Greek culture,[5] but by the end of the third century B.C. Greeks could hardly tolerate the Egyptians. Yet Hellenizing efforts met with some success and became sufficiently attractive that Egyptians soon found that if they aspired to rise in society, they would need to learn the Greek language and adopt Greek dress. Some even assumed Greek names. Those of the lower class without such ambition continued to talk their native language of which we have ample evidence in the demotic papyri, but it never figured prominently in the culture and education of the Delta, at least as the Greeks saw it. Greek thus became the normal written language in Ptolemaic Egypt, as well as that spoken in the classroom, from the pulpit, and on the street corner. The native speaker/reader of that language neither

[3] Pierre Jouguet, *Macedonian Imperialism and the Hellenization of the East* (New York, 1928), pp. 323-34.

[4] Edwyn Bevan, "History of Egypt under the Ptolemaic Empire," pp. 39-41, Vol. IV in *History of Egypt*, ed., Flinders Petrie (London, 1927).

[5] Colin H. Roberts, "Literature and Society in the Papyri," *Museum Helveticum* X (1953), 264-66.

heard nor read any real differences between the variety used in his motherland and in his new home. A few inflected forms did change from Attic Greek, but these one found elsewhere in the Mediterranean world. So the transition proved relatively easy.[6]

When Alexander died, Egypt fell to Ptolemy Soter who along with his descendants ruled the country for nearly three hundred years—until Rome's claim and influence were more fully achieved with the defeat of Antony and Cleopatra at Actium (31 B.C.) and after Octavian made Egypt his private domain. In turn the Romans held sway until the conquering Moslems laid Egypt to the sword and subdued the city and countryside in 640, long after Greece and Rome had ceased to exert a continuing literary significance. During this nearly 1000 years Egypt and Alexandria passed through many social revolutions and changes, rising to impressive heights in the third and second centuries B.C., lapsing for a couple of hundred years, emerging again in the second to third centuries A.D., and later declining, never again in the Greco-Roman era to exert a commanding force on the literary world.

Before he died, Alexander the Great built seventy cities scattered throughout his conquered lands in his brief twelve years as emperor. Each had a constitution, an assembly,[7] and a council of free citizens who made their own laws and elected their own magistrates. The Greek language was spoken in all, and neither in Alexandria (one of the seventy) nor in any of the others was it ever replaced by Latin in business and literary circles.[8] Each of the cities made some contribution to Greek civilization; Alexandria's most important tribute was its economic support and learning.[9]

Encouraged in a dream to found a city at the mouth of the Nile—if we may believe Pseudo-Plutarch—Alexander commissioned Dino-

---

[6] Arnold H.M. Jones, *Greek City from Alexander to Justinian* (Oxford, 1940), pp. 292-93. P[eter] M. Fraser's *Ptolemaic Alexandria*, 3 vols (Oxford, 1972) is the best and latest general study of the city but he (1) has little to say about its rhetorical training and practice, and (2) virtually ignores, perforce, Roman times.

[7] The thorny question of Alexandria's senate (boule) we shall take up in a later chapter.

[8] Ernest C. Moore, *Story of Instruction: The Beginnings* (New York, 1936), I, 278.

[9] For an able account of the social and economic life of Egypt, see Mikhail Rostovtzeff, *Social and Economic History of the Hellenistic World* (Oxford, 1941), 3 vols.

crates to lay out plans for the city[10] which was magnificently located with a pleasant northwest breeze, commerce by land and sea, and rich in fertile ground from the annual floods of the Nile. Like Antioch (Syria), later founded by Seleucus I, one of Alexander's generals, the city was divided into four quarters occupied by various groups, a division which would figure prominently in later persecutions. Its total circumference of some nine miles anticipated vast concourses of people. Excavations have found that the main street traversed the entire length of the city from east to west, was nearly 100 feet wide, and was intersected by another nearly half as wide. Seven parallel streets ran the length of the city, and twelve its width.[11]

The houses had a modern appearance not only because many were recently built to accomodate the influx of newcomers, but also because few if any were constructed of wood due to so few trees in the area. Stone was almost exclusively the building product both at the outset and even into the Roman era.[12]

When Ptolemy I (Soter) came to power in 323 he and his son, Philadelphus, developed the administrative machinery for one of the most rigidly controlled bureaucracies the world had seen, simply because of the independence both Alexandria and Egypt claimed. Every official down to the village scribe held appointments directly or indirectly from the civil government.[13] This personal hegemony exercised by the Ptolemies and later Roman emperors would have vast implications for the theory and practice of rhetoric not only while the Greeks held power, but for setting the intellectual tone later under the Romans who permitted Alexandria much less freedom than it had known under the Ptolemies.

[10] Ps-Plutarch, *Lives*, "Alexander," XXVI. 3 (London, 1919), trans. Bernadotte Perrin (Loeb); Vitruvius, *De Architectura*, II, Pref. 4, trans. F[rank] Granger (London, 1931) (Loeb); Pliny, *Historia Naturalis*, V, xi (Cambridge, Mass., 1942), trans. H[arris] Rackham (Loeb); and Edward A. Parsons, *Alexandrian Library* (Amsterdam, 1952), pp. 54-55.

[11] Strabo, *Geography*, V. 1. 7 and XVII. 1. 6, 8 & 13 (London, 1928), trans. Horace L. Jones (Loeb); and Auguste Couat, *Alexandrian Poetry under the First Three Ptolemies* (London, 1931), pp. 3-4, trans. James Loeb. See also chapter I, "Fondation de la Ville" in Max de Zogheb, *Études sur L'Ancienne Alexandrie* (Paris, 1909), pp. 7-43.

[12] Cf. Julius Caesar's "Alexandrian War," I in *Commentaries on the Gallic and Civil Wars* where he states that all the houses were built without wood (*materia*).

[13] Arnold H.M. Jones, *Cities of the Eastern Roman Provinces* (Oxford, 1937), pp. 297-98.

Alexandria was not the capital of Egypt. It did not lie *in* Egypt, but *by* it. Along with Naucratis and Ptolemais, it was an independent city state (πόλις), in something of the same way that Washington D.C. is today in the United States.[14] It grew rapidly and importantly so that by 200 B.C. it was the greatest city in the world, though later surpassed by Rome. By Caligula's time (A.D. 37-41) it probably had a population of nearly one million.[15] One papyrus claimed that Alexandria *was* the world; other cities were only villages of her.[16]

Not only because of its strategic location did Alexandria own a diverse and alien population, but also because of what it offered. One found here officials, magistrates, priests (of both indigenous and foreign gods), rhetoricians, poets, philosophers, philologists, businessmen, soldiers, sailors, slaves—virtually every segment of Mediterranean society—who nationally were Greek, Egyptian, Jewish, Persian, Italian (Roman), Cretan, or Cypriotic, all of whom had come for diverse reasons.[17]

Only Greek citizens however were eligible for the "better life" in cosmopolitan Alexandria, and citizenship came by one of two means: either one was born of Greek citizen-parents, or he obtained it by official grant.[18] The Greeks wished to perpetuate not only Hellenistic culture and tradition, but also retain the government in the hands of loyal Greeks. Hence, the gymnasium, ephebate,[19] and

[14] H. Idris Bell, "Alexandria ad Aegyptum," *JRS*, XXXVI (1946), 130 ff; Rostovtzeff, *Social and Economic History*, I, 415; and Jouguet, "Vie Municipale," p. 483.

[15] Philo, "In Flaccum," *Philo*, IX (London, 1941), trans. F[rancis] H. Colson (Loeb), William W. Tarn, *Hellenistic Civilisation* (London, 1953), p. 185; and Rostovtzeff, *Social and Economic History*, II, 1139.

[16] P. Berlin 130451. 28, cited in Tarn, *Hellenistic Civilisation*, 2nd ed. (London, 1936), pp. 160 and 185.

[17] Rostovtzeff, *Social and Economic History*, I, 419 and II, 1054-55, and Arthur Weigall, *Life and Times of Cleopatra, Queen of Egypt* (New York, 1924), pp. 36-37. Polybius, visiting Alexandria during the reign of Ptolemy VIII (Euergetes, 145-117 B.C.), saw only three groups from all that met his eye: (1) the native Egyptians, civilized and perceptive ἐπιχώριον φῦλον ὀξὺ καὶ πολιτικόν; (2) the mercenaries, soldiers; and (3) the Alexandrians, not so civilized, but more so than the mercenaries and who had not forgotten their Greek customs. *Histories*, XXXIV. 14. Cf. Strabo, *Geography*, XVII. 1. 12 for the same categories.

[18] Herbert A. Musurillo, *Acts of the Pagan Martyrs: Acta Alexandrinorum* (Oxford, 1954), pp. 89-90.

[19] Since the teaching of rhetoric in the ephebic institution is at most tenuous with no solid date available on the subject, we shall have no further recourse

educational training generally, were all conceived for the cultivation and perpetuation of Greek ideas and to provide Greek leadership. Ethnic rivalry and jealousies soon developed, as one would expect.

ECONOMIC PROBLEMS

In addition to population problems Alexandria also suffered from economic difficulties. The country at large had sunk to a low level due to neglect when the Romans assumed responsibilities in 30 B.C., but it would drop even lower by the end of the fourth century. Its general decay under the Ptolemies could be seen in the large tracts of land lying waste (or under the jurisdiction of the temples or in the hands of court favorites), depopulated villages, dishonesty in government, and a debased currency.[20] Augustus restored some of its former prosperity, but ere long this posture changed and the few alien Romans proved ruthless in their taxation and administration, viewing the country as the breadbasket to feed the homeland. Economic revival came again in the third century,[21] but subsided by the end of the fourth. Rostovtzeff has remarked that

Egypt's role in the Roman Empire was to serve, to toil, and to suffer for the Roman people, for the *annona populi Romani*, and, if the Roman people were interested in the prosperity of Egypt, it was exclusively because the Roman people had a large stake in this prosperity.[22]

Although other Roman provinces were governed by the Roman senate after 30 B.C., neither Alexandria nor Egypt were. Nor were they fully integrated into the Empire until Diocletian's reign. The city itself saw its local prefect exert enormous influence in applying and administering Roman law.[23] Roman senators for a time, as in

to it in this study. For facets of the ephebate, see H. Idris Bell, "Records of Entry among the Ephebi," *JEA*, XII (1912), 245-47; BGU 1084 and PSI 777 both deal with Alexandria; Raphael Taubenschlag, *Law of Greco-Roman Egypt in the Light of the Papyri* (Warsaw, 1948), II, 22-24; and Dio Cassius, *Roman History* (London, 1914-27), LXXVIII. 9, trans. Earnest Cary (Loeb).

[20] Mikhail Rostovtzeff, "Roman Exploitation of Egypt in the First Century A.D.," *Journal of Economic and Business History*, I (1929), 345, and Tenny Frank, "On Augustus and the Aerarium," *JRS*, XXIII (1933), 147.

[21] Allan C. Johnson, "Roman Egypt in the Third Century," *JJP*, IV (1950), 158.

[22] Rostovtzeff, "Roman Exploitation of Egypt," p. 343.

[23] For the authority of the Egyptian prefect see Hugh Last, "*Praefectvs Aegypti* and His Powers," *JEA*, XL (1954), 68-73.

the era of Marc Antony, were even prohibited from setting foot on Egyptian soil without imperial leave—one of several facts which permitted Alexandria to develop along different lines from other parts of the Empire. The government resembled more an oriental private estate than a republic.[24]

Following an economic revival beginning with Augustus and extending for nearly a century, the country at large declined economically, probably due to the enormous tax drain of the emperors. By the end of that century they had pauperized the middle class, and by the close of the second century A.D. many peasants, economically stripped, fled from their farms taking with them such property as they could.[25] Caracalla's Edict of 212 made Roman citizens of all free inhabitants of the Empire, abolished the old dichotomy of citizens-subjects, increased significantly the emperor's tax base in Alexandria and Egypt generally, and created a virtual commonwealth of free citizens, making international travel easy.[26] With this measure came also Latin as the official court language so that for the first time the country was integrated into the Empire's legal system. But the Latin language, essentially alien to Egyptian culture and mentality, never really took root, hence one finds few papyri of the works of Cicero, Catullus, Horace, or Ovid. Alexandrians did not wish to appear to forsake the culture of their motherland, so they steadfastly clung to her tongue, even though Koine had now largely replaced Attic Greek.

In the fourth century economic conditions worsened, a situation which complicated but did not arrest the growth of the famous Library and education in Alexandria. Yet significantly the papyri of speeches and rhetorical treatises from this and the following century are much fewer than in the second and third centuries. (See Table in Chapter 5.) If Alexandria gained the autonomy other cities enjoyed, it did so only to better serve the central government's

[24] Jones, *Cities of the Eastern Roman Provinces*, p. 305, and Jouguet, "Vie Municipale," pp. 71-72. See also Fraser, *Ptolemaic Alexandria*, I, 237.

[25] Jones, *Cities of the Eastern Roman Provinces*, p. 316; Margaret E. Larson, "Officials of Karanis (27 B.C.-A.D. 337): A Contribution to the Study of Local Government in Egypt under Roman Rule," PhD diss. (University of Michigan, 1954), p. 5; Naphtali Lewis, *"ΜΕΡΙΣΜΟΣ ΑΝΑΚΕΧΩΡΗΚΟΤΩΝ*. An Aspect of the Roman Oppression in Egypt," *JEA*, XXIII (1937), 67-68; Tenny Frank, "On Augustus and the Aerarium" p. 148; and J[oseph] G. Milne, "Ruin of Egypt by Roman Mismanagement," *JRS*, XVII (1927), 7-8.

[26] Charles P. Sherman, *Roman Law in the Modern World* (Boston, 1917), I, 53-54, and II, 31, and Fraser, *Ptolemaic Alexandria*, I, 121 and 319.

financial ends.[27] As a hub for tourists, traders, and students, the city must have been well equipped with inns, guides, and interpreters to accomodate those who emigrated to it. "The schools of medicine, rhetoric, and other arts, the Museum and Library attracted their quota of students and scholars, who probably spent money liberally as they represented, for the most part, the wealthy aristocracy of the Empire."[28] Philo tells us that in his time almost every day Alexandria's lecture halls and theatres were crowded with auditors of discourses on virtue and other topics, and further notes that their thirst for morality and knowledge was superficial—a characteristic they carried with them for centuries and which other ancient authorities amply verified.[29] But in the fourth century a general demise had set in from which the city never recovered.[30]

CULTURAL AND SCIENTIFIC GROWTH

Related to the economic conditions, though not in a precise linear fashion, the cultural and scientific growth of the city, became particularly well known under the first three Ptolemies.[31] Cyrene, Cos (the birthplace of Philadelphus), and Samos not only provided immigrants but also helped forge the intellectual products for the next generations. With its two state libraries and Museum the city for centuries was a think-tank of the world, and for a while surpassed all other cities.

The Alexandrian literary circle of the third century B.C. was the most brilliant of the post-classical schools; ... Alexandrian scholarship and literary criticism were epoch-making in the development of knowledge. Moreover, just as in a geographical sense, standing as she did at the meeting place of several trade routes, so also in the world of the mind Alexandria was a great clearing-house where various currents of thought and feeling met and mingled.[32]

[27] Jones, *Cities of the Eastern Roman Provinces*, p. 343, and Milne, "Ruin of Egypt by Roman Mismanagement," 5-12 and *passim*.

[28] Allan C. Johnson, "Roman Egypt to the Reign of Diocletian," p. 342, Vol. II of *Economic Survey of Ancient Rome* (Baltimore, 1936), ed. Tenny Frank.

[29] James Drummond, *Philo Judaeus* (London, 1888), I, 5. We shall later examine Dion Chrysostom's Oration XXXII which in the second century speaks pointedly of the superficial, riotous traits of the city's residents.

[30] Economic hard times affected the Library, gymnasium, and education generally, hastening their demise.

[31] Karl O. Müller, *History of the Literature of Ancient Greece* (London, 1858), II 418-19.

[32] H. Idris Bell, "Hellenic Culture in Egypt," *JEA*, VIII (1922), 140.

The city could boast far into the Roman Empire of its primary and pure research. Scholars developed a system of accents in the Greek language—though not the present form—to guide the pronunciation of the many foreigners who emigrated to the city's shores.[33] Here the Septuagint (LXX), the Greek translation of the Hebrew Bible, came to fruition in the late third century B.C. to accomodate the local Jews who had comfortably settled down and had virtually forgotten their ancient tongue. Here in the centuries to come theological heresies would spin off from orthodoxy in quantity and quality rivaled nowhere else in the ancient world. And here religious councils and debates sought to resolve the diverse philosophical and theological ideas of its people.[34] In the second century the civil war which forced Ptolemy VIII to flee to Cyprus (131 BC) due to his misrule, persecutions, and arrogance, coincided with (or followed closely) the exodus from Alexandria of some of its great men of letters. Thus scholarship languished in the late decades of that century.

Tarsus, Rome, and Athens, with their many rhetorical schools and scholars, surpassed Alexandria in learning from time to time, but the Delta City, like some of the twentieth century, fluctuated so that it periodically reasserted itself.[35] Cicero expressed to Atticus (*Epistles*, II,5) that he was and had been eager for a long time to visit Alexandria, but he had nothing to say of its literary role in his time. It continued to ride on its past glories as it entered the Roman Empire, though rivaled by Pergamum which also boasted a fine library.[36] Yet in the late fourth century A.D. when the gymnasium was passing from the scene the Roman historian Ammianus Marcellinus, writing from Antioch, declared that Alexandria was still the crown of all the cities (*Alexandria enim vertex omnium est civitatum*), and that its teachers continued to show signs of life (*Nam et disciplinarum magistri quodam modo spirant*).[37] Shortly after the beautiful

---

[33] Basil F.C. Atkinson, *Greek Language*, 2nd ed. (London, 1933), pp. 265-66.

[34] For a fuller indication of the scholarship at Alexandria in the second century A.D. see Eric G. Turner, "Érudition Alexandrie et les Papyrus," Ch. d'Ég., XXXVII (1962), 135-52 where he discusses P. Oxy 2455 and other discoveries as examples of Alexandrian learning, and the documentation they provide for its erudition.

[35] Strabo, *Geography*, XIV. 5. 13: in the whole realm of education (παιδείαν ἐγκύκλιον ἅπασαν).

[36] G[eorges] M.A. Grube, *Greek and Roman Critics* (London, 1965), p. 132.

[37] *Op. cit.*, XXII. 16. 7 & 17.

and competent Alexandrian philosopher, Hypatia, daughter of Theon, was murdered (415) by religious fanatics of the local Christian church, the city ceased to function as a center of thought and learning. With its demise Jews too were expelled soon from the city.[38]

Nothing served to set the intellectual and scholarly life of Alexandria apart from most other cities of the East more than its Library and Museum. Ancient authorities cannot agree on the identity of the founder, but it probably was Demetrius of Phaleron who prompted Ptolemy I to establish it, and Ptolemy II who extended what his father began.[39] Greece enjoyed public libraries before Alexander sailed to the Nile Valley, so it is no surprise to find them in the new city.[40] Alexandria boasted two libraries under the Ptolemies, as well as the Museum: the larger of them was located in the Brucheum sector while the smaller was built in the native Egyptian quarter.[41] With Aristotle the whole Greek world passed from oral to written instruction, thus encouraging the establishment of a Library and Museum in concert with a change of literary habits.[42]

Demetrius of Phaleron, an Athenian statesman of high order, fled his native country when political upheaval threatened his life. He settled in Alexandria, thus becoming an important cultural link between the two cities. Ptolemy I unsuccessfully teased Theophrastus to emigrate from Athens, while Strato, the scientist, came and remained for a while but returned to Athens at the death of Theophrastus and assumed the directorship of the Lyceum.[43] But Demetrius stayed and brought with him his great talent (*multum ingenii*, so Quintilian)[44]

---

[38] Davis, *Race Relations*, p. 123.

[39] Vitruvius (*De Architectura* [London, 1934,] VII. Pref. 4; trans. F[rank] Granger [Loeb]) credits the foundation to Ptolemy II (Philadelphus) out of jealousy for the great repository the Attalid Kings founded at Pergamum. For much of the discussion of the Library in this essay I am indebted to Parsons, *Alexandrian Library*, *passim*.

[40] James W. Thompson, *Ancient Libraries* (Berkeley, 1940), p. 21.

[41] R.M. Blomfield, "Sites of the Ptolemaic Museum and Library," *BSA*, VI (1904), 27-37. Blomfield seeks to refute the traditional locations of the libraries, but ends up admitting he does not know where they were built.

[42] Frederic G. Kenyon, *Books and Readers in Ancient Greece and Rome* (Oxford, 1932), p. 25.

[43] Rudolph Pfeiffer, *History of Classical Scholarship* (Oxford, 1968), p. 96.

[44] *Institutio Oratoria*, X. i. 80, trans. H[arold] E. Butler (Cambridge, Mass., 1958) (Loeb). Josephus (*Contra Apionem*, II. 46) described Demetrius as the most learned man of Demetrius' era.

and encouraged Soter to establish a library. Athenians earlier had recognized his political ability and leadership by erecting hundreds of statues in his honor, only to pull them down when he fled the city in 307 B.C.[45]

Like Cicero later, Demetrius was both an orator and rhetorical theorist. He had hob-nobbed with Dinarchus, last of the Ten Orators,[46] and had heard Demosthenes say that the great Athenian ran up hills to improve his ability to project and spoke with pebbles in his mouth to improve articulation.[46a] While Demetrius could not match Demosthenes' eloquence, Cicero thought that he was the foremost representative of the intermediate style with a minimum of force and maximum of charm, and is said to have modeled his style after Demetrius.[47] As a theorist, Demetrius authored a belletristic treatise, On Style (περὶ ἑρμηνείας), only fragments of which have survived.[48] We know, however, that it examined in detail the art and technique of Demosthenes' speaking.[49]

The prestige and influence of Demetrius on Ptolemy Soter moved the king to establish a library on a solid footing,[50] but after it opened its doors not Demetrius but Zenodotus of Ephesus served as the first librarian. Demetrius in the meantime had lost popularity and favor with Ptolemy II, and was banished to Upper Egypt where he died from a snake bite.[51]

---

[45] Dion Chrysostom (*Oration* XXXVII. 41) says 1500 statues, but Diogenes Laertius (V. 75-81) puts the figure at 360. Probably Diogenes refers to Athens alone, while Dion included those elsewhere in Greece.

[46] See Franz Susemihl, *Geschichte der Griechischen Litteratur in der Alexandrinerzeit* (Leipzig, 1891-92), 135-42 and 338, and Parsons, *Alexandrian Library*, pp. 131 ff for facets of Demetrius' life.

[46a] Thus Ps-Plutarch (*Lives*, "Demosthenes," XI) was dependent on Demetrius for this legend which has come down to us.

[47] *De Oratore*, II. 95 and *Orator*, 92.

[48] For a variety of reasons it should not be identified with the one which has come down to us by the same name and by another Demetrius. G[eorges] M.A. Grube, *Greek and Roman Critics*, p. 120.

[49] Jacques Matter, *Histoire de L'École d'Alexandrie*, 2nd ed. (Paris, 1840), III, 81.

[50] R.M. Blomfield, "Emplacement du Musée et de la Bibliothèque des Ptolémées," *BSA*, I (N.S.) (1904), 15. Eusebius Pamphilus (*Evangelicae Praeparations*, VIII. 2 [Oxford, 1903] ed. E[dwin] H. Gifford) echoes that Demetrius was appointed over the library.

[51] The correct ordering of the first several librarians long baffled scholars

As a scholar-statesman, former disciple of Phocion, and student of Theophrastus, Demetrius showed great interest in learning and books. We can not determine from extant evidence if it was he who urged the Septuagint translation for the local Jews, but his intellectual curiosity and high motivation would have supported this kind of literary venture.

The Library's manuscripts were catalogued ultimately accordingly to Callimachus' eight compartments of oratory, rhetoric, poetry (two parts), law, philosophy, history, and miscellaneous. After the age of originality in the period of Aristotle and the Ten Orators came the age of classification and criticism. It was only natural that as a Greek bastion of learning the Alexandrian school should examine carefully the Athenian practice of the literary arts. In arranging speeches the scholars apparently noted every speech of which they had a copy and gave it a title. Callimachus, the poet, may never have served as librarian, but his systematic cataloguing of literature (in his *Pinakes*) with biographical details of its authors and (probably) placing speeches into Aristotle's three divisions[52] of political, forensic, and epideictic, greatly helped classification for centuries to come.

As a state institution, unlike the private libraries in Greece,[53] the large Alexandrian Library had three functions. First, the directors were commissioned to build the number of holdings as rapidly and systematically as possible by both fair and foul means. The state not only provided money for this task, but it also engaged in questionable practices to achieve its end. Ptolemy III (Euergetes) required, for example, that all merchant ships anchoring in the Alexandrian harbor must loan their literary manuscripts to the Library for copying. The institution then supplied copyists for transcribing them, but

until P. Oxy 1241 finally resolved the matter whether Apollonius of Rhodes served twice. It turns out that two men named Apollonius served, and not one serving twice. The correct sequence starting with Zenodotus reads: Zenodotus, Apollonius of Rhodes, Eratosthenes, Aristophanes, Apollonius (the compiler: ἰδιογραφος), Aristarchus, and Cydas (an army officer).

[52] *Rhetoric* 1358b6.

[53] An inscription found on Cos (Rhodes) in 1912 indicates a widespread practice of wealthy or private supporters making gifts to the state for library purposes. Louis Robert, "Notes d'Épigraphie Hellénistique," *Bulletin de Correspondence Hellénique*, LIX (1935), 421-23, and William A. Oldfather, "Maintenance of Ancient Greek Public Libraries," *Library Quarterly*, VIII (1938), 287.

returned the duplicate to the ship, keeping the original. The prototype carried the inscription "a book from the ships" (τὸ ἐκ τῶν πλοίων).[54] Hardworking directors were so successful in their efforts to augment the collection that it reportedly reached a figure of 700,000 volumes,[55] achieved in part because papyrus grew freely in Egypt, thus making raw materials plentiful for the work. The second task for the directors was to catalog the manuscripts. As previously noted, Callimachus' *Pinakes* with its eight categories afforded a systematic approach to the job. This classification played an important role in the third and final function of the Library, that of serving as a repository for works in textual criticism, an area in which it surpassed all others of antiquity. In working with the texts the Library Fellows concerned themselves with (a) standardizing orthography, (b) explaining words or other oddities in texts (scholia), (c) subjecting the work to critical judgment to determine which texts were authentic and which spurious, and (d) determining what portions likely belonged in the originals and which were inserted by later scribes.

The names of the librarians who directed this work rank among the greatest known in Alexandrian scholarship: Zenodotus of Ephesus, Apollonius of Rhodes, Eratosthenes, Aristophanes of Byzantium, and Aristarchus of Byzantium—to name five.[56] Aristophanes' ability proved so impressive that the King of Pergamum tried to spirit him out of the country to serve in his court in Asia Minor. Ptolemy V (Epiphanes), learning of it, put Aristophanes in safe keeping—in prison—and placed an embargo on exports of papyrus.[57]

THE ALEXANDRIAN CANON

In such an atmosphere with its impressive collection, systematic classification, and leisure time, one would expect to find a canon

[54] Müller, *History of the Literature of Ancient Greece.* II, 419.

[55] So Ammianus Marcellinus (XXII. 16. 12-13), but he probably was including both libraries (*bibliothecae*).

[56] Couat, *Alexandrian Poetry*, p. 35; Grube (*Greek and Roman Critics*, pp. 129 f) called Aristarchus the "greatest of all Alexandrian scholars." See ftn 51 for the correct sequence of the first several librarians.

[57] Kenyon, *Books and Readers*, pp. 87 ff. This prohibition turned out a blessing, for King Eumenes (according to a story no longer provable), deprived of an adequate supply of paper, was forced to find another source for literary purposes— vellum.

of authors whom scholars and intellectuals—even the public at large—"ought" to know. Such a one is the "Alexandrian Canon of the Ten Orators" which encompassed Demosthenes, Lysias, Hyperides, Isocrates, Aeschines, Isaeus, Antiphon, Andocides, Dinarchus, and Lycurgus. Unfortunately several facets of this register of greats persist as imponderables, and for several reasons. First, although the group is named after Alexandria, some have conjectured it was actually composed at Pergamum which also boasted a fine library with first-rate scholars. But if it originated in Asia Minor, why was it called the Alexandrian Canon? Names are usually assigned to those activities and products where either they originate or with which they are primarily concerned, as the Peloponnesian War or Doric Temple. Second, we do not know whom to credit for the table, and hence are uncertain when it came to light. If Caecilius of Calacte's lost work, *On the Character of the Ten Orators*, provided the basis for Ps-Plutarch's *Lives*, this would establish the late first century B.C. as the *terminus ad quem*. But this is uncertain. One must recognize, however, that Zenodotus, the third century B.C. Director of the Library, worked diligently on the manuscripts and on a canon of prose authors. He could, then, have come up with this kind of table. Third, if the Canon had been drawn up perhaps by the second century B.C. why did Cicero and Quintilian not know of it, while Ps-Plutarch apparently did? True, the latter does not mention the Ten specifically, but he wrote sketches of them, suggesting that by then the listing had found favor with scholars. By the second century of the Roman era the inventory had circulated widely enough to permit Herodes Atticus (100-179) to be labeled, due to his eloquence, "one of the Ten" orators.[58] In sum, the name of the catalog of orators and the available facilities and scholars all suggest Alexandria, but no primary evidence so identifies it. The problem, as with many others of Ptolemaic Egypt, cannot be resolved with the available data.[59]

We have no documents to show that the Alexandrian Library,

[58] Philostratus, *Lives of the Sophists*, 564, trans. Wilmer C. Wright (London, 1922) (Loeb).

[59] See the following which in greater or lesser degree speak to the issue of the Canon: A.E. Douglas, "Cicero, Quintilian, and the Canon of the Ten Orators," *Mnem.*, 4th ser., IX (1956), 30-40; Parsons, *Alexandrian Library*, p. 226; Susemihl, *Geschichte der Griechischen Litteratur*, II, 484; and George A. Kennedy, *Art of Persuasion in Greece* (Princeton, 1963), p. 125.

unlike, perhaps, Rome's, opened its holdings generally to young students who journeyed to the city.[60] We can with fair certainty believe that the native Egyptian, always a second-class resident under Greco-Roman domination, had no access to the Library, and probably did not much care for its foreign manuscripts—except for those individuals trying to break out of their lower-class existence. Moreover, even the average Greek probably could not walk in and ask for a copy of Demosthenes' "On the Crown," or Isocrates' "Helen," simply because general circulation or even reference would not become a reality for centuries; nor was the Library intended for such. Its purpose was more archival and critical than it was for the general education of the resident students.

In the Roman Empire the situation changed for at least two reasons. First while the Library with its huge collection drew many scholars to peruse its holdings—men like Timagenes and Alexander of Seleucia—some not only forsook Alexandria for the greater lure of Rome, but others spurned the journey from the chora to the city altogether.[61] Moreover, as previously hinted, Roman libraries, more than those of Alexandria, took more seriously the general education of the population, or so the twenty-eight libraries there in the fourth century of the Empire would suggest.[62] This greater access to books, as well as the greater popularity of Rome, caused many students to sail west rather than east. Secondly, the Roman siege of Alexandria by Julius Caesar destroyed hundreds of thousands of volumes. Whether or not the fires set by the Romans actually consumed the great library or the lesser one is not completely settled. Ps-Plutarch declares that Caesar's ships caught fire when the Egyptians attacked the Roman force and the flames spread to the city, burning the Library. Seneca adds that 400,000 books burned.[63] With no coverings

[60] Clarence E. Boyd, *Public Libraries* and *Literary Culture in Ancient Rome* (Chicago, 1915), p. 61. But Pfeiffer (*History of Classical Scholarship*, p. 103), citing no evidence, holds that both the large and small library opened its doors to whoever could read.

[61] "The learned Alexandrian of this time became a sort of 'jointure' of Greek science, worthy of respect and useful, but of no pervading influence on the great movement of culture or mis-culture of the imperial period." Theodor Mommsen, "Provinces of the Roman Empire," p. 296, Vol. II of *History of Rome* (New York, 1899), trans. William P. Dickson.

[62] Boyd, *Public Libraries and Literary Culture*, p. 3.

[63] See the discussion in Tarn, *Hellenistic Civilisation*, pp. 269 f; Frederick J. Teggert, "Caesar and the Alexandrian Library," *Zentralblatt für Bibliotheks-*

over the windows of the building, a hot, dry climate, and the breeze off the sea (its usual direction) it would not be difficult for sparks from a great fire to blow through and ignite the scrolls. The buildings themselves however, would likely have withstood the conflagration because virtually all were fireproof. Oddly enough, Caesar makes no mention in the *Civil Wars*[64] of destroying any library in the Alexandrian campaign, an entry one would expect if in fact it happened. But since Domitian sought to restore the institution (probably not the structure) in his own reign by sending scribes to Alexandria to copy and correct those it still had, it is likely that a large quantity of books were in fact destroyed in the earlier Roman sacking.[65] With Theodosius I's destruction in the late fourth century of the Serapeum the temple which for hundreds of years had served Alexandrian polytheists, the Library slips from view and significance.[66]

The Museum sprang up in association with the larger of the two libraries, that in the Brucheum. Together with the Library it formed a kind of university of the Oxford type where learned men were invited to take fellowships and devote their leisure time to science and learning.[67] Not surprisingly, an atmosphere of leisurely scholarship prevailed, for had not Demetrius, its scholarly founder, known in Athens of the Peripatetics at the Academy and Lyceum, and tasted their intellectual fruits?[68] The Museum, known as a σύνοδος (assembly), provided the sort of community of scholarship which one found in the Athenian Peripatitikos of Aristotle's day, so much so that some think (but without adequate foundation) that we can trace uninterruptedly the line of succession from the Athenian to the Alexandrian school.[69] Professional scholars wanting to teach did

---

wesen, XVI (1899), 470-75; and Blomfield, "Sites of the Ptolemaic Museum and Library," pp. 30 f.

[64] See especially III. 111. But we should be wary of putting too much emphasis on the argument *ex silentio*.

[65] Suetonius, *Lives*, "Domitian," XX (London, 1914), trans. John C. Rolfe (Loeb).

[66] Müller, *History of the Literature of Ancient Greece*, III, 289.

[67] Eric G. Turner, *Greek Papyri: An Introduction* (Oxford, 1968), pp. 102-03, and John P. Mahaffy, *Alexander's Empire* (New York, 1906), pp. 142-43.

[68] Henri-Irénée Marrou, *Histoire de L'Éducation dans L'Antiquité*, 4th ed. (Paris, 1958), p. 262 and *passim*. I have also used the English translation by George Lamb (New York, 1956).

[69] K[arl] O. Brink, "Callimachus and Aristotle: An Inquiry into Callimachus' *ΠΡΟΣ ΠΡΑΞΙΦΑΝΗΝ*," *Classical Quarterly*, XL (1946), 11.

so—unlike in the Library which was for research purposes—while others immersed themselves in intellectual pursuits and debates. The instruction and research were so spiritedly and thoroughly conducted that the Museum produced rival schools in philology and medicine.[70] Professors and non-scholar members dined together in large halls, while seats were scattered around the grounds for the doctors and students to engage in dialogue.[71] Small wonder that Timon of Phlius, the third century B.C. satirist, called the Museum a bird-cage ($\tau\acute{a}\lambda\alpha\rho\acute{o}\nu$), ridiculing the quarreling philosophers who got their living by others feeding them like choice birds.[72] But the quarreling factions do suggest an enclave of considerable academic freedom in an empire which repressed much debate. The scholars held their property in common,[73] had a priest to care for certain spiritual needs—as in offering sacrifices[74]—and were free of certain taxes.

Within the Museum teachers of all disciplines could be found: rhetoric, philosophy, and medicine—to name three.[75] The authors, scholars, sophists, and teachers of the Museum taught and intellectually stimulated students who came from near and far to pursue their professional work in an unregimented atmosphere.[76]

The Museum seems to have grown from its original function as purely a research institution—perhaps like Dumbarton Oaks today—to a university with research and teaching responsibilities later in the Empire.[77] Museum Fellows employed three means in their literary work, as do scholars in the twentieth century: Monographs explicating in depth single questions; lexicons listing in semi-alphabetic order those terms established in authentic texts; and commentaries

[70] Marrou, *Histoire de L'Éducation dans L'Antiquité*, p. 262.

[71] Blomfield, "Sites of the Ptolemaic Museum and Library," p. 27. We know the names of eleven third century A.D. non-scholar members—men awarded membership because of their public service. See Naphtali Lewis, "Non-Scholar Members of the Alexandrian Museum," *Mnem.* XVI, 4th ser. (1963), 257-61.

[72] Athenaeus, *Deipnosophistae*, I. 22d (London, 1927), trans. Charles B. Gulick (Loeb).

[73] Strabo, *Geography*, XVII. 1. 8.

[74] Edwyn Bevan, "History of Egypt under the Ptolemaic Empire," p. 124, and Pierre Jouguet, "Vie Municipale," p. 101.

[75] Marrou, *Histoire de L'Éducation*, p. 293. One inscription of the late fourth to early fifth century tells of scholastic rhetoric ($\sigma\chi o\lambda\alpha\sigma\tau\iota\kappa\acute{o}s$ $\rho\epsilon\tau o\rho\iota\kappa\acute{o}s$ [sic]). *PW*, "Museion."

[76] Couat, *Alexandrian Poetry*, pp. 18-19.

[77] Marrou, *Histoire de L'Éducation*, p. 262.

explaining an author or his works.[78] We know of no rhetorical textbook emanating from the Museum, though Theon's *techne* will be discussed later.

Considerable ambiguity surrounds the actual rhetorical teaching which took place at the Museum, for there we have no hard evidence of any speech instruction—unlike that of poets, grammarians, and philologists—despite the interest and competence in eloquence held by the founder, Demetrius of Phaleron.[79] Probably declamations of which we have ample papyrological testimony from elsewhere in Egypt were also used in the government-owned classrooms of the Museum, much as they were in private school. But we can not be sure.

Changes came to the Museum during the Roman Empire. Claudius provided an addition to the Museum and kept in constant touch with its writers and scientists.[80] Hadrian granted professorships to wandering sophists, e.g., Dionysius of Miletus and Polemon, who were not required to take up residency at the Museum, but could draw salaries simply by lending their prestigious names to the institution.[81] The consequent feelings of rivalry and jealousy which sprang up between those with and those without professional duties caused unrest among the staff.[82] Caracalla in the early third century scorned the Museum and what it sought to do and talked of burning its books, though apparently all that he finally did was purge the Fellowship of the philosophers.[83]

From the second century B.C. the Museum with its interest in a wide variety of disciplines plowed new ground from which ulti-

---

[78] Turner, "Érudition Alexandrie et les Papyrus," p. 147. For a helpful introductory statement of the textual criticism and method of the Alexandrian scholars see Turner's *Greek Papyri: An Introduction*, pp. 100 ff.

[79] For views on the possibility and subject of rhetoric at the Museum see John E. Sandys, *History of Classical Scholarship* (Cambridge, 1903-08), I, 106; Brink, "Callimachus and Aristotle," p. 26; Ernest C. Moore, *Story of Instruction: The Beginnings*, I, 295; and George S. Bey, "Education in Egypt during the Christian Period and Amongst the Copts," *Bulletin de la Société d'Archéologie (Copte)*, IX (1943), 111.

[80] Vincent M. Scramuzza, *Emperor Claudius* (Cambridge, Mass., 1940), p. 44.

[81] Philostratus, *Lives*, 524 & 532.

[82] J[oseph] G. Milne, *History of Egypt under Roman Rule*, 3rd ed. (London, 1924), p. 47, and Bernard W. Henderson, *Life and Principate of the Emperor Hadrian*, A.D. 76-138 (London, 1923), pp. 129-30.

[83] William W. Capes, *University Life in Ancient Athens* (New York, 1877), pp. 88-89.

mately sprang the modern university. Earlier in Athens and Rome one found separate schools of rhetoric, philosophy, and the various arts, but as entities in themselves. Now in the Museum he could find for the first time not simply schools but one institution devoted to many disciplines: *e pluribus unum*.[84] It significantly guided ancient scholarship for at least 400 years, but fades from the scene in the third century A.D., and has certainly disappeared by the late fourth century after the demise also of the Library.[85] Perhaps the Christian Catechetical School which originated no later than the late second century was conceived as a counterpart to the pagan instruction of the Museum.

In sum, the establishment of the city with its Library and Museum attracted the notice of scholars throughout the Mediterranean world. Poets, philologists, dramatists all used the huge holdings for lasting achievement in literary criticism. Influential in either institution were the public orators, sophists, and teachers who catered to students and general public. Most of these depended, as they have always done, on their knowledge of people and the times, leaving technical work to the scholars more suited to such activities. We shall see in subsequent chapters not only the raw materials with which they worked, but something of their mode of operation.

[84] James H. Oliver, "*MOYΣEION* in Late Attic Inscriptions," *Hisperia*, III (1934), 193-94.

[85] Milne, *History of Egypt under Roman Rule*, pp. 252-53. Marrou (*Histoire de L'Éducation*, p. 293) believes the Museum persisted until the fifth century, but if so, it certainly exercised little influence on scholarship.

CHAPTER II

TEMPERAMENT AND AUDIENCES OF ALEXANDRIA

With Alexandria firmly settled and its educational institutions established for Greek young men, ethnic problems were certain to develop. And they did, not only because of different national loyalties of the people, nor their cultural differences, but because of the general character of those who irrespective of family background became "Alexandrians."

The Greek orator had his boule and the Roman senator his senate before whom each could argue his cases and whose membership he could analyze for greatest rhetorical effectiveness. But Alexandrians were not so blessed. True, in the Delta the street orators could often predict the kind of listeners they would have, based on ethnic biases. But compared to Western haranguers, they found little common-ground among the high-strung listeners for their lines of argument. A proper understanding of the city's inhabitants, then, is essential to grasping public oratory, particularly that slanted to the rabble.

ETHNIC DIFFERENCES

Audiences in any era largely determine the kind of speech an orator can give on specific occasions, and ancient authorities repeatedly struck the note of the riotous, jealous, and superficial character of Alexandria's population. Egyptians, Jews, and Greeks required little provocation for melees which in their wake frequently left many dead. Egyptians saw the Greeks as ravagers and coveters of anything good the Egyptians held. Jews reckoned the Egyptians as peasants with an unenviable culture, while Greeks perceived the Jews as holier-than-thou exclusivists holding themselves aloof from Alexandrian life. Moreover, the Jews had been permitted a self-governing gerousia (γερουσία) but Augustus denied a boule (βουλή) to the Alexandrians—those who were Greek citizens and not merely Greek inhabitants of the city. Jews, on the other hand, saw the Greeks as intolerant bigots unable to come to terms with other nationalities or races who did not conform to Greek culture and religion.[1] None of the three factions ever served in any way as an intermediary between the other two in times of crisis. Each either remained neutral in a particular fracas, or sided with one of the two parties.

Specifically, Greek jealousy of the Jews leading to periodic social eruptions stemmed from several agents. First and most important was the fact that the Sons of Israel could not, by virtue of their religion, enter fully into the life of the community. Monotheism and (to non-believers) peculiar modes of worship prevented their participation in the idolatrous activity centered around the Serapeum. Under Gaius the issue became particularly acute when he tried to have his statue erected in the Temple, a blasphemous act to the Jews. Second, the Jews had been largely confined for centuries to first one, then two sections of the four part city. While growing numbers—perhaps 200,000 by Vespasian's time—and social acceptance of some Jews permitted limited mobility to other sections, they largely remained in the same quarters, thus polarizing ethnic factions.[2] Third, compared with their cousins elsewhere, Alexandrian Jews were first in independence, repute, culture, and wealth. Most were not affluent, yet some were and their economic and cultural success as merchants, smiths, and industrialists issued in jealousy by others.[3] Then, too, the Jewish γερουσία could rule its own people to a large degree, while the Greeks, as we shall see later, could not

---

[1] Abundant literature supports these general statements. See, *inter alia*, Strabo, *Geography*, XVII. 1. 6; Juvenal, *Satires*, XV. 45 (London, 1918), trans, G[eorge] G. Ramsey (Loeb); Dion Chrysostom, "Alexandrian Speech" (Oration XXXII) in *Dion Chrysostom* (London, 1932), trans. James W. Cohoon and H. Lamar Crosby (Loeb); A.C. Johnson, "Roman Egypt," pp. 335-36; and Philostratus, *Life of Apollonius of Tyana* (London, 1912), 26, trans. Frederick C. Conybeare (Loeb).

[2] Salon W. Baron, *Social and Religious History of the Jews* (New York, 1937), I, 133, and H. Idris Bell, *Jews and Christians in Egypt*, pp. 10-11.

[3] H. Idris Bell, "Anti-Semitism in Alexandria," *JRS*, XXXI (1941), 2, and Theodor Mommsen, "Provinces of the Roman Empire," Vol. II in *History of Rome* (New York, 1899), 291.

claim a senate for at least 200 years into the Empire,[4] and even then it lacked significant autonomy. The large measure of Jewish independence in political matters constantly irritated the Greeks here and elsewhere in the Empire. Finally, but on the negative side, Alexandrian Jews surely lacked full citizenship in the *polis*, though Josephus and others later insisted they did possess it.[5] Those Jews willing to pay the price of idolatrous worship likely were citizens, but surely the majority of them would never have gone this far.[6] When Philo says (*In Flaccum*, 53) that Flaccus destroyed their citizenship ($\pi o \lambda \iota \tau \epsilon i a s$), he probably means the Roman prefect interfered with their common rights, not, however, because they were Alexandrian citizens. Moreover, they could not participate in the city's athletic events; they were simply to enjoy a city not their own, as Claudius set forth in one rescript.[7] In short, bitter feelings ran deep and wide between Jews and Greeks, and needed little provocation to spill over into violence.

Jews and Greeks, then, despised those who did not share their particular beliefs and god(s), even though each had more civic responsibility and liberty than did the native Egyptians.[8] The lower-class immigrant, unlike the literati and upperclass Alexandrian, had few enviable conventions and cared little for the motherland. Neither they nor the more intellectual Greeks made any study of themselves, with the possible exception of Satyrus, nor wrote any histories of their city, leaving it largely to outsiders, like Strabo, to profile their culture.[9] They could not boast of a Herodotus or Thucydides, a Tacitus or Livy who sprang up among them.

[4] Bell, *Jews and Christians in Egypt*, pp. 12 & 16, and Philo, *In Flaccum*, 74.

[5] *Antiquities*, XIV. x. 1 and XIV. xii. 8 (Cambridge, Mass., 1965), trans. Louis H. Feldman (Loeb). But his statement that they had $i \sigma o \pi o \lambda i \tau a s$, equality of rights, does not mean they were Macedonian citizens. See also Victor A. Tcherikover and Alexander Fuks, *Corpus Papyrorum Judaicarum* (Cambridge, Mass., 1957 and later), I, 63-64.

[6] BGU 1140 may suggest some were citizens, but P. Brit. Mus. 2248 with its note that the Jews lived in a foreign city ($\epsilon \nu \ \dot a \lambda \lambda o \tau \rho i a \ \pi o \lambda \epsilon \iota$) implies they were not, on the whole, full citizens. Bell, *Jews and Christians in Egypt*, pp. 14-15 and 29. This issue of citizenship, still the subject of lively debate, is fully discussed in Bell, *supra*, pp. 10-21.

[7] P. Brit. Mus. 2248.

[8] É[mile] Amélinea, *Résumé de L'Histoire de L'Égypte* (Paris, 1894), p. 193.

[9] Satyrus' second century B.C. work, *On the Demes of Alexandria* ($\pi \epsilon \rho i \ \tau \hat \omega \nu \ \tau \hat \eta s$ $'A \lambda \epsilon \xi a \nu \delta \rho \epsilon i a s$), has been found in twenty-one fragments, P. Oxy 2465. Born in the Pontus, he later emigrated to Alexandria where he settled. His work, of narrow

Incapable of reflecting on their future and scorning the past, the rabble of Alexandria spent their strength on the present moment so that when they disliked an event or situation the normal procedure called for rioting and mob force. The largest contingent of Roman soldiers in all Egypt was billeted at Alexandria, a fact doubtless related to the blustering and ebullient people. "The city was constantly disturbed by street rioting, and there was no great regard for human life," observes one modern writer.[10] Ammianus Marcellinus also noted the frenzied minds (*efferatis hominum*) of the people and that they frequently were aroused to rebellion and rioting (*agitatur et turbulentis*).[11]

The view the Alexandrian held of his past, the indifference with which he regarded his heritage, the insecure anchors he felt in life, the unconcern with which he treated the social evolution of society account in large part for the unsettled feeling many had as they walked its streets, and watched the teaming thousands. They could not be certain what might happen, given the necessary conditions.

While intermarriage barely touched the problem of ethnic tension between Jew and Greek—Jews seldom intermarried with Gentiles—it helped modestly in issues between Greek and Egyptian, as it had taken place between them since at least the third century B.C.. Such domestic contracts, considered legal, granted Egyptians Greek nationality, whatever that would mean, but not necessarily citizenship. The Ptolemies administered two different legal systems, depending on whether one was Greek or Egyptian, but the more such wedlocks occurred the more confused and complicated became this double standard. The Romans continued these marital contracts, but placed certain limitations on them. Yet the situation did not significantly cement the badly divided city over the 700 years of Greco-Roman domination. Despite this volatile atmosphere, the Alexandrians seldom attempted an overthrow of their government—they never assailed it under the Ptolemies—chiefly waging mayhem among themselves.[12]

---

scope, is the monograph most closely approaching a self-study of the local political scene. Perhaps P. Oxy 2820, a first century B.C. fragment, comes also from an historical treatise, but we cannot be sure.

[10] Arthur Weigall, *Life and Times of Cleopatra, Queen of Egypt*, p. 41. See also J.G. Milne, *History of Egypt*, p. 23.

[11] *Op. cit.* XXII. 11. 4-5.

[12] Davis, *Race Relations*, pp. 50-55; Taubenschlag, *Law of Greco-Roman Egypt*, I, 77 f gives a full discussion of the intermarriage situation. In speaking

Oddly, Alexandria, Naucratis, and Ptolemais, though cosmopolitan, did not view intermarriage as liberally as did the chora ($\chi\acute\omega\rho\alpha$), the countryside, and probably because the education and literature helped to entrench Greek separatism and national purity rather than break down such barriers.

DION'S DESCRIPTION OF THE ALEXANDRIANS

So, the Alexandrians were divisive, jealous, and riotous, and over a long period of time. One of the best descriptions is set forth in a speech by Dion Chrysostom of Prusa (45-115) in his "Oration to the Alexandrians" (Oration XXXII).

He spoke in the large Greek theatre of Alexandria on an unknown, but important occasion probably in the reign of Trajan (98-117)[13] with whom he had been on good terms. Thousands came to hear him deliver his epideictic speech, including perhaps visiting ambassadors then in the city (40) and Roman soldiers quartered in the city. Although the speech condemned the townspeople in summary language, the normally boisterous residents listened attentively to the long address, a fact which suggests he was specifically commissioned on this occasion by the emperor and not invited by the city. Interspersing a few complimentary remarks—the people are quick-witted, their city is second only to Rome, and its merchant marine is internationally important—with those of another sort, Dion proceeds to tell the Alexandrians what he (and probably the emperor) really thinks of them. They are frivolous and heedless, never at a loss for fun-making and laughter, with many entertainers (speakers?) who cater to such whims (1). Orators who speak to them fear to treat their topics frankly because of the impatience and turbulent character of the populace. Despite these criticisms, Alexandria is lucky ($\epsilon\mathring{v}\tau\upsilon\chi o\mathring{v}s$ $\pi\acute o\lambda\epsilon\omega s$) that he (Dion) speaks so candidly, unafraid

---

of Greek nationality, Taubenschlag probably means Egyptians were more fully accepted into the Greek culture and received greater privileges, yet still short of citizenship ($\pi o\lambda\iota\tau\epsilon\acute\iota as$).

[13] See the Cohoon-Crosby edition (Loeb) for items which follow here in the speech text. E.K. Borthwick's analysis of the situation ("Dion Chrysostom on the Mob at Alexandria, *Classical Review*, N.S. XXII, No. 1 [1972], 1-3) characterizes the Alexandrian populace as much like that found at late twentieth century rock music festivals.

as he is of the mob and its uproar (11) and without benefit of song and lyre ($\chi\omega\rho\grave{\iota}s$ $\mathring{\omega}\delta\mathring{\eta}s$ $\kappa\alpha\grave{\iota}$ $\kappa\iota\theta\acute{\alpha}\rho\alpha s$, 20). Their public display of hysterics and dissiliency at meetings militates against their intellectual, religious, and far-sighted improvement. Rather it encourages stupid wrangling ($\check{\epsilon}\pi\iota\nu$ $\delta\grave{\epsilon}$ $\mathring{\alpha}\mu\alpha\theta\mathring{\eta}$), covetousness ($\phi\iota\lambda o\tau\iota\mu\acute{\iota}\alpha\nu$), and extravagance ($\delta\alpha\pi\acute{\alpha}\nu\eta\nu$).

Unlike Athenians of yore, Alexandrians have no one to reprimand them when they get out of hand, perhaps a reference to their great measure of autonomy under both the Ptolemies and the early Romans. So they should welcome his forthrightness. Their behavior is uncontrolled and inappropriate. They throw objects ($\tau\grave{\alpha}$ $\check{o}\nu\tau\alpha$) into the air (probably substantial outer garments, not just handkerchiefs). The fault may be with those who call themselves philosophers, for some of them stand at street-corners, alley-ways, and the temple gates to prey upon unsuspecting listeners. They do great harm for they teach thoughtless people to deride philosophers generally when they really should eradicate insolence from their audience (8-9).

Most of their theatrical events are sheer buffoonery and useless, he continues, as shown by the epideictic declamations of some orators, as well as by speakers reading their own poetry. Such activity reminds one of a doctor who treats a patient with flowers, courtesans, and perfume: it ignores the real cause of an illness (10). Alexandrians are interested only in food for the body and entertainment for their diversion (31-32)—much as one sees women of ill repute who though wanton at home should behave with decorum outside the house, but do not. They do anything in public they want (41). The city is mad over music and horse-racing, is weak ($\mathring{\alpha}\sigma\phi\epsilon\nu\acute{\eta}s$), and its people's character, shallow ($\kappa o\acute{\upsilon}\phi os$) (43,48). In some cities men are remembered for their heroic deeds as they gave their lives for the fatherland, but Alexandrians are concerned with cat gut ($\chi o\rho\delta\mathring{\eta}$)—music. They are cowards and slackers ($\delta\epsilon\iota\lambda o\grave{\iota}$ ... $\kappa\alpha\grave{\iota}$ $\mathring{\alpha}\sigma\tau\rho\acute{\alpha}\tau\omega\nu\tau o\iota$). When the concert harpist is out of tune the audience immediately discerns it, but when the people fail to live in harmony with laws of nature, they are indifferent to it (46). They act like men suffering from a hang-over ($\kappa\rho\alpha\iota\pi\mathring{\alpha}\lambda\acute{\alpha}\omega$). They don't respect themselves, so neither do others respect them (52). Their use of drugs and inhaling of fumes cause their immoderate conduct (56). Whereas music was invented to calm men and harmonize their lives with nature, Alexandrians have reversed all this (58).

How did they become this way? It is as a friend of Aesop once said: sheep and birds tagged after Orpheus, the legendary Greek poet, to hear his music. After he died Zeus changed them into human beings, and these same creatures migrated to Alexandria and settled there!

What will come of their disorderliness? The emperor [?] will not accede to their more important requests because he believes their utter lack of self-control does not merit them, declares the Bithynian.[14] It is tragic that when people abroad speak of the city, they say good things of the Museum, Library, and metropolis generally, but regard the people as worthless and fools (86). Indeed, they seem like a concentrated manure pile ($\kappa \acute{o} \mu \pi o s$) where everything is brought together (87). It is one thing to observe varieties of human weakness seen anywhere; it is quite another when it persists regularly. When that happens it becomes a civic issue ($\delta \eta \mu \acute{o} \sigma \iota o s$) (91). Do not think that you will emerge from all this with no price to pay. Wickedness grows from stage to stage until finally it is harvested in destruction (74). It is not laughter that is good for man but what makes him joyful ($\dot{\alpha} \lambda \lambda \grave{\alpha} \ \tau \grave{o} \ \chi \alpha \acute{\iota} \rho \epsilon \iota \nu$) that is important. When men lack joy and are ignorant they seek laughter, sometimes by drugs ($\sigma \alpha \rho \delta \acute{o} \nu \iota o \nu$, 99).

Dion's speech lacks the conclusion we might expect to find in an earlier Attic orator. He opines that his plight may be that of another (proverbial) speaker of whom it was predicted that he would sing in an ass' ($\ddot{o} \nu o \upsilon$) ears. But since he does not desire that, he stops abruptly!

Like epideictic oratory from of old, the sort that Lysias gave at Olympia, Dion's speech dealt mostly with the present, but catalogued some of the disgraceful past, and implicitly hoped for a better future. It was delivered more to spectators than to judges, more for censure and help than for determining critical points at issue.[15] In this hour-long speech—if the text is accurate and complete[16]—and as expected of any epideicticist, Dion did not simply display his rhetorical ability as an itinerant sophist might have done,

---

[14] Perhaps referring to a repeated request for a senate which may have been abolished by one of the Ptolemies. But the evidence is inconclusive. See Bell, *Jews and Christians in Egypt*, pp. 8 f for a fuller discussion of this point.

[15] On the general theme of epideictic oratory see the able treatment of George A. Kennedy, *Art of Persuasion in Greece*, pp. 152 ff.

[16] At one point he says $\mu \acute{\iota} \alpha \nu \ \ddot{\omega} \rho \alpha \nu \ \sigma \omega \phi \rho o \nu \hat{\eta} \sigma \alpha \iota$. The Loeb text, about 8700 words in length, suggests this time limit if the speaker's rate approximated 150 words per minute, a "normal" speech rate.

but immersed himself in the occasion and developed a significant line of thought which essentially condemned the public demonstrations so often seen in the city. The structure in the speech does not resemble that prescribed by Aristotle (*Rhetoric*, 1366ᵃ24ff) for ceremonial and vituperative speeches, indicating he in no discernible way was indebted to that earlier theorist. On the other hand, the discourse more neatly fits into that pattern provided by the *Rhetorica ad Alexandrum* (1441ᵇ14ff) where the author suggests that speakers ridicule their opponents on those matters on which the latter pride themselves and anticipate the audience's objections or show the issues are grave. This, of course, Dion amply does. But such instructions are so general, so commonplace, as to prove of little value in ascertaining whether or not Dion was in any way indebted to the earlier work. Dion's was a prophetic voice, not a *vox populi*, nor even a *vox viri*, but more a *vox dei*! If they did not listen to one physician and pay heed to his remedies, they would perforce visit a different kind of physician whose treatment would be more drastic (οἱ δὲ τοιοῦτοι παρ᾽ ἑτέρους, ἴασιν ἰατροὺς οὐχ ἑκόντες ἰσχυροτέρους, 17).

Other ancient authorities also testify to the same characteristics of the people. Caesar's *Commentaries* picture them as having a temperament making them the fittest sort for treason.[17] Philo, the Alexandrian Jewish philosopher who sought to accomodate Neoplatonism to the Mosaic law, characterized the Alexandrians (though not the Jews) as adept at flattery, bewitching, and hypocrisy (κολακείας καὶ γοητείας καὶ ὑποκρίσεις), ready to charm with words (θῶπας λόγους), all of which brings disaster with their unbridled lips,[18] while Quintilian later saw them as boastful and boorish (*inflati ... et inanes*).[19] Hadrian reportedly wrote a letter describing the Alexandrian Jews, Christians, and everyone there as factious, vain, unruly—worshippers of only one god, money.[20] Eunapius portrayed them as loud and demanding,[21] while in the late second and third century Athenaeus characterized them as rowdies at dinner

---

[17] *Op cit.*, "Alexandrian War," VII.

[18] Philo, "De Legatione ad Gaium," XXV. 162, *Philo*, X (London, 1962), trans. F[rancis] H. Colson (Loeb).

[19] He saw the difference between Asians and Athenians as the cause for Asians liking a florid style more than did the Athenians. *Institutes*, XII. x. 16.

[20] Cited by A.C. Johnson, "Roman Egypt," pp. 335-36.

[21] *Lives of the Sophists*, 463 (London, 1961), trans., Wilner C. Wright (Loeb).

parties: they shout, brawl, abuse the wine-pourer, and buffet the slaves to the point of tears.[22] Apollonius of Tyana, who flourished in the late first century, condemned (in a speech to the Alexandrians) their passionate love of horse-racing, and admitted he would "like to call down fire upon such a city as this."[23] Like Antioch (Syria), Alexandria was filled with factious, riotous residents who lived only for the day.[24] This restless disposition provided an intermittently active volcano of emotion from which seething hatred periodically erupted into violent destruction. On many such occasions the residents did not await the harangue of the orator to rise against their enemies. Schooled by years of bitterness and daily friction, they needed few words to prepare the city for a *coup de main*.

Undoubtedly small knots of Jews, Greeks, Egyptians and others were not of this character, just as differences obtain everywhere. But the majority and the power structure were of this sort, so much so that ancient authorities admit no exceptions.

PERSECUTION AND VIOLENCE

Irritable and volatile, Alexandrians saw repeated violence and rioting take place over a period of centuries. Not only did their nature lend itself to such disorder, but political conditions left the city unsettled. During the 200 year period from 30 B.C. to A.D. 170, for example, fifty-two men held the prefecture of Alexandria, providing little continuity of administration and giving a general kaleidoscopic sense among the restless people.[25] The Greeks, always inclined to live for the moment, pandered to their emotions *vis à vis* the short-lived administrations.

So riots occurred, and several of them. Primary evidence does not reveal the identity of the agitators whose oratory precipitated the recorded crises, but since the inflamatory spoken word always arouses and is the instrument by which harbingers of ill-will marshall forces in hours of crises, we can be certain that politico-religious

---

[22] *Deipnosophistae*, X. 420e.

[23] Philostratus, *Life of Apollonius*, XXVI. Only a fragment of this speech has come down to us.

[24] R.W. Pounder, *Saint Paul and His Cities* (London, 1913), p. 71.

[25] Harold T. Davis, *Alexandria, the Golden City* (Evanston, Illinois, 1957), II, 285.

demagogues played a significant role. Given the temperament of Alexandria and of man generally, the city would inevitably have witnessed periodic outbreaks of violence without such harangues, but not on the scale she did had she relied on the ink of the papyrus alone.

The tongue of the orator wielded its power. A simple outcry from an anonymous hate-monger enflamed the smoldering embers of hatred within a blood-thirsty, highly factious people. Four such outbreaks should be noted, for they suggest not only the kind of audiences speakers addressed, but a particular species of deliberative oratory. We shall leave until later those pogroms instigated by the government itself when the imperial policy forbade the worship of God in certain ways.

The first paroxysm of violence, A.D. 38, occurred when the Jewish king Herod Agrippa passed through Alexandria enroute to his new assignment in Judea. His march through the streets, to the delight and cheers of the Jews, inflamed jealous Greeks who scarecrowed the new king by dressing a local moron like a monarch and paraded him down the main thoroughfare, and in addition erected imperial statues in Jewish synagogues. The Jews retaliated but, hopelessly outnumbered, suffered a great massacre.[26] Later when they were confined to their ghetto and faced starvation, they sneaked out to replenish food supplies but were pursued, physically flogged in much the same way the Egyptians were for criminal infractions, and even slaughtered. Flaccus, the Roman prefect, did nothing to help the Jews or to maintain order; on the contrary—if we can believe Philo, and no evidence contradicts him—he encouraged the Greeks in their melee by giving tacit permission for the anti-semitic attacks. His labeling them foreigners and aliens ($\xi\acute{\epsilon}\nu o\upsilon\varsigma$ $\kappa\alpha\grave{\iota}$ $\grave{\epsilon}\pi\acute{\eta}\lambda\upsilon\delta\alpha\varsigma$) in Egypt, although they had lived there for hundreds of years, further aggravated the situation. The hemorrhage of human, social, and political forces deeply wounded the city. Not until many Jews were beaten, dragged through the streets, compelled to eat pork, and finally killed did Flaccus seek to restore law and order. So serious

[26] For this riot in A.D. 38 see Bell, "Anti-Semitism in Alexandria," 1-18; Josephus, *Antiquities*, XVIII. vi. 1 ff; Bell, *Jews and Christians in Egypt*, pp. 16 ff which leans heavily on P. Lond 1912; Tcherikover and Fuks, *CPJ*, I, 66; and Emil Schurer, *Geschichte des Judischen Volkes im Zeitalter Jesus Christi* (Leipzig, 1901), trans. John MacPherson, Sophia Taylor, and Peter Christie. I have used both the German and English editions.

was his dereliction of duty to maintain the *pax Romana* that Caligula finally executed him.[27]

The second riot, that of the Jewish revolt of A.D. 115-17, is curious because its precipating cause is difficult to pinpoint. True, the special poll tax (λαογραφία), required for years, was a constant source of irritation, along with other minor factors, but one can discover no sufficient reason for the putsch which came about the same time as the generalized outbreaks on Cyprus and in Mesopotamia. Probably the Jews saw a small incident as a chance to lash out against their long-time enemies, the Greeks. Whatever the catalyst, it resulted in the most cruel and ruthless of all Jewish revolts in Alexandria, and nearly annihilated the entire Jewish population throughout the province,[28] but not before the sons of Abraham largely destroyed the city, its roads, buildings, and property. In turn the great Synagogue was razed. Unlike in the riots under Flaccus when Jews still saw Rome as basically their friend, in this rebellion the Jews were pitted against both Greeks and Romans, for the Roman government in the previous century had plundered the sacred Temple at Jerusalem, an unforgivable trespass to international Jewry. Intermittent persecution thereafter brought the virtual expulsion of the Jewish community from the Delta city finally in the fifth century.[29]

In 248-49 an anonymous rabble-rouser—Alexandrians commonly did not wait for formal protest meetings—stirred up the Alexandrian mob to frenzy and hate, this time against Christians who were insulting local gods by declining to worship them. Those refusing to pay homage were tortured and stoned to death during the six-month outrage. Christians, following the example of their Savior, on the whole offered no resistance, turning the other cheek as their household goods were thrown into streets and set afire, and their persons and families brutally tortured.[30] The Egyptian prefect, probably Aelius

[27] The embassy to Gaius Caligula will be taken up in Chapter III.

[28] For a complete history of this revolt see Alexander Fuks, "Jewish Revolt in Egypt (A.D. 115-117) in the Light of the Papyri," *Aegyptus*, XXXIII (1953), 131-58; Fuks, "Aspects of the Jewish Revolt in A.D. 115-117," *JRS*, LI (1961), 98-104; Tcherikover and Fuks, *CPJ*, I, 63-64 and 91 f.; and Hugh McLennan, *Oxyrhynchus: An Economic and Social Study* (Princeton, 1935), p. 20.

[29] Bell, "Anti-Semitism in Alexandria," 17.

[30] Stewart I. Oost, "Alexandrian Seditions under Philip and Gassienus," *Classical Philology*, LVI (1961), 4-6; and John M. Neale, "Patriarchate of Alexandria," pp. 41-42, Vol. I in *History of the Holy Eastern Church* (London, 1848).

Appius Sabinus, like Flaccus two centuries before, did nothing to stem the outrageous massacre, but unlike Flaccus he was later elevated to senatorial rank and in no way reprimanded.[31]

In 361 Christians, cleaning up an area formerly used by the polytheistic Greeks in their religious ceremonies, discovered human skulls which indicated pagan human sacrifice. The workers, shocked at such bestiality, paraded them through the streets, showing the results of heathen rites. The Greeks were enraged at this blasphemy and interference in their religious traditions—though without denying them—tore into the Christians, seized Bishop George of the city, trampled him, and after dragging him about like a spread eagle (*divaricatis pedibus*, so Ammianus Marcellinus), tore his body to pieces and burned its members. The Apostate Julian, himself no friend of the Christians now, refused to take any action, placating his conscience with a strongly worded letter to the Alexandrians.[32]

A later chapter will treat the founding of the Christian church in Alexandria and of the preaching of its bishops and priests. We should at this point, however, indicate something of the persecution of the Christians which transpired as a direct result of imperial decree, as differentiated from pogroms which broke out due to the paroxysmal behavior of the inhabitants. Both types of oppression affected the quantity of preaching one could hear in the city. Neither Rome nor the Alexandrian Greeks would have persecuted Jews or Christians for worshipping their peculiar God, if they had included him among several others. But the monotheism of the Judeo-Christian tradition with its concern for moral character, self-discipline, and a changed life was too much for pleasure-seeking, blustering Alexandria. The issue, then, was Christianity vs *Romanitas* (the Roman way of life), for inevitably the two life styles conflicted. The former, as a radical movement, rejected much of the past and present as they related to idolatry. The latter, a conservative defender of the status quo, upheld both as legitimate and good. Christianity injected into Roman life the belief that one's primary allegiance belonged to God, and secondarily to man, thus denying the absolute power of the state. The lines were clearly drawn.

No urban settlement in the entire ancient world, apart from Jerusalem, so affected the development of Christianity as did Alexan-

---

[31] Oost, "Alexandrian Seditions," 6.

[32] Ammianus Marcellinus, XXII 11. 3 ff, and Socrates, *Ecclesiastical History* (London, 1853), III. ii-iv. (No translator listed).

dria.[33] The Gospel came here perhaps in the mid-first century, grew and flourished, but as one would expect in its variegated atmosphere, numerous heresies sprang up, each with its own coterie of followers.[34] While we have considerable information in theological treatises on the controversies, little of the spoken word surrounding the debates has survived.

The Greco-Roman world was never free of prejudice and muzzling of free speech whether in church or out. Had not Socrates demonstrated the danger of unpopular ideas, and in the Roman Republic had not the Censors in 92 B.C. closed down rhetorical schools taught by Latin rhetoricians because they dared to put Greek rhetorical principles into Roman dress? Neither Grecian nor Roman mentality encouraged those who longed for or sought to practice freedom of expression. But when pressure came Christians, unlike their Jewish neighbors, declined to revolt against persecution of their religion; some fled while others willingly gave their lives. They welcomed neither cruelty nor martyrdom but determined by life or death to honor their God.[35] Yet for many of them, at least in the West and probably in the East as well, the doctrine of free speech ($\pi\alpha\rho\rho\eta\sigma\acute{\iota}\alpha$) had not meant what it had for secular politicians or lawyers. To the former it signified, among other things, liberty to preach about their new faith and to put man into proper relationship with his Creator. On the other hand, the normal Greek or Roman insisted

---

[33] J[ohn] M. Creed, "Egypt and the Christian Church," p. 300 in *Legacy of Egypt* (Oxford, 1942), ed., Stephen R.K. Glanville.

[34] Abel F. Villemain, *Tableau de L'Éloquence Chrétienne au IVe Siècle* (Paris, 1851), p. 87.

[35] Jules Lebreton and Jacques Zeiller, *History of the Primitive Church* (New York, 1949), II, 1225-26, trans. Ernest C. Messenger. A qualification should be made to the statement, however. Some Montanists, a schismatic "Christian" group, may have welcomed death since they held that flight under persecution was a form of apostasy, but they had only a modest following in Alexandria. Clement writes of them, but he is not overly concerned with their importance. But more significantly, both Clement and Origin spoke favorably of martyrdom, though neither ever directly urged that the faithful put their head on the block. They simply could see that death would end the sufferings and duress they all experienced. See the *Stromata* passage (IV. iv. 206B) in Migne, *Patrologiae Graeca*, VIII (the full statement of the "perfection" Clement saw in the consequent sacrifice for one's faith: Αὐτίκα τελείωσιν τὸ μαρτύριον καλοῦμεν,οὐκ ὅτι τέλος τοῦ βίου ὁ ἄνθρωπος ἔλαβεν, ὡς οἱ λοιποί, ἀλλ᾽ ὅτι τέλειον ἔργον ἀγάπης ἐνεδείξατο.) and Origin's "Exhortation to Martyrdom," 47 ff, and *passim* in Migne, *Patrologiae Graeca*, XI. 563 ff.

on it as an inherent right of all men to be heard on important issues. He saw it as the right to declare anything, the right to speak the plain truth, the courage to express one's conviction, especially on political matters.[36]

Christians found distressing conditions during the reign of Marcus Aurelius (161-80), but the difficulties seemed to stem not so much from an imperial policy as from crowd violence typical of Alexandria against any noncomformists. "Tertullian, in fact, roundly declared [the emperor] to be a protector of the Christians," asserts one author.[37] But sometime between 200 and 202, perhaps immediately after granting Alexandria a senate, Septimius Severus levied heavy penalties on anyone converting to Christianity, prescribing official witch hunts especially of catechumens and neophytes. The interdict, however, probably affected more the place of public preaching than personal conversions, but to what extent we have no record. After the death of Severus his son Caracalla, following a visit to Alexandria, treated its traditional restiveness and free speech as rebellion which he suppressed by executions and loss of special privileges.[38] This muzzled religious as well as political speaking, driving preachers and Christian laymen underground.

Riots under Philip in 249 soon led to another persecution under Decius, Philip's successor and the first emperor to persecute systematically Christians. The new emperor reacted against the permissive attitude of Philip and issued an edict (in 250?), the text of which has not survived, which called for searching out and making as many apostates from the Christian religion as possible. He rightly saw the movement as a threat to *Romanitas* and the state. Anyone, clergy or layman, suspected of seditious allegiance to the sect was dragged to a statue of the emperor where he was compelled to pay homage. So widespread was the resulting slaughter of those who

[36] W[illem] C. Van Unnik, "Christian's Freedom of Speech in the New Testament," *Bulletin of the John Rylands Library* (Manchester), XLIV (1962), 469-77. The German scholar Erik Peterson first traced the linguistic history of παρρησία in a fifteen page monograph, and promised a fuller essay on the subject later, but it never appeared. "Zur Bedeutungsgeschichte von ΠΑΡΡΗΣΙΑ," *Rheinhold-Seeberg-Festschrift* (Leipzig, 1927), pp. 283-97, cited in Van Unnik, 469, who makes a stronger case for the religious dimension that I have set forth here.

[37] Paul Keresztes, "Marcus Aurelius a Persecutor?" *Harvard Theological Review*, LXI (1968), 321-22.

[38] Edward R. Hardy, *Christian Egypt: Church and People* (New York, 1952), pp. 9 and 82, and *SHA*, "Septimius Severus," XVII. 1.

would not thus worship that Dionysius, Bishop of Alexandria, could cite Exodus XII.30 when another great scourge had swept the nation: "For there is not a house in which there is not one dead."[39] However respectful they were of the laws, obedient to the emperor, loyal to Rome, and devoted to the common good, Christians were still viewed with suspicion simply because of their positive monotheism and their refusal to enter fully into questionable urban affairs. Persecutors beat, imprisoned, starved, and stoned their victims, deriving sadistic pleasure out of administering the punishment themselves rather than leaving it to the creatures of nature, for unlike at Rome, one heard no cry in Alexandria of "Christianos ad Leonem!"

In 257 Valerian, frightened by unrest on the frontier, promulgated an edict of *recognoscere romanas ceremonias* (recognizing Roman ceremonies) and prohibited the public worship by Christians. Later the noose was further tightened to include not just clergy but others as well. While technically they were trying to stamp out Christianity, and not Christians per se, actually the only way to attack the former was to besiege the latter. Moreover, since Christians could not worship publicly, sinister rumors circulated about their clandestine meetings: sexual orgies, incest, assassinations, ritual cannibalism all were alleged to take place. So the unknown spawned greater fear and hatred.

Later that same century Diocletian (284-305) ordered the widespread destruction of Christian churches and the burning of their Scriptures. Preachers were incarcerated but as always could secure release by offering sacrifices to pagan gods, a route few chose. Throughout North Africa a large number of believers suffered martyrdom by every imaginable means as the search and seizure policy continued for a quarter-century before the Edict of Milan (313) relieved the pressure.[40] Some Egyptian pagans were so shamed and sorrowed by the government's intolerance that they risked their own lives and property to hide the Christians from the marauding troops.[41]

---

[39] Dionysius of Alexandria, "Epistle XII: To the Alexandrians," 1, trans. S[tewart] D.F. Salmond, in Vol. VI of *Ante-Nicene Fathers* (Buffalo, 1886), eds. Alexander Roberts and James Donaldson.

[40] Eusebius, *Historia Ecclesiastica*, VI. 41; Charles L. Feltoe, "Letters and Other Remains of Dionysius of Alexandria," *Cambridge Patristic Texts* (Cambridge, 1904), p. 14, ed. A[rthur] J. Mason; and Lebreton and Zeiller, *History of the Primitive Church*, II, 791-92 and 1218.

[41] Maude A. Huttman, "Establishment of Christianity and the Proscription

But corporal persecution subsided, though other duress replaced it, with the conversion of Constantine. The apostate Julian (360-63) had grown up under the hardship incurred by his devoutly Christian mother dying a few months after his birth, and his father, the half-brother of Constantine the Great, falling at the hand of Constantius (337-61) who feared any pretenders to the throne. The lad studied at Constantinople under the Christian sophist Hecebolius whom he greatly respected and loved in later life. Imprisoned for six years, he turned his back on the religion of his mother and teacher, a fact which significantly affected Christian rhetoricians. In 362, two years after he came to the throne, he expelled Christian instructors from state classrooms because they could not teach Greek and Roman literature and mythology with the commitment and surety required. Their presuppositions would lead to academic hedging. Further, their children could no longer receive instruction in the Greek orators and poets because "such studies [were] conducive to the acquisition of argumentative and persuasive powers,"[42] and these he did not wish the Christians to have. Julian perceived that every effective teacher had a knot in his thread before he began to sew, that no one taught his subject "objectively." Granting his bias, one sees that he carried to a logical conclusion the arguments of Decius and others, and thus the emperor took the only feasible course open to him. Several Christian rhetoricians, including Eusebius of Alexandria, lost their positions as a result of the imperial injunction.[43]

So, in whatever realm one looks, the atmosphere in Alexandria was an unsettled one: the temperament of the populace boisterous, riotous, and factious gave place to intermittent outbreaks involving

---

of Paganism," *Studies in History, Economics and Public Law* (New York, 1914), 31-34; Neale, "Alexandrian Patriarchate," I, 93 ff; Lebreton and Zeiller, *History of the Primitive Church*, II, 1200; and E[rnest] G. Sihler, "In the Era of Diocletian," *Biblical Review*, V (1920), 274-75. See also Joseph Plescia, "On the Persecution of the Christians in the Roman Empire," *Latomus*, XXX Fasc. 1 (1971), 120-32, for this and related observations.

[42] Sozomen, *Ecclesiastical History*, V. xviii (London, 1855), trans. Edward Walford, and Julian, *Epistles*, 376c (London, 1913), trans. Wilmer C. Wright (Loeb).

[43] Eunapius, *Lives of the Sophists*, 493 and *PW*, "Eusebios" (36). While other evidence is scanty on the religious commitment of Eusebius, the fact that he lost his job is strong evidence that he was numbered among the believers.

CHAPTER III

SPOKESMEN FOR TRUTH: THE SECULAR SPEAKERS

With the loss of Greek independence and the consequent sub-jugation of Egypt in the East, one would not expect to find in Alexandria the sort of oratory heard in Athens in the days of Demosthenes. Secular or sacred oratory, the concern of this and the following chapter, simply could not flourish in an oppressive atmosphere as it did in a freer society. But given Alexander's opening of the lands to the East, and the tumultuous nature of the Alexandrians, one would hope to uncover more specific mention of it than in fact occurs.[1] If some citizens received their education in whole or in part at the hands of rhetoricians in the Ptolemaic kingdom, why have we no greater knowledge of it? The answer lies in several areas: (A) soil conditions have dissolved many papyri which must have existed earlier; this is particularly true with the high water table in the Delta itself. Prolonged existence of papyri demands hot, dry conditions like those found in Upper Egypt. (B) Contemporaries omitted notice of the rhetorical theory and training because of its commonality—much like what happens today in university senates, religious meetings, and other situations where one normally expects speeches of varying length and quality; it goes unnoticed by the public, and for much the same reason: mediocre quality. And (C) many books and speeches do not enjoy wide circulation, due to cost or publication, even though their ideas should command more than passing interest. This limitation particularly obtains in a society whose written and spoken word must first be handcopied, even though the raw material may be relatively cheap.

---

[1] S[imon] Davis, *Race Relations in Ancient Egypt*, p. 72n.

WELL-KNOWN ORATORS

Specific names, with a few exceptions, are hard to come by when one examines the orators and oratory of Greco-Roman Alexandria, unlike in Rome and Athens where he finds a long history of oral discourse. Alexandrian Greeks and Romans not only felt little urge to write accounts of their speaking, either past or present, but probably heard less formal speaking than the more stable centers to the West. Limited practice prompted little indigenous criticism by contemporaries.

Several speakers can be noted, however. Demetrius of Phaleron, the orator-statesman-general and Library-founder, migrated to Alexandria from Athens where he seems to have studied under Theophrastus, Aristotle's pupil, and provided Alexandria its chief link with Athens. Cicero centuries later admired his oratory and ranked him as the best in style of the "Intermediate" school, patterning his own speaking after the ex-Athenian.[2] His encomium on Socrates, as well as his popular and ambassadorial speeches,[3] prompted Josephus to call him the most learned man of his day.[4] When Cicero tells us that Demetrius was highly accomplished in speaking, that he gave the discipline of oratory softness and pliability, and that he won his audience without overpowering it, he likely was recalling the Athenian's career prior to his coming to Alexandria,[5] but a man of his reputation and ability doubtless continued his public speaking in Alexandria, yet nothing of it has come down to us. The simple trip to the East would not in itself have muzzled Demetrius, but we are hard pressed to characterize his oratory after he left Athens.

Then, there was the iconoclastic and epideictic speech of Dion Chrysostom (Oration XXXII) given in the large Greek theatre probably during the reign of Trajan, as already noticed.[6] Unlike most Alexandrian speakers treating a controversial topic, Dion held the attention of his listeners and departed without an ensuing riot. In keeping with the city's concern for the present and his own knowledge of the requirement of an epideictic oration, he confined himself to their contemporary mode of conduct, relating how they appeared

[2] *De Oratore*, II. 95 and *Orator* 92.
[3] Susemihl, *Geschichte der Griechischen Litteratur*, I, 135-42.
[4] "Contra Apionem," II. 46 (London, 1926), trans. Henry St. Thackeray (Loeb).
[5] *Brutus*, IX. 37 f.
[6] See Chapter II.

to outsiders. Probably the occasion was one of the few in Greco-Roman Alexandria that the residents listened to a public speaker profile their negative appearance without venting their emotions.

The public career of Theodotus of Chios (or possibly Samos) has largely escaped us, but we do know that as tutor and counselor to Ptolemy XIV he carried much weight. Quintilian saw his oratory as a mixture of the deliberative and judicial which he learned and practiced in the rhetorical schools probably prior to his emigration to Alexandria. The most important speech, so far as we know, he gave to Ptolemy, perhaps in the form of counsel in which he urged the king to put Pompey to death if the latter should flee to the city ahead of Julius Caesar. Theodotus' "godless advice" ($\dot{a}\theta\dot{\epsilon}\mu\iota\sigma\tau o\nu$ $\dot{\epsilon}\iota\sigma\eta\gamma\epsilon\hat{\iota}\tau o$,, so Appian) led to Pompey's death and prompted his own assassination some years later in Asia.[7] The death of the Roman general and the subsequent murder of Theodotus so profoundly impressed the city and world that they were used as themes in declamations in Quintilian's day a century later.[8]

P. Aelius Aristides visited Alexandria sometime during the period A.D. 149-54 and, unlike Dion Chrysostom, charmed the people so that shortly after his speech they erected an inscription (CIG 4679) in his honor.[9] We know neither his topic on this occasion or on most others, but in his panegyric "Roman Oration" (Oration XXVI), given during the reign of Antoninus Pius (138-61), he praised many things in the Empire, but none of which lauded the eloquence in Alexandria. Such an omission suggests its spoken discourse had reached no significant height nor deserved any special notice. Since his surviving rhetorical works indicate his indebtedness to both Isocrates (for his ethical position) and Demosthenes (for oratory generally), we can assume a broadness of vision and effectiveness in delivery, as indeed the inscription suggests.

In the late fourth century (c. 394) when he was perhaps thirty years of age, Synesius of Cyrene journeyed to Alexandria for further

[7] Whether by Cassius (*Roman History*, "Civil Wars," II. 90) or Brutus (Plutarch, *Lives*, "Pompey," 80. 6) is not clear.

[8] Quintilian, *Institutes*, III. viii. 55-58, and *PW*, "Theodotus" (14), 2nd ed.

[9] The original inscription may be found in the Vatican Museum. See also *PW*, "P. Aelius Aristides" (24). August Boeckh-Ioannes Franz (*Corpus Inscriptionum Graecarum* [Berlin, 1953]) argues for a little earlier date, 145-47, in discussing CIG 4679. BGU 588, an anonymous fragment of a possible speech by Aristides, and variously dated from the first to the third centuries, is too meagre and uncertain to command further attention here.

study at the Museum-University.[10] He became disciple and friend of Hypatia, the beautiful and brilliant philosopher and to whom he wrote several extant letters. That he lectured in the city we know because his public discourse commanded sufficient attention to earn him an embassy to Arcadius in Constantinople in 397, though on behalf of his native town and not that of the Delta city.[11] His themes in Alexandria have not survived, but one can assume that the extant Eulogy on Baldness (φαλάκρας ἐγκώμιον), a panegyric responding to an earlier encomium of Dion Chrysostom on the hair, was fairly typical.

While one is left to speculate on Alexandrian speeches of Synesius, we do know something of his rhetorical theory. Like Plato he held philosophy superior to rhetoric because it taught a different way of looking at life: more analysis, wider perspective, and less contention. It was the queen of all the disciplines, making its devotees useful in society—so he wrote to his friend Pylamenes (*Epistle* 103)— though rhetoric was helpful as a liberal training and preparation for philosophic study. Only as the handmaiden of philosophy could rhetoric best operate: as mental relaxation for serious philosophers; it deserved little more. So as an aristocrat, a man of leisure, Synesius allegedly scorned the sophistic movement and those who made their livelihood by their mouths. Yet he only appears to dislike them and perhaps only some of them, for he himself was a sophist, though he would (unconvincingly) deny its trivia. *Baldness*, as much as anything else, provides classic proof of the sophistic mentality and practice he allegedly disliked.[12] Notwithstanding, he almost surely used this lecture-hall variety of speech when he spoke to the Alexandrians and probably to the Cyrenians.

In addition to known itinerant speakers, others also spoke in various capacities to the people. One third century papyrus, P Oxy 1612, hints at the issue of a cultic worship of the emperor, a practice

---

[10] The best biography in English is W[illiam] S. Crawford's *Synesius the Hellene* (London, 1901), but José C. Pando's monograph, "Life and Times of Synesius of Cyrene as Revealed in His Works," *Catholic University of American Patristic Studies* (Washington, D.C., 1940) in places is more critical and incisive.

[11] His speech on that occasion, "On Kingship" (περὶ βασιλείας), pled for a citizen army, a unique plea for the ancient world, in order to thwart the political crises he saw looming both in Cyrene and in the empire at large.

[12] Crawford, *Synesius*, p. 170. See also Augustine Fitzgerald. trans., *Letters of Synesius of Cyrene* (Oxford, 1926), pp. 14, 67, and *passim*.

which was probably widespread.[13] The speaker boldly handles the veneration of the ruler, and decries its method of practice in his own city, almost surely Alexandria, but he does not oppose the devotion itself—only its deviations. Perhaps a sophist, whether Roman or Nicomedian we do not know, he addresses the audience spiritedly and bravely declaring (as modern editors have translated it):

I am referring to the rites which they say that they perform to Caesar. It was not we who originally invented those rites, which is to our credit, but it was a Nicaean who was the first to institute them. The character of the man need not be described: in any case let the rites be his, and let them be performed among his people alone, as the Eleusinian rites are among the Athenians, unless we wish to commit sacrilege against Demeter also, if we performed to her the ritual used there; for she is unwilling to allow any rites of that sort (?). As a proof that you will not be depriving Caesar of the glory of immortality, if you listen to me, I will tell you ...

While details do not complete the picture as we should like, this fragment seems to describe differences on certain rites of emperor-worship, perhaps as to what and where it should properly be observed. Presumably various sectors of the Empire performed their homage in different ways, based upon variant cultures and people, so that one should not seek to transport an indigenous rite to another and alien area. That the whole issue of cult-worship profoundly affected the political condition of both Jews and Christians we have already seen from several persecutions.

A lesser known vehicle than the sophist for encouraging public discourse was the literary group. By reading aloud the works of various scholars and the vanity productions of some of the emperors, a common practice in the ancient world, it fostered the study of literature and brought listeners together over an indeterminable period of time. We know of two such groups, one from Ptolemaic Egypt, the other from the Roman era. In the late third or early second century B.C. Aristophanes of Byzantium, the learned Librarian, embarrassed one poet reading his "original" work to several scholars at the Library. The Byzantian recognized it as plagiarized from an earlier scholar, produced the papyrus from the Library's holdings, compelling the interpreter to admit his deception. The poet was tried, convicted, and dismissed in shame. Because of his professional alertness, Aristophanes was elevated to the post of Director of the Library.[14]

[13] See also the commentary in *Archiv*, VII (1924), 226-27.

[14] Vitruvius, *De Architectura*, VII. Pref. 6 & 7 (London, 1931-34), trans. Frank Granger (Loeb).

Later under the Roman principate there appeared at Alexandria another courtly reading club which read aloud Claudius' writings on various topics. The group met in conjunction with the Museum or smaller library where scholars gathered, and was perhaps organized and perpetuated under pressure of the emperor who had acquired some thoroughness in Roman learning.[15] Whether, however, it grew out of the emperor's interest in history, gaming, or autobiography, all of which intrigued him, we do not know. But reading groups generally appealed to few scholars, as they do in any age.

THE BOULE

A question larger than mere names or small reading circles, is the secular oratory of ancient Alexandria, particularly when juxtaposed to that of Rome and Athens. Did the Delta city enjoy political speaking at any time from the founding of the city to the opening of the fifth century? We have already noticed in the preceding chapter the important political speech of Dion Chrysostom sometime during Trajan's reign, hence negating summary statements such as Matter's that panegyric oratory alone was tolerated,[16] but we do not encounter a quantity like that in Greece. To state it did not exist at all, however, as does Matter, leans too heavily on the argument *ex silentio* and thus claims too much. True, one discovers no political speaking as free, elevated, and copious as that of Demosthenes, Aeschines, or Cicero. But this hardly denies all political suasion.

Egyptologists have long debated whether or not Alexandria had a senate ($\beta o \upsilon \lambda \acute{\eta}$) prior to Emperor Severus' visit in A.D. 199-200 and his subsequent establishment of it.[17] Did it have a senate in

---

[15] W[illiam] W. Capes, *Roman History: The Early Empire* (New York, 1888), p. 87.

[16] "En effet, le gouvernement des Ptolémées, aussi absolu dans les nouvelles institutions qu'il fît que dans des usages anciennes qu'il conserva, ne toléra aucun genre d'éloquence politique, pas même le panégyrique des rois morts." Matter, *Histoire de L'École d'Alexandrie*, III, .79.

[17] Arguing for the probable existence of a senate in Ptolemaic Alexandria: Taubenschlag, *Law of Greco-Roman Egypt*, II, 13, Jouguet, "Vie Municipale," pp. 25-33 and 161-62, and Fraser, *Ptolemaic Alexandria*, I, 95. Those who believe we cannot know include, Bell, *Jews and Christians in Egypt*, pp. 8-10, and Jones, *Cities of the Eastern Roman Provinces*, pp. 304 and 471n, although both equivocate on the matter. Those opposing the idea of a senate include Edwin R. Bevan,

which political figures of the day could debate current issues and which students of rhetoric could attend to observe the rhetorical gladiators in combat? Scholarly opinion divides into three camps: yes, no, and we can't be certain. Briefly the affirmative arguments may be summarized as follows: Since Ptolemais had its own boule and ecclesia (ἐκκλησία) in the third century B.C., it is highly unlikely that Alexandria, the most important cultural outpost for Greek paideia, did not have one as well. Further, PSI 1160, while fragmentary, suggests Alexandria had a senate at the time of the city's capture in 30 B.C.,[18] and that the delegation mentioned in the papyrus is trying to forestall its threatened abolition by Octavius. Moreover, when the Alexandrian mission appears before Claudius in A.D. 41, it seems to ask for the re-instatement of what it had known centuries before, even though it does not openly request it.

The second group, disavowing the existence of the boule, contends that of the thousands of documentary papyri now discovered and published, if Alexandria had had a senate the fact would have come to light. Moreover, the mutinous nature of the residents made a power-wielding body incompatible with Greco-Roman government; they simply could not be trusted. Did not Dion, confidant of Vespasian and Trajan, and good friend of Nerva, tell them (Oration XXXII, "To the Alexandrians," 73-74) that their lack of self-control prevented the emperor's giving serious consideration to their important requests? Cautions about arguing *ex silentio* notwithstanding, one may conclude that at no time prior to A.D. 200 did the city have its own boule.

The third group, torn between the lack of specific evidence, yet wary of arguing from silence, admits its ignorance and declares that we simply do not know. Why do the papyri, inscriptions, and contemporary accounts make no mention of the matter, if Alexandria did in fact have one? Was the senate so emasculated that it accom-

---

House of Seleucus (London, 1902), I, 223 and 280 (although on p. 101 he is less certain), Max Radin, *Jews among the Greeks and Romans* (Philadelphia, 1915), p. 107, and Herbert A. Musurillo, *Acts of the Pagan Martyrs*, pp. 83 f. Bell, "Acts of the Alexandrians," *JJP*, IV (1950), 21, with the benefit of an additional quarter-century of reflection, combined with an open mind, moved from an earlier position of doubting the city's owning one to strongly suspecting it not only had one, but that one of the Ptolemies, perhaps Euergetes II (170-116 BC), abolished it.

[18] Bell, *Jews and Christians in Egypt*, pp. viii, and 8-9, Jouguet, "Vie Municipale," p. 349, and Scramuzza, *Emperor Claudius*, p. 70.

plished nothing significant, hence deserved no mention by anyone? Hardly, because even in the everyday accounts of activities we should encounter some word about it. Why have no private memoirs described or at least noted it in passing, since we can document the fact that some Alexandrians served in the Roman senate in the second century? The whole situation is baffling, and defies solution at this time.

Weighing all the arguments, we make three observations: (A) the Ptolemies recognized the explosive character of the people, but would not summarily have denied this thriving city a senate before it had a chance to prove itself; (B) the argument *ex silentio* must be used cautiously, especially when one recalls that excavators have discovered about as many papyri which editors have not yet published as those they have. Nearly every papyrus contains some kind of new information, and we may soon learn of this political body when more primary documents are published. And (C) P Oxy 2465, fragments of Satyrus' second century (B.C.) work on the demes of Alexandria, notes that Alexandria had a prytanis ($\pi\rho\acute{u}\tau\alpha\nu\iota\varsigma$). Since one of the prytanis' tasks in Athens and presumably in Alexandria as well, was to preside over the boule, we can infer the presence of an Alexandrian senate at least by the second century B.C. Moreover, Dion (Orat. XXXII) spoke of the $\delta\hat{\eta}\mu\sigma\varsigma$ and equates this body with the Alexandrians themselves (25). It had the power of a potentate and authority over a large number of people. The demes had certain police powers, their members owned land and held office, and could debate and pass bills in their meetings. In any event, Alexandria had some kind of democracy though it lacked the power of an Athenian boule. We conclude that in all likelihood the city did have a senate during Ptolemaic days, but that sometime prior to the Roman conquest, it was abolished probably because of the unpredictability of the citizens who made up its membership. That it had none for the first 200 years of the Empire we can be certain, for the emperor saw it not only as too risky to his program of *pax Romana*, but also he conceived of the city and chora as his own private domain. Moreover, Marc Antony compelled Alexandria to conduct its business without a senate and excluded all Egyptians (presumably including Alexandrian Greeks) from the Roman senate, though in the second century A.D. this restriction no longer held.[19]

[19] *Dio's Roman History*, LI. 17. 2, and Mason Hammond, "Composition of the Roman Senate, A.D. 68-235," *JRS*, XLVII (1957), 79n.

Why is the issue of a senate important to a study of rhetoric in Alexandria? What does it matter whether or not the citizens there achieved this political tool? It is important, first, for the same reasons that the congress and legislatures constitute essential elements in twentieth century America serving under a president and governors. While individuals make decisions in every republic and democracy, normally the popular representatives or the people themselves decide political matters based largely on deliberative discourse at one level or another. This was as true in the Greco-Roman world as in modern times, though the later Ptolemies were more subservient to Rome than, say, Soter or Philadelphus. But the issue of the existence of a senate is important, secondly, because the observation of model speeches formed an important link in the chain of education for young men in the gymnasium and rhetorical schools, as we shall see in a later chapter.[20] Students of Cicero's time and in the later rhetorical schools in Rome commonly visited the Roman senate to hear its members argue and expound on the issues of the day. If Alexandria had no such deliberative body, clearly other means would need to be substituted, for not until at least A.D. 202 could its students attend senatorial speaking.[21]

Granted the strong probability of a senate in the early Ptolemaic period and the certainty of it from the beginning of the third century, were Alexandrians sufficiently concerned about its importance to seek its re-instatement prior to Septimius Severus? The evidence shows that they were. Soon after Claudius assumed the purple, the city commissioned an embassy to approach him asking for the establishment of a boule. He refused to grant her one not only because he feared her inability to govern responsibly, but also for the reason that he wished to retain the city for his personal gain. P. Lond. 1912 (P. Brit. Mus. 2248) leads one to believe that if the city had a senate prior to the departure of its embassy to Rome, surely Claudius would have pointed it out, for it would have strengthened his case.[22] At the same time, if the ambassadors had done their homework and had known of a previous senate, would they not have mentioned it? Perhaps. But they may have wished to avoid

[20] See Chapter V.

[21] Jouguet, "Vie Municipale," pp. 345 f. and Larson, "Officials of Karanis," pp. 7 f.

[22] Musurillo, *Acts of the Pagan Martyrs*, pp. 1-3 and 83-88.

embarrassment at their recent political history and instability, and found it less awkward to avoid the past than to risk the possibility of imperial rebuff for their earlier conduct. Scramuzza argues, without excepting Alexandria, that "all Hellenistic cities were organized on the pattern of the old Greek cities with demes, tribes, a council and an assembly, these institutions being integrated with one another like the woof and web of a fabric."[23] If such was the case in the early decades of Alexandria, it clearly was not throughout, as we have already seen.

PSI 1160, found in Abusir-el-Meleq (costal Egypt), provides suggestive information on the city's attempt to persuade the emperor Claudius to revive its senate.[24] The document probably dates from 20-19 B.C., was written perhaps by the rhetorician-spokesman of the embassy, and handed to Augustus with a request for re-establishing the political body. Some scholars contend it strongly implies Alexandria had a boule prior to its subjugation by the Romans in 30 B.C., and that the delegation simply wished to forestall its abolition which in fact finally took place under Augustus. The fragment declares that the proposed senate could, among other things: (1) ascertain who should be enrolled in the ephebi, thus limiting the number of those exempted from paying taxes; (2) guard Alexandrians against extortion by tax-collectors; and (3) make certain that future embassies fell on the rich, so the city would not bear the expense of them.

Two documents reveal the result of the mission. P. Lond. 1912, the "Claudian Letter," indicates that the emperor denied their request. This papyrus of A.D. 41, a copy of the original, indicates that while the emperor was uncertain whether Alexandria had a senate under the Ptolemies, he does know that it has had none under the Empire.[25] Claudius must have replied to the embassy something to the effect that while Alexandrians argue they had a senate under former rulers, those times and all their arrangements are ended, done. New conditions and persons reign now in a new empire. Clearly, neither Augustus, Tiberius, nor Caligula allowed them to

[23] Scramuzza, *Emperor Claudius*, p. 70.

[24] See not only the original text in *Pubblicazioni della Società Italiana. Papiri Greci e Latini*, X (Florence, 1932), 95-101, but also the discussions in *CPJ*, II, 150, Musurillo, *Acts of the Pagan Martyrs*, pp. 1-3 and 83-84, James H. Oliver, "βουλή Papyrus," *Aegyptus*, XI (1931), 161-68, and *Archiv*, IX (1930), 253-56.

[25] This embassy will be considered in greater detail later in this chapter.

have a senate, so their request lacks precedent under the present system of government.[26] *Scriptores Historiae Augustae* strikes the same refrain: that the city had no public council in Roman times prior to Severus, (and adds) just as it had none under the Ptolemies (*sine publico consilio ita ut sub regibus ante vivebant*).[27]

Why did Severus finally reinstate the senate shortly after his visit in A.D. 199-200? Several factors, all largely selfish, account for it. First, previously miffed at the city of Antioch for its anti-Severian feelings,[28] the emperor wanted to create jealousy between the two literary centers and remove Antioch from the focus of the Mediterranean world. Two cities each with a senate would deprive either of uniqueness. Second, several other cities received the same privilege at that time, so that the Delta city was simply numbered among others. Thus, no particular love for Alexandria prompted the move. Third, a senate with a broad tax base (determined by citizenship, not simply residence) would more nearly guarantee the emperor his revenue, for well-to-do persons were required to serve in the senate with its membership becoming an hereditary obligation. Consequently, the senate could serve as a watchdog in matters of citizenship. Finally, the fact that Alexandrians had served in the Roman senate during previous decades[29] might have proved that some of them at least could take on the political responsibility of self-government. We have little grounds for believing that Severus' early interest in oratory—he declaimed as a young man—prompted his establishment of a senate as a rhetorical and public forum[30] any more than a twentieth century ruler would endow a chair of mathematics because he had studied arithmetic when a schoolboy. Emperors like Severus, Julian, and others—Hadrian excepted—easily forgot their earlier training when expediency dictated another policy.

With a senate the Alexandrians would assume a larger share of

---

[26] Thusly, J. Grafton Milne (*History of Egypt*, p. 284) sees the likely response of the emperor.

[27] *SHA*, "Septimius Severus," XVII. 2.

[28] Antioch had preferred Pescennius Niger, competitor to Severus, for the throne, as well as ridiculed Severus when he was stationed in the city (A.D. 179) in command of the Fourth Legion.

[29] Hammond, "Composition of the [Roman] Senate, A.D. 68-235," 79n; Jouguet, "Vie Municipale," pp. 345-46, Margaret E. Larson, "Officials of Karanis (27 B.C.-A.D. 337)," Ph.D Diss. (University of Michigan, 1954), pp. 7-9, and Arthur E.R. Boak, *History of Rome to 565 A.D.* (New York, 1922), p. 282.

[30] Statius, *Silvae*, IV, proem (London, 1928), trans. J[ohn] H. Mozley (Loeb).

self-government through its deliberations, though if they had wild hopes that it would follow the pattern of the earlier Athenian boule they were destined for serious disappointment. Political speaking since at least Isocrates and Aristotle had dealt with future events, on what should or should not be done in given situations. Should taxes be raised or the gymnasiarch be permitted to avoid the usual financial obligations falling on his office? Who should care for the housekeeping duties of the local temple, or be invited to address the city in the Theatre? Whom should the fathers commission to represent the city's grievances before the prefect or perhaps the emperor? How much money should be set aside for the annual games, and when should they be scheduled? These and similar topics concerned the deliberative (political) speaker. In treating such topics he would argue their expediency or inexpediency, values, justice or injustice, honor or dishonor for his listeners and society at large. Increased political autonomy did not greatly augment the Alexandrians' power, for jurisdiction and enforcement still lay in the hands of the prefect or his delegates.

The boule of Alexandria presumably was charged with administrative duties of the city such as devolved around the treasury or providing leaders for the city's highest posts. We know there must have been debates over such nominations, just as there were elsewhere in Egypt,[31] because civic leaders often did not wish the jobs thrust upon them due to resulting financial obligations. Unfortunately, speeches in the senate for whatever the case have not survived.

But from elsewhere in Egypt we know something of what other senates discussed from time to time, and can draw parallels for the Delta. All the evidence reveals that they were limited to municipal affairs, except for resolutions or special greetings to the emperor; hence they would minimally interfere with matters of the empire. They debated (1) whether or not one should be obliged to assume the duties of a civic leader;[32] (2) care of the local temple; (3) economic matters (as transportation of animals down river, perhaps to Alexandria);[33] (4) nomination of one to take charge of transportation

---

[31] E[efje] P. Wegener, "ἀρχαί and the Nomination to the ἀρχαί in the μητροπόλεις of Roman Egypt," Mnem., 4th ser., I (1948), 15-42, 115-32, and 297-326.

[32] Ibid., 15-17 and 115-117.

[33] P. Oxy. 1414.

of military supplies;[34] (5) arranging local festivities (as those sponsored by the gymnasium); (6) negotiating loans for the city; (7) maintaining the public baths;[35] (8) advancing funds from senatorial reserves; (9) appointing a spokesman to invite the local Roman military commander to a forthcoming festival; (10) urging someone to assume the office of the steward of the games; (11) nominations to the gymnasiarchy; (12) postponing the petition of local priests until a subsequent meeting; and (13) electing a substitute cosmetes (of the gymnasium) for a certain number of days.[36] Doubtless Alexandria's boule concerned itself with these and similar matters peculiar to its cosmopolitan atmosphere. All the topics, however, appear strictly local in nature[37] and on the surface at least, would not elicit the spirited and lofty debates such as we find on international policy in earlier Greece.

Arguments whether in the demos or boule must have centered around one's ability to handle the job, his administrative capacity, his oratorical and negotiating power, his financial resources, and the justice and mercy of a proposal, particularly when one did not desire a job like the gymnasiarchy which would drain him financially.

Some evidence has accumulated indicating certain legislative proceedings in Roman Egypt—whether in the boule or not, remains uncertain—were reported verbatim. Speed writing was devised sometime in Cicero's period and by the mid-first century A.D. at the latest senatorial proceedings of Latin deliberations were taken down by shorthand.[38] Some speeches were reported with "he said" ($\epsilon\hat{\iota}\pi\epsilon\nu$), suggesting partial verbatim accounts, while others constitute *oratio oblique*—all, however, brief in nature.[39] The account of one

---

[34] P. Oxy. 1415.

[35] P. Oxy. 1413 and 1416; and MacLennan, *Oxyrhynchus*, pp. 47-48. Some indication of discussions in the boule in several Egyptian towns can be found in Jouguet's chapter, "Réformes au début du IIIᵉ Siècle," in "Vie Municipale," pp. 334-98, though he neglects for the most part mention of Alexandria.

[36] B[ernhard] A. van Groningen, "Pap. Oxy. 1416 and the History of the Gymnasiarchy," *Acts du Vᵉ Congrès International de Papyrologie* [*1937*] (Brussels, 1938), p. 509.

[37] See P. Ryl. 77, P. Oxy. 2407, and PSI 1396 for illustrations of the strictly municipal concerns of the senates.

[38] Revel A. Coles, "Reports of Proceedings in Papyri," Pt. IV in *Papyrologica Bruxellensia* (Brussels, 1966), pp. 10-13.

[39] See P. Ryl. 77 and PSI 1396 as providing summary statements of what occurred.

late third century public body (σύλλογος) contains verbatim utterances of an advocate whose remarks are so enthusiastically received by the crowd as to drown him out.[40]

The procedure for the senate appears simple and straight-forward. The president (prytanis) called the body together at no regularly fixed hour. He took an active part in the debates, unlike his modern counterpart, and was responsible for appointing certain individuals to particular civic duties. Senators could read items into the record, much as Demosthenes did in *De Corona*, thus influencing the amount of memorization necessary for speaking.[41] The altercation must have become heated at times, for one fragment, P. Oxy. 1406, contains a rescript of Caracalla, A.D. 213-17, forbidding Oxyrhynchus senators' striking one another or using indecorous language toward the president or other members: "If a senator strikes or censures (in an unseemly manner) the (prytanis) or another senator, he shall be deprived of his rank and set in a position of dishonor."

In sum, we must content ourselves at this juncture to understanding how the senate came into being, what it was designed to do, and portions of what in fact it did, leaving to others at a later date when more information comes to light the task of profiling in greater detail its political oratory.

THE EMBASSIES

Another type of deliberative oratory, ambassadorial speaking, constituted an additional kind of secular discourse, and typically dealt with what should or should not be done in regard to local grievances or needs. Emperors made decisions by listening to speakers bring petitions from their constituencies. They did not rely on discussion with a cabinet-level group to the extent that modern rulers do, particularly when deciding matters relating to outlying regions of the Empire. Frequently, therefore, provinces and cities sent embassies to Rome or elsewhere to present their positions on important matters. Sophists, rhetoricians, and leading scholars made up the embassy's personnel, traveling to various parts of the Empire where the emperor might be visiting on particular occasions. The

---

[40] P. Oxy. 2407.
[41] P. Oxy. 1412, 1413, 1414, and 1415, and P. Erl. 23.

idea, then, of resident ambassadors at the royal court was unknown in the ancient world.

Many and varied occasions called Greek and Roman delegations to the imperial city. They included an emperor's inauguration ("assumption of the purple"), concluding peace treaties; mediating provincial differences; appealing for financial or military aid; presenting gifts for services rendered; delivering prisoners or demanding prisoners; and arranging for burial of the war-dead. The number of ambassadors on a particular mission ranged from three to ten, with a minimum age of fifty in some Hellenic communities, but forty for the Romans.[42] The emissary could never predict the reaction of the emperor to his speech and mission generally, though he could always presume that he would be placed on the defensive before he finished. Sometimes the ruler operated as both accuser and judge between disputing parties, as P. Lond. 1912 suggests.

The *Acta Alexandrinorum* concerns ambassadors and gymnasiarchs of the first to second centuries A.D. sufficiently sympathetic with the city's causes to speak and even to die for them, much as Christians and Jews died under persecution for their faith. The altercation between emperor and accused reached fever-pitch at times as each openly charged the other with partisanship, incompetence, or insolence. We are, however, hard pressed for satisfactory rhetorical data to draw any general conclusion on such official business other than to note that unlike rhetoricians and students in schools, as we shall see later,[43] these spokesmen were much bolder in their challenge of Roman authority. But the meagre remains which have survived provide too little data to grasp the speakers' theory of rhetoric. Musurillo has rightly said, "the various speeches in the *Acta* offer little enough scope for the student of ancient rhetoric; but one can sometimes detect the influence of the so-called 'progymnasmata' writers, e.g., Hermogenes and Theon ...."[44] Probably most speakers sought to conciliate and ingratiate—fawning before some emperors was common—in their opening remarks, but as the ruler challenged, interrupted, and levied counter arguments, organization would flounder, tempers would flare, and voice levels rise.

---

[42] Coleman Phillipson, *International Law and Custom of Ancient Greece and Rome* (London, 1911), I, 321-25.

[43] See Chapter V.

[44] Musurillo, *Acts of the Pagan Martyrs*, p. 249n.

This is precisely what happened, as far as we can tell, in a trial before a Roman emperor (probably Marcus Aurelius), as described in P. Oxy 33 and discussed more fully later.

Of the Alexandrian embassies of which we have record the most famous and perhaps most completely reported is that of Philo to Gaius Caligula in A.D. 38-39. Philo was born of distinguished Jewish parents in Alexandria where not only his parents commanded respect, but where his brother was an alabarch, the chief administrative officer of the Alexandrian Jews. Philo touched on rhetorical studies in his education, but devoted himself intensively to Greek philosophy. In his mature years he sought to combine his philosophic and religious interest to prove that the Mosaic teachings contained the highest philosophic truth. He wrote no rhetorical works, but quotations and passages in his "Concerning the Special Laws" indicate his probable knowledge of Cicero's *Pro Ligario* and Demosthenes' *Contra Aristocratem*, both of which he likely read in school.

Why would Philo, a Neoplatonist and scholarly recluse, represent his people before the emperor? His active public life—probably mostly in judicial capacities—and attempts to harmonize Mosaic Law with Hellenistic Law in Alexandria commanded local Jewish respect, so that Josephus surely expressed a majority opinion of the Jewish community when he called Philo famous (τὰ πάντα) on all accounts.[45]

What precipitated this *cause célèbre* and what resulted from it? The Philonic embassy grew out of the carnage (described in the previous chapter) in the reign of Caligula and the prefecture of Flaccus when Herod Agrippa visited there. The two Alexandrian groups, Greeks and Jews, most intimately involved sailed west to Rome to plead their cause before the emperor. Philo headed a delegation of five Jews while Apion was the chief spokesman for the three men of the Greeks.[46] After arrival in Rome and securing

---

[45] Cited in Edwin R. Goodenough, "Philo and Public Life," *JEA*, XII (1926), 77-79. See also Eusebius, *H.E.*, II, 4, 5, and 18, James Drummond, *Philo Judaeus* (London, 1888), I, 1, and Josephus, *Antiquities of the Jews* (New York, 1810), XVIII. 257 f, trans. William Whiston. For Philo's attention to the biblical literalists of various shades, see Montgomery J. Shroyer, "Alexandrian Jewish Literalists," *Journal of Biblical Literature*, LV (1936), 261-84.

[46] Josephus (*Antiquities*, XVIII. 257 f) says that Philo and Apion both headed groups of three each, but Philo specifically states in the *Legatione* (370) that his group totaled five—evidence which we should take in preference to Josephus'.

an audience with Gaius, Philo presented his case. His lengthy speech with its historical narrative reminds us of a speech by another Jew, Stephen (Acts vii), when the latter spoke in defense of himself some decades earlier in Jerusalem. Standing before the emperor, the Alexandrian began by describing Flaccus' prefecture over the Delta city the last six years. While he can praise the prefect, he does so, admittedly, only to portray his villainy in sharper relief (7). When imperial friends came to Flaccus offering to support him in a forthcoming governmental shakeup—the prefect was not on good terms with Gaius—if in turn he would close his eyes to their treatment of the Jews, he consented (21-24). The climax came when Herod Agrippa, enroute to a new imperial assignment in Judea, visited Alexandria. Greek jealousy ($\phi\theta\acute{o}\nu o\varsigma$), intense at a Jewish king parading in the streets, incited Flaccus to take action against the royal visit, precipitating the resulting pogrom. Alexandrians crowned one Carabas, a local moron, and paid him honors, mocking the Agrippa ceremony. They further ingratiated themselves with Gaius and infuriated the local Jews by setting up statues of the emperor in local synagogues.

Why did the prefect act thusly? Philo hedges, but sees anti-semitism at the roots. Later Flaccus abolished their citizenship ($\pi o\lambda\iota\tau\epsilon\acute{\iota}a$) in Alexandria thus removing Jewish guarantees to civil and criminal rights (53).[47] He also drove all Jews from other parts of the city

---

[47] Philo cannot mean that Jews had the same citizenship privileges as Greeks, but that they had some rights to keep and observe their own customs and traditions.

The question of Jewish citizenship does not properly fall within the scope of this work, but one must note the issue in passing. The evidence for the debate is less specific in Ptolemaic Egypt than in the Empire. Schürer (*History of the Jewish People*, 2nd ed. [New York, 1910?] II, ii, 271-72) declares that Alexander the Great conferred on the Jews equal rights with the Macedonians, as these same rights were granted to the Jews in many Greek towns. But such a statement does not quite make them citizens. Under the Principate Josephus (*Antiquities*, XII. viii. 1 ff) says they had equal rights ($\iota\sigma o\pi o\lambda\acute{\iota}\tau a\varsigma$) with the Macedonian citizens. This has been interpreted by Tcherikover and Fuks (*CPJ*, I, 63-64) as alleging that Alexandrian Jews were Greek citizens, although admittedly they had many civic privileges (Josephus, *Antiquities*, XIV. x. 1, Bell, "Anti-Semitism in Alexandria," *JRS*, XXXI [1941], 2, and Schürer, *Geschichte des Judischen Volkes*, III, 79). But it stretches the evidence and language too far to equate civic privileges with citizenship. Nor can we believe Josephus (*Antiquities*, XII. 121) that they were citizens under Vespasian and Titus ($\delta\acute{\iota}\kappa a\iota a\ \tau\grave{a}\ \tau\hat{\eta}\varsigma\ \pi o\lambda\iota\tau\epsilon\acute{\iota}a\varsigma\ \mu\eta\kappa\acute{\epsilon}\tau\iota$). He may be suggesting here, as in *Contra Apionem* (11. 38 ff), that they were "Alexandrians," because they lived there, and not because they owned equal political rights.

into a crowded ghetto, leaving Greeks to plunder and confiscate their property. Poverty broke out because of no opportunity to practice their trades.[48] The physical violence and suffering which followed (58-72) became so intense that the policy of conquering kings on a conquered people seems mild in comparison. Famine spread, and people were dragged through the streets, trampled under foot, stoned, clubbed, stabbed, burned, and crucified. Moreover, Flaccus had 38 members of the Jewish gerousia ($\gamma\epsilon\rho ov\sigma i\alpha$) publicly flogged in a manner suggesting they were the lowest type of trash, rather than with the kind of scourge ($\mu\acute{a}\sigma\tau\iota\xi$) their political status merited (72-80). The whole affair was a malicious plot ($\dot{\epsilon}\pi\iota\beta ov\lambda\dot{\eta}$ $\tau\hat{\eta}s$ $\dot{a}\pi o\tau o\mu i\alpha s$) of Flaccus (95). When the Jews (probably in their council of elders) passed a resolution praising Gaius, Flaccus rather than relaying their tribute to the emperor, pocketed it, thus implying Jewish hostility to the crown. The rest the emperor knows.[49]

The speech focused on two main points following the prooemium which contains ingratiating materials designed to win the emperor's good will:[50] Alexandrians had great expectations of Gaius' reign (8-13), were saddened at his illness (14-17), and rejoiced at his recovery (18-21). But having proceeded along these lines, Philo (a) depicts Gaius' true character (22-196) and (b) shows how it was revealed with his crowning insult by trying to introduce his statue into the Temple at Jerusalem (197-338).

Perhaps as Bell has suggested, part of Alexandria's anti-semitic problems stemmed from the Jews seeking full citizenship when Greeks felt Jewish separatism and peculiarities accounted in part for the city slipping from a first- to a second-class metropolis. It kept the city in constant ferment (*Jews and Christians in Egypt*, pp. 10-11). Further, P. Lond. 1912 strongly implies that Alexandrian Jews in the first century lacked full citizenship in the Empire: they could not participate in athletic events, and, as Claudius saw it, they lived in and could enjoy a foreign city ($\dot{\epsilon}v$ $\dot{a}\lambda\lambda o\tau\rho i\alpha$ $\pi\acute{o}\lambda\epsilon\iota$). Finally, following Caracalla's edict (212), Jews along with most other Gentiles received full citizenship, erasing the previous official discrimination. See also Scramuzza, *Emperor Claudius*, pp. 74 f., and BGU 1140.

[48] They normally occupied two of the five quarters (55), though probably sharing it with some of the lower-class Greeks or Egyptians living there. CPJ, I, 4.

[49] See the text in "In Flaccum," *Philo*, IX (London, 1941), trans. F[rancis] H. Colson (Loeb), the commentary by Ulrich Wilcken, "Alexandrinische Gesandtschaften vor Kaiser Claudius," *Hermes*, XXX (1895), 481-98, and additional observations by Bell, *Jews and Christians in Egypt*, pp. 25 and 28, CPJ, II, 153, and Musurillo, *Acts of the Pagan Martyrs*, pp. 18 ff.

[50] See the critical introduction by Colson (Loeb) for possible lacunae and what part the embassy had in the proposed *Palinode* of Philo.

Examples were common in deliberative oratory, but narration was not, yet Philo felt sketching the past could better show the emperor what should be done in the future. The first main point he proves by tracing in five steps the sacrilegious attempt, detailing suicides and murders which were either engineered by the emperor or committed by him (22-73). Moreover he has been hostile to the Jews when they had done nothing deserving it, as even his predecessors knew (115-61). The second mainpoint, the introduction of his statue into the Jerusalem Temple and demanding that it be venerated, Philo traces in six steps (200-334) from that of the Jammeians' first erection of it through Gaius' orders to Petronius, governor of Syria, to re-instate it, and finally to the emperor's ultimate acquiescence under the influence of Herod Agrippa not to place the statue in the Temple.

The epilogue is inadequate and relates the ambassador's attempt to seek a sympathetic hearing from the emperor and the latter's derisive reaction. It likely was appended later, for its content does not relate to the original speech. The embassy finally departed Rome with a sense of hopelessness for the cause (349-67).

When we try determine Philo's rhetorical indebtedness for both the content and the organization of the speech we proceed along uncertain lines. Several theorists of the ancient world prescribed the kind of procedure Philo echoed. Aristotle (*Rhetoric*, 1377^{b}1ff) suggested virtue, wisdom, and good will which the speaker would want to exude, while the *Rhetorica ad Alexandrum* (1426^{b}23ff) indicates that for a vituperative ceremonial speech the speaker should recite the errors and offenses committed, and show that the accused's actions are dishonest and detrimental to the mass of citizens. Moreover, one should distinguish offenses whose punishment is fixed by law from those decided by juries. In the former, as before an emperor, one must simply prove the act was committed.

All these things, of course, Philo does. And so we should expect of him.

When, however, we look more closely at the structure we see that while the *Legatione* is similar to the treatise to Alexander (1436^{a}34ff) with its conciliatory introduction and narration, it is less akin to its suggestions for a forensic speech (1441^{b}33ff). The conclusion is that probably neither Aristotle nor the *ad Alexandrum* influenced Philo in his preparation or delivery of this oration—at least not directly.

A better case can be made for his indebtedness to Isocrates, though the speaker was probably not aware of it. Analysis of the plea shows that it more nearly follows Isocratean divisions of the judical speech—proemium, narration, proof, and epilogue[51]—than any other available systematic theory. Moreover, since Isocrates did not clearly distinguish the three kinds of oratory which Aristotle later delineated, and since Philo here treats a forensic speech on a deliberative occasion, we have further evidence for this influence. Finally, we have some papyrological confirmation of Isocrates before Philo's time,[52] and even more during the first and second centuries, giving the speaker access to earlier Greek thought. We can then better credit the ancient Greek teacher's ideas filtering down to the first century than we can any other source.

We have evidence elsewhere for this same embassy of Philo's, a papyrus which sheds a little more light surrounding the personalities involved. P. Oxy. 1089, a third century copy of a first century event, records certain events of the prefecture of L. Avillius Flaccus, the subject of Philo's mission, but does not clarify all details. Philo relates that Isidorus, surely the gymnasiarch of Alexandria and once the confidant of Flaccus, later became estranged from the ruler, and thereupon the piqued Isidorus stirred up the rabble against Flaccus at the Gymnasium. Some demonstrators were arrested, confessed, and fled,[53] as did the rabble rouser (ἄνθρωπος ὀχλικός) Isidorus who was implicated through the confession of one of the rioters. He was later caught and condemned to death, an event still remembered in the reign of Commodus (180-92), nearly a century and a half later.[54]

Naturally, Josephus had little regard for Philo's Gentile opponent, Apion, rightly accusing him of turning his back on his countrymen from Upper Egypt by posing as an Alexandrian and in fact becoming

---

[51] Kennedy, *Art of Persuasion in Greece*, p. 72.

[52] P. Hib. 229.

[53] The papyrus which resembles the *Acts of the Pagan Martyrs* indicates that Isidorus met Flaccus in the Serapeum temple. They talked, but we do not know the tenor of their conversation. The motive for the Greek hostility to Rome is more anti-Rome than anti-semitic; that is, the Alexandrian Greeks if they were anti-semitic were so at least in part because the Jews were so pro-Rome. See a cautious analysis in Musurillo, *Acts of the Pagan Martyrs*, pp. 96-97.

[54] Philo, "In Flaccum," 135 ff, Tcherikover and Fuks, *CPJ*, II, 156, and *PW*, "Isidoros" (8).

a citizen.[55] That Apion misrepresented the Jews when he told Gaius that they neglected honors due the emperor by refusing to erect statues in his honor is both true and false. Obviously no practicing Jew could have permitted such statuary in his house of worship, so in this sense the Jews could be accused of eroding the emperor's respect. Jews and Christians, as earlier noted, frequently locked horns with Rome not because they worshipped Yahweh but because they would not also tolerate other gods in their religious schemes. On the other hand, Alexandrian Jews for the first 200 years of the Empire were largely on good terms with Rome, seeing the imperial capital as their only protector when all else failed, and the emperor knew this. Apion clearly wished to present the Jewish case in the worst possible light.

Following the embassy Philo returned and spent the rest of his days in Alexandria in various public and philosophic capacities, while Apion, perhaps after reporting to the Alexandrian Greeks, returned to Rome where he lived during most of the remainder of his life teaching as a grammarian. Like some other teachers of his day, he appears to have been a vain man, for Tiberius earlier had called him a cymbal of the world (*cymbalum mundi*) because he boorishly liked to call attention to himself.[56]

Lesser embassies can be quickly mentioned. One first century delegation journeyed to Rome perhaps for the purpose of requesting Augustus to grant Alexandria a senate. P. Oxy. 2435, highlighting it, notes two speakers, Alexander and Timoxenus. The first appears to conciliate the audience, while the second makes some sort of request. But the papyrus breaks off before we learn much of either rhetorical effort. BGU 511, written about A.D. 200 but depicting a first century embassy to Claudius, contains part of the emperor's oration and notes the protocol of negotiations of the Jewish and anti-Jewish embassies. The document may well relate to the same embassy depicted in P. Lond. 1912.[57]

---

[55] Josephus, *Contra Apionem*, II, 29, 30, and 32. Whether Apion was born in Upper Egypt (ὀάσειτῆς Αἰγύπτου) or came from Lower Egypt (βαθυτάτῳ τῆς Αἰγύπτου), both of which Josephus asserts, we can be certain he was not a native Alexandrian, as he sorely wished to be, and in fact later became. Such social climbing would certainly cause ill-feeling with those not so successful.

[56] *PW*, "Apion" (3).

[57] See also the commentary in Wilcken, "Alexandrinische Gesandtschaften vor Kaiser Claudius," 481-98.

Sometime during the reign of Trajan embassies from both Jewish and Greek elements of Alexandria again journeyed to Rome to present their case this time on an unknown issue. According to P. Oxy. 1242, our source for this second century occasion, distinguished individuals composed the Greek delegation including two gymnasiarchs, one gymnasiarch-elect, a distinguished ex-official, and one Paul, the advocate-spokesman who volunteered his services. The Jewish mission was made up of seven members, the number perhaps having a mystical significance, whose spokesman was one Sopater born in Antioch. The delegations, we are surprisingly told, carried with them "their own gods" (τοὺς ἰδίους θεούς). This must mean some religious symbols in the case of the Jews who would hardly have transported any idols or tangible images. But we know from elsewhere in the document that the Greeks had brought a bust of Serapis. Trajan gave the Jews a warm greeting, but, influenced by the empress who favored the Jewish position, he scorned the Greek commission. The debate became so heated and the atmosphere so charged with emotion when the Alexandrian Greek speaker accused the emperor of Jewish bias that sweat broke out on the image of Serapis carried by the Alexandrians (ἡ τοῦ Σαράπιδος προτομὴ ἣν ἐβάσταζον οἱ πρεσβεῖς αἰφνίδιον ἵδρωσεν), a phenomenon which amazed even the emperor. While the account does not reveal the outcome of the embassy, it does prove, as we have seen elsewhere, that some advocates spoke boldly to the reigning monarch, well aware of the penalty it might carry.

Thus taken together, the rhetoric of the boule, the itinerant sophists, and the embassies to the emperor constitute a substantial portion of the secular speaking for Greco-Roman Alexandria.[58] While the papyrological accounts always break off before we learn all we should desire of either the substance or the rhetorical theory, they do reveal that speakers sometimes heatedly debated municipal issues in the senate, fearlessly attacked the puerile and unrestrained conduct of the people, and ingratiated or insulted the emperor to his face. Such acts demanded no small quantity of fortitude. Moreover, some speakers like Philo came to their task well prepared with an abundance

---

[58] I am omitting here E[mile] Egger's interesting discussion of another oratorical fragment because of uncertainty if it deals with Alexandria in particular or Egypt generally. It may be found in his "Observations sur un Fragment Oratoire en Langue Grecque," *Revue Archéologique*, VI (1862), 139-52.

of information and narrative ability. Unfortunately, we cannot assay the effect of the major portion of such oratory on either imperial or common audiences.

Alexandria seems to have been only modestly influenced if at all by the extant theories of rhetoric, as we shall see later. Aristotle had set forth in his *Rhetoric* (1358ª1ff) the three genera of speeches, deliberative, ceremonial, and forensic, yet while one finds ample evidence for the first and third types, he sees little of the second (Dion's Oration XXXII excepted) and no funeral orations at all. This species had formed an integral part of Greek culture at least since the time of Pericles, and undoubtedly long before, but there is no indication of any given in Alexandria. One papyrus of a *Laudatio Funebris* (P. Colon. inv. 4701) given by Caesar Augustus at Rome on the death of Marcus Agrippa has come to light, and is a translation from the Latin (itself the product of Augustus) into Greek for the koine-speaking Alexandrians, but no such panegyric for Alexandrian ears has been found.[59] We may assume, however, that orators did praise the dead not only because of the long-standing practice, but also because Christians saw death as a triumphant entry into eternity.

THE COURT ROOM

The final area to concern us here, the courtroom, provides as many obstacles to investigation as does that of the political arena.[60] For again we have knowledge of certain acts and edicts, as well as actual pleadings, but as always the spoken word is treated so sketchily as to leave many lacunae in the documents.

Under Ptolemy II (Philadelphus) and later under the Roman

---

[59] For an extended treatment of this document see L[udwig] Koenen's "Die 'Laudatio Funebris' des Augustus für Agrippa auf einem neuen Papyrus," *Zeitschrift für Papyrologie und Epigraphik*, V (1970), 217-83, and additional commentary by E.W. Gray, "Imperium of M. Agrippa," *ibid.*, VI (1970), 227-38 and Koenen, "*Summum Fastigum ...*," *ibid.*, VI (1970), 239-43.

[60] For the discussion of Alexandrian law and particularly its legal pleading I have supplemented my own research with a helpful doctoral dissertation by Herwald Schmidt, "Der Einfluss der Rhetorik auf das Recht der Papyri Äegypten" (Universität Erlangen, 1949). Schmidt argues that (1) rhetoric exercised a strong influence on law not only in the pre-classic and Byzantine periods, but continuously throughout the Greco-Roman period, and (2) it served as the fountain of law in Roman Egypt.

Empire Alexandria had its own autonomous law courts where plaintiff or defendant, Greek or Egyptian, had the right to use his mother tongue and to employ interpreters when needed.[61] In the third century A.D. special tribunals were set up to judge disputes between Greeks and Egyptians, taking into account both Greek and local Egyptian law. Jews not only had their own courts based on the Mosaic law, but could, when the need arose, go before the Greek courts where Ptolemaic advocates, paid by state-regulated fees, pleaded cases on behalf of clients.[62]

As was true in the West, so it appears in the East: Hellenism introduced into Alexandrian legal practice the art of forensic discourse with all the attendant abuses of oratorical display. Egypt seems to have had no experience with lawyers until the arrival of the Greeks who brought with them their long history of law and pleading. Advocates were often not skilled in the law, and thus were forced to consult with those who were. In classical Athens the synegoros (συνήγορος) chiefly praised the character of his client, taking little part in the case itself. When, however, in Hellenistic Egypt he spoke more to the issues involved, he was obliged to learn more law.[63] For a while the courts did not limit the number of advocates a client might use in a single case, but in time this license got so out of hand that restrictions later were placed on them.[64] The number of legal counsel on the prosecution's side often exceeded those on the defense not only because the Empire stressed prosecution of the law, particularly in tax cases, but also because many criminal cases involved high treason (*crimen majestatis*) and persons of the aristocracy—conditions which discouraged defense counsel, as the emperor could take umbrage at too vigorous efforts in defense.[65]

Egypt, and surely Alexandria, saw three kinds of lawyers in its legal system. The first two, the syndicus (σύνδικος) and ekdicus

---

[61] Taubenschlag, *Law of Greco-Roman Egypt*, II, 35-36, and Tcherikover and Fuks, *CPJ*, I, 33.

[62] Taubenschlag, *Law of Greco-Roman Egypt*, I, 387.

[63] Schmidt, "Einfluss," pp. 8-9 and 30.

[64] Anton-Hermann Chroust, "Legal Profession in Ancient Republican Rome," *Notre Dame Lawyer*, XXX (1954), 119-20. P. Strass. 41 and P. Tebt. 287 indicate at least two lawyers for the plaintiffs.

[65] E. Patrick Parks, "Roman Rhetorical Schools as a Preparation for the Courts under the Early Empire," *Johns Hopkins University Studies in Historical and Political Science*, LXIII (1945), 38-54. See the whole of Parks' study for the place of legal pleading in the Western Empire.

(ἔκδικος), corresponded to the *defensor civitatis* elsewhere in the Empire and developed much the way their Latin counterparts did in the West. The former officially represented the town in its external dealings with the imperial government, and internally in the city's dealings with private individuals. The ekdicus was retained by private people and, among other duties, served as legal advisor to the city in fourth century Egypt. We do not know when either appeared, but they were very active in the era of Constantine and Julian.[66] The third, the synegoros (συνήγορος), was more a character-speaker than a lawyer, often represented the plaintiffs, and sometimes so identified (μετά) with his client as to speak as if he were the party at bar, rather than simply appearing on behalf of (ὑπέρ) his client.[67]

Trials were open to the public, with both accuser and defendant normally present in Roman Alexandria, though in Ptolemaic Egypt they ofttimes absented themselves.[68] Proceedings began with the accuser making the opening remarks, charging the defendant with the act, and sometimes seeking to discredit opposing counsel. The defendant followed and tried to abjure or soften the accusation,[69] and probably did so in part by praising his client's patriotism and love of people. Name-calling was part of the game in the West, found its place even in litigation before the emperor,[70] and must have been even more so in the flamboyant atmosphere of Alexandria. While there was a significant degree of freedom in the courts, the Roman advocate could not say everything on his mind, as Tacitus reminds us.[71] But this limitation was designed to curb excessive *ad hominem* attacks more than to restrict legitimate argument.

Court procedure for the first three centuries of the Empire was based on a formulaic system not greatly unlike twentieth century American law, but it may have applied only to Roman citizens. Evidence is inconclusive at this point. After preliminary hearings determined if evidence was sufficient to warrant litigation, the case

---

[66] B[rinley] R. Rees, "Defensor Civitatis in Egypt," *JJP*, VI (1952), 80-81 and 87, and Ludwig Mitteis and Ulrich Wilcken, *Grundzüge und Chrestomathie der Papyruskunde* (Leipzig-Berlin, 1912), II, Pt. 1, 31.

[67] Schmidt, "Einfluss," pp. 11 and 28.

[68] P. Mich. 365 of the late second century shows that parties were not always present in the imperial courts.

[69] Sherman, *Roman Law*, II, 487-91.

[70] See P. Oxy. 33.

[71] *Dialogus de Oratoribus*, 38.

went to trial before the court-referee (*judex*) who was bound by a formula composed normally of four parts: *demonstratio* setting forth the statement of facts, and cause of action; the *intentio* containing the plaintiff's claim, and the *exceptiones* (arguments) of the defense; and finally, the *condemnatio* empowering the judex to condemn or acquit. Occasionally the procedure included a subsequent *adjudicatio* investing the judex with the power to make ad hoc decisions, as in partitioning property held in common by two or more persons,[72] but its implementation was sporadic. Later changes in Diocletian's reign abolished the centuries-old practice of dividing the task between the magistrate (praetor) and judex, henceforth permitting the magistrate to handle all matters, but the basic system continued throughout the Empire until the Turkish conquest in the fifteenth century. Under such a routine, the defendant could argue his own case, hire a member of the bar to represent him, or in the event of indigent litigants, the court could assign a lawyer to the action.[73]

In all the quackery and superficiality of the inhabitants with their love for the poetic arts and showmanship one would expect to find hired claques for orators and entertainers of the sort Pliny described in Rome, but the evidence is silent on the matter. Students in the sophistic schools used them (as we shall see in a later chapter), but Alexandrian lawyers were not so vain, so far as we know. Probably the Alexandrian mentality and disposition made such expenditures of funds unnecessary in the courts and political arena, for the residents were naturally endowed, and willingly encouraged display without the need of money to prompt them. At times, the situation got out of hand and the people became so intoxicated with merriment that Dion said (Orat. XXXII) that if one passed a courtroom he could not determine whether a trial or drinking party was in progress (οὐκ ἂν γνοίη ῥᾳδίως πότερον ἔνδον πίνουσιν ἢ δικάζονται, 68). P. Lond. 2565 shows something of rhetorical flourishes in a third century A.D. prefect's court in Memphis as three villagers seek relief from serving as cosmetes, not unlike that style found in some sophistic rhetoric.

---

[72] Sherman, *Roman Law*, II, 401-03. Perhaps future research will prove that the description noted here applies only to Roman law under the *ius civile*. If so, as Professor Eric Turner has pointed out to me, Alexandrians and others in Egypt would not have been subject to it.

[73] *Ibid.*, 406-11.

There was available however to *advocati* in the West (at least by Nero's time) another kind of applause devised by the residents. It consisted of rubbing tiles or sherds together to effect a particular sound variously described as bees (*bombi*), roof-tiles (*imbrices*), and bricks (*testae*). But we find no mention of this device in Alexandria either in the courtrooms, churches, or popular discourse.[74]

Legal training for Jewish immigrants included rhetoric and logic in addition to Mosaic and Greek law, but for the most part the works they used remain a mystery. We know of the availability of Aristotle's *Rhetoric*, the *Rhetorica ad Alexandrum*, and certain Isocratean works, but whether these were used in the law schools one cannot say. Judges were to be on guard against specious arguments of advocates,[75] as the ancient theorists clearly warned. The rhetorical, logical, and legal study of Greek institutions likely held for Gentiles as well, though how they were handled in legal education has yet to be learned fully. Surely they studied Draconian laws and their later revision by Solon, procedures of public and private suits ($\gamma\rho\alpha\phi\acute{\eta}$ ... $\delta\acute{\iota}\kappa\eta$)—we have evidence of this sort of litigation in the papyri—as well as particular cases which came to bar. Later under the Empire the XII Tables, that collection of principal rules of ancient Roman law which form the basis of Roman Civil jurisprudence, would have found its way into the student's preparation. Some used the $\delta\iota\kappa\alpha\iota\acute{\omega}\mu\alpha\tau\alpha$, the most informative text of Alexandrian civil law of Ptolemaic times, as we find in P. Hal. 1, which provided legal maxims and instructions for the lawyers[76] while others, like the synegoroi of Ptolemaic Egypt, would not have encumbered their speaking with such matters, wishing greater freedom in the development of their lines of thought. Native Egyptian lawyers who presided over special Ptolemaic tribunals would be expected

---

[74] Suetonius, *Lives of the Caesars*, "Nero," XX. 3 (London, 1914), trans. J[ohn] C. Rolfe (Loeb).

[75] Erwin R. Goodenough, *Jurisprudence of the Jewish Courts in Egypt* (New Haven, 1929), pp. 251-52. Sherman (*Roman Law*, I, 148) appears not to have understood the importance of rhetorical training for the Roman Lawyer, for he omits any mention of it when outlining the five-year course of study for the law school student.

[76] See a full account of this in *DIKAIOMATA: Auszüge aus Alexandrinischen Gesetzen und Verordnungen in einem Papyrus des Philologischen Seminars der Universität Halle* (Berlin, 1913) (no author), and discussed in Schmidt, "Einfluss," pp. 11f.

to understand both Greek and local Egyptian law,[77] but in time these judges were replaced by Greeks more conversant with Greek and Roman legal practice.

The lawyers' role varied from Ptolemaic to Roman Egypt. In the former times counsel often identified closely with their clients, speaking as if they themselves were called to the bar to answer accusations. This in part stemmed from the fact that the parties involved often did not appear in court when summoned or when suing. In Roman times, however, when litigants more commonly accompanied their counsel into the courtroom, lawyers frequently spoke on behalf of (ὑπέρ) their clients, as we learn from P. Tebt. 287 and P. Oxy 237, rather than in place (μετά) of them. P. Oxy 2340, containing the record of a hearing in A.D. 192, shows an advocate picturing his client as a much abused foreman in a textile shop who cannot afford to participate in the liturgy of an assistant strategus in Alexandria. Always in Alexandria, though, as in Athens, Rome, and elsewhere, the nature of judicial oratory was such that it concerned itself with the past, as Aristotle had earlier set forth.[78]

We can discover certain characteristics of legal pleading by examining several cases in Greco-Roman Egypt with the understanding that what occurred in the chora likely did in Alexandria as well.

The "Hermias Case" of the second century B.C.,[79] is important as a legal document from Upper Egypt not only because of the rather full account it provides of one hearing, but because of the insights one can get of the advocates. Hermias, the plaintiff represented by Philocles, alleges that he has been deprived by the defendants (represented by Deinon) of a house occupied by one Horos. The papyrus sketches the minutes of the action, but does not tell us precisely what the legal issues were. Deinon's speech, more fully reported than Philocles',[80] is well-reasoned and systematic. It follows four or five divisions of a speech we would expect to find in either a Greek or Roman oration,[81] suggesting rhetorical training based

---

[77] Tarn, *Hellenistic Civilisation*, 2nd ed., pp. 71-72.

[78] For his description of the three kinds of oratory—deliberative, judicial, and epideictic—see the *Rhetoric*, 1358b.

[79] Pap. 161/162 is discussed by Ulrich Wilcken (*Papyri aus Oberägypten*, I Berlin/Leipzig, 1935) and Schmidt, "Einfluss," pp. 14ff.

[80] Whether from the bias of the court reporter or the presiding judge who may have dictated the account, we do not know.

[81] Greeks: exordium (προοίμιον), statement of the case (πρόθεσις), proof (πίστις), and conclusion (ἐπίλογος)—so Aristotle, *Rhetoric*, 1414b5ff. But the *Rhetorica*

on earlier principles, but we have no way of discovering where in fact he learned his theory. He denounces the empty claims of Hermias and, by *ad hominem* arguments, accuses Hermias of injuring (black-mailing) the defendants who earlier bought the house. His introduction of a bill of sale which serves as evidence for much of his plea, and the use of documents to prove that the parents of the defendants had earlier agreed on the purchase are themselves prima facie evidence. But even without these tangible proofs, the clemency edict of Ptolemy Euergetes II of 145/144 B.C., he contends, would give the defendants the homestead. On the other hand, Philocles and his client, Hermias, produce no proof he has ever lived in the house, and have no documentary evidence to substantiate his prior ownership of it. In the end the judge decides for the defendants, since Hermias has only empty charges, and no proof (τεκμήριον), as pointed out by Deinon.

Two years later Hermias tried his luck again, using the same counsel. Philocles' plea, this one superior to his earlier effort, contained more carefully reasoned arguments than before as well as documentary proof which he read into the record. This time he has thoroughly researched the law and included evidence from a wide variety of sources, as well as maxims of the former trial two years earlier. Deinon, again counsel for the defendants, refutes the "empty accusations" of Philocles, denies his stock maxims, and points out that neither Hermias nor his father had lived in the required area to get squatters' rights to the house. Deinon's arguments have a powerful effect on the presiding judge who again decides in his favor.

But other facts we also know about legal pleading. P. Amh. 33 of the same period as the Hermias Case reveals that in early Ptolemaic Egypt lawyers were deemed untrustworthy, particularly in tax cases since the state's financial concerns were of highest importance. The emperor feared the agility of and the retaining fee for the synegoros would deprive the state of needed tax revenue, and so in tax cases lawyers could not appear. This papyrus depicts five farmers of the mid-second century who complain that the komarch, the village head, has hired a professional pleader to defend him against charges

---

ad Alexandrum (1443ᵇ25ff) does not closely approach this format for the defense. The Romans structured such speeches with *prooemium, narratio, probatio, refutatio*—Aristotle combined the proofs and refutation—and *peroratio*, or so Quintilian conceived of most of the writers prior to his time (*Institutes*, III.ix.1).

of fiscal irregularities. Yet, contend the plaintiffs, by imperial decree such suits permit no hired advocates because earlier experience has shown that they proved unsatisfactory (to the state). Presumably the lawyer did not participate.[82] Indeed, to have done so would have meant disbarment and confiscation of his property. In Roman times however no such injunction held against lawyers in tax cases.

Several second/third century A.D. documents deserve attention for light they too shed on forensic oratory. In the first, P. Oxy. 2464,[83] another inheritance claim whose setting takes place in an Attic courtroom sometime after 402 B.C., shows the speaker's opponent as one Demeas, perhaps an adopted son, who earlier served as the speaker's guardian. The plaintiff, an heiress come of age, sues for the return of her property, alleging that Demeas, who argues the suit is inadmissible, has misappropriated the estate. We do not know the outcome of the case, but it is important because it may be a lost one by Hyperides, "On Behalf of Demeas" ($\pi\rho\grave{o}s\ \delta\eta\mu\acute{e}a\nu$), cited by Pollus[84] and Harpocration's *Lexicon*.[85] If so, it would suggest not only that it was sufficiently worthy of preservation and possible use in legal training (formally or informally), but more significantly, it augments Hyperides' corpus, for the speech hitherto has been known only by secondary sources.

P. Oxy. 471 contains an excerpt of an advocate's violent speech accusing one Maximus, probably the high government official Vibius Maximus (Prefect, 103-07), of unnatural sexual relations with a seventeen year-old boy.[86] The prosecution details how witnesses saw (in Oxyrhynchus?) the

---

[82] The same distrust for lawyers in such cases obtained also in Athens. Cf. George A. Kennedy, "Rhetoric of Advocacy in Greece and Rome," *AJP*, LXXXIX (1968), 421.

We shall here pass over P. Giss. 46 and P. Hamb. 145 of the first and second centuries of the Empire because each is too meagre and uncertain to gain much information for legal pleading.

[83] See a brief review of it in Hugh Lloyd-Jones, "Oxyrhynchus Papyri, Part 27. Edited by E.G. Turner, John Rae, L. Koenen, and José Maria Fernandez Pomar. London, 1962," *Gnomom*, XXXV (1963), 450-53.

[84] *Iulii Pollucis Onomasticon*, X. 15, ed. G. Dindorf (Leipzig, 1824).

[85] See the *Lexicon*, "*ΛΟΥΣΙΕΥΣ*."

[86] It should be recalled that one function of the pedagogue in Greek education was to protect the lad from sexual deviates, including teachers. On the problem of homosexuality in ancient education see Henri-Irénée Marrou, "De la Pédérastie Comme Éducation," Chapter 3 in his *Histoire de L'Éducation dans L'Antiquité*, 4th ed., pp. 55-67.

shameless look and shameless goings to and fro of the lovers ... For when once accustomed to his shame this handsome and rich youth gave himself airs and became so impudent that he sported with and clasped hands of ... the chamberlain in the presence of everyone ... This still beardless ... and handsome youth you kept all day in the praetorium and did not send him any longer to the schools and the exercises proper for the young ... You travel about the whole of Egypt with the youth. [Indeed], did not a boy of seventeen years accompany you to the judgement-seat in the public court?

What if any defense the official made is not clear, but we see a lawyer fearless in his denunciation of ranking politicians.

Another fragment of an advocate's speech (P. Oxy. 472) given about A.D. 130 shows the anonymous defense counsel arguing that his client, a woman, is not guilty as charged of attempted homicide (poisoning), but, turning the tables, the plaintiff is guilty of self-inflicted poison. The plaintiff leveled no complaint, counsel contends, when he came from the defendant's house, whereas when he emerged from that of his own son and heir he complained of it. "He had indeed reasons for administering poison to himself which many others have had, preferring death to life; for he was ruined by creditors and at his wit's end; but if anyone really plotted against him, his son is the most likely person."[87] Again, the outcome of the trial is uncertain.

P. Athen. 58 reads like a second century Greek advocate's speech against official charges. The terms of "excellent prefect" and "blameless guards" suggest flattery, while the whole of the contents may relate to the Hadrianic troubles of A.D. 119-20 when the emperor summoned Jewish and Greek delegations from Alexandria to Rome. But we cannot be certain.[88]

Litigation of the late second century is further depicted in a third century fragment, P. Oxy. 33, which covers part of the trial of an Alexandrian gymnasiarch, one Appian, standing before the emperor in Rome for an unknown crime. The defendant is represented by

---

[87] See P. Oxy. 486 which may deal with the same dispute.

[88] I here pass over PSI 1222 from Oxyrhynchus of the second/third century which notes a defense lawyer named Didymus arguing his client's case on an unknown offense. It seems to be an actual speech and not one designed for classroom purposes, but its nature and a host of other questions do not provide us with enough information to merit further consideration. Cf. Deborah H. Samuel, "Rhetorical Papyrus in the Yale Collection," Ph.D Diss. (Yale, 1964), p. 152.

counsel who, rather than pleading on Appian's behalf, urges him to die like a true patriot! Appian, not content with such heroism, violently and abusively scores the ruler and then exits to his doom. The emperor, probably Marcus Aurelius, fuming at such insolence, recalls Appian and asks him to show greater respect hereafter when he speaks to him. Does Appian know to whom he is speaking? "Yes," replies the prisoner, "to a tyrant" ($\tau\acute{\nu}\rho\alpha\nu\nu\sigma$)! "No!" retorts the emperor, to "a king" ($\beta\alpha\sigma\iota\lambda\acute{\epsilon}\alpha$)! Appian continues his scornful diatribe, and is ordered out for his execution. In the streets, hoping to arouse the people, he cries out that he is of noble birth and a gymnasiarch ($\epsilon\dot{\nu}\gamma\epsilon\nu\eta\varsigma$ $\kappa\alpha\grave{\iota}$ $\gamma\nu\mu\nu\alpha\sigma\acute{\iota}\alpha\rho\chi\sigma\varsigma$), and thereby nearly incites a riot. The military escort hurries back to the emperor to report the explosive situation, and the ruler again recalls the prisoner who renews his jibes, but later calms down. But the papyrus breaks off before the outcome becomes clear.[89] This speech situation resembles the *Acta Alexandrinorum* and shows character attacks fully in keeping with what we know of Alexandrians over an extended period of time.

In the third century two court documents lend further insight into vibrant legal pleading. P. Lond. 2565 shows a flourishing court system of the prefect in Egypt about the time of Decius. The speeches it includes are short and stacatto, perhaps derived from shorthand notes. Three villagers have been nominated by the senate to the office of prytany but do not want it, perhaps because of its financial obligations. On appeal they finally argue the case before the prefect who seems to take an active part in the proceedings. Aside from noting, however, that one of the senate's counsel cannot answer some of the plaintiff's arguments and so resorts to *ad misericordiam*, the text does not permit any extended reconstruction of the drift or force of the arguments.[90] The second fragment, P. Oxy. 2690, reveals a harsh rebuke of a political/legal official—whether of the emperor, such as those found in the *Acta Alexandrinorum*, or a judge (perhaps a Roman prefect in Egypt) is unclear. But in either case friendship has been confused with justice, and the speaker demands that when one sits in the judge's seat he must forget any friendships with the litigants so as not to compromise the judical process. The attack

---

[89] See also a commentary on the document in Musurillo, *Acts of the Pagan Martyrs*, pp. 65-70 and 207-11.

[90] For plate, text, translation, and commentary see T.C. Skeat and E[efje] P. Wegener, "Trial before the Prefect of Egypt Apius Sabinus," *JEA*, XXI (1935), 224-47.

at the top level of government is a significant bit of information on legal pleading.

Names of *advocati* in Alexandria are exceedingly difficult to come by during the 700 years here under discussion, though several in Egypt at large are known. One, probably from Alexandria, was Lampon the former gymnasiarch who appeared before Claudius in A.D. 41 on behalf of Isidorus who then headed up the gymnasium, and who probably can be identified with the Isidorus in P. Oxy. 1089. Philo describes him as dishonest, a fraud and cheat, and a mediocre record-dredger (γραμματοκύφων), responsible for countless deaths in his record-manipulation stemming from bribes. The allusion to his work with documents suggests he was a kind of historical chronicler who either wished to be objective and hence took no position on data he found, or was so ill-prepared to generalize on the materials that his writing served little purpose beyond that of recording.[91] In any event, Philo had no use for him, yet he hides details of his life.

We know of two lawyers in the late Byzantine period, Dioscorus,[92] the sixth century lawyer also acclaimed for his literary ability, and Theodorus of Alexandria of the same century who studied at Constantinople, later practiced law in Asia Minor and was called a σχολαστικός.[93] Both men, however, fall beyond the period here under discussion. The Eulalus of P. Giss. 46 may be an Alexandrian lawyer (ῥήτωρ), but the fragment is too sketchy to be certain.

Where we have evidence of Attic court oratory in Alexandria and Egypt generally we should recognize that the fragments have come from private libraries—often of wealthy residents—as well as from the schools where they were used in teaching. It is significant that some speeches, such as the probable Hyperides speech in P. Oxy. 2464 and the cultic speech in P. Giss. 99 were thought important

---

[91] But the papyri at large contain the names of numerous lawyers in Egypt itself. See Schmidt, "Einfluss," pp. 51 ff, 64 ff, and *passim*, and P. Lond. 2565. For a fuller discussion see Tcherikover and Fuks, C.P.J., II, 154; Philo, "In Flaccum," 130 ff; Clark Hopkins, "Date of the Trial of Isidorus and Lampo before Claudius, B.G.U., II, 511 and P. Cair. 10448," *Yale Classical Studies*, I (1928), 171-77; and Anton von Premerstein, "Zu den Sogenannter Alexandrinischen Märtyrakten," *Philologus*, Supp. xvi, No. 2 (1923), 15-27.

[92] Georgy S. Bey, "Education in Egypt during the Christian Period and amongst the Copts," *Bulletin de la Société d'Archéologie (Copte)*, IX (1943), 106-07.

[93] *PW*, "Theodoros," (43).

enough in Egypt either for simple preservation or perhaps use in rhetorico-legal training centuries after they took place.[94]

The available evidence provides no indication that sophists, students, or lawyers in other than official capacities ever served as spokesmen for any of the oppressed ethnic groups of the city, as Philo did for the Jews in the first century, or as Libanius did for Antioch in the fourth. All seemed more concerned with their own interests or with the problems of daily living than they were with any long-range plans to alleviate duress and hardship of others. It remained for Jewish and Christian spokesmen, though from quite different vantage points, to carve out a world-view of life with the determination to implement it in the Delta. The normal secular speaker had difficulty seeing beyond the demands of immediacy.

How did the lawyers act in the cases they argued? Extant evidence suggests several characteristics of their work. They (1) took care not to alienate the judge in the introduction of their speech, and often engaged in flattery;[95] (2) could number two or more in a particular litigation, the second speaker complementing the first;[96] (3) could be either thorough in preparation, or slip-shod, and sometimes differed in the quality and completeness of their prior research from one case to another;[97] (4) read Latin legislation into their Greek oral arguments;[98] (5) made impromptu adaptations to the judge and their own opponents, and could turn the tables unexpectedly on opposing counsel;[99] (6) appeared for ($\upsilon\pi\epsilon\rho$) their parties and spoke on their behalf,[100] or they spoke as if they were the party at bar, identifying with ($\mu\epsilon\tau\alpha$) them;[101] (7) engaged in *ad hominem* arguments against their opponents,[102] and even criticized the judge's

---

[94] This problem receives fuller treatment in a subsequent chapter dealing with Greco-Roman education. For the speech on the cult of Apollos see Ernest Kornemann and Paul M. Meyer, *Griechische Papyri in Museum des Oberhessischen Geschichtsvereins zu Giessen* (Berlin and Leipzig, 1912), I, Pt. iii.

[95] P. Strass. 41, cited in Schmidt, "Einfluss," p. 55, and P. Athen. 58.

[96] P. Strass. 41, cited in Schmidt, *loc. cit.*, p. 57, and P. Tebt. 287.

[97] P. Strass. 41, cited in Schmidt, *loc. cit.*, p. 58, P. Oxy. 237, 899, and 2565, and Schmidt, *loc. cit.*, pp. 16 f.

[98] P. Bour. 20 and Schmidt, *loc. cit.*, pp. 16 f.

[99] Schmidt, *loc. cit.*, p. 58, P. Oxy. 472, and P. Bour. 20.

[100] P. Strass. 41 cited in Schmidt, *loc. cit.*, pp. 54 ff, P. Oxy. 37, and P. Hal. 1.

[101] Schmidt, *loc. cit.*, p. 28.

[102] Wilcken, *Papyri aus Oberägypten*, Pap. 161/162, cited in Schmidt, *loc. cit.*, pp. 16 f, and P. Oxy. 471.

biases;[103] (8) sometimes spoke at length, particularly in Roman Egypt, though later restrictions were placed on them;[104] (9) depicted their clients as much abused, and resorted to *ad misericordiam* arguments when they could not answer the opposition;[105] (10) often had well-arranged, systematic speeches, following the kind of *dispositio* (with adaptations) that one knows from Corax's forensic speeches;[106] (11) assumed responsibility for a wide variety of cases, as one would expect in any culture; (12) appeared to have memorized collections of apt quotations for use at bar;[107] and (13) even forsook their client's cause altogether.[108]

In summing up we should make four observations concerning the politico-legal speaking in Alexandria, assuming that it mirrors in certain respects what we find elsewhere in Egypt.[109] First, rhetoric influenced not only the decisions of the judges, but even the very way in which they worded their decisions, based as they sometimes were on legal maxims used by the speakers. Not simply the naked and written law alone, but also the issues of equity and natural, "higher," law of man figured into the decisions. These matters provided particularly attractive opportunities for speakers since often the two were separated by a wide gulf. Then, the oratory of social disruption, of the embassy, and of the courtroom was fertilized from practical life as well as from the rhetoric of the problems of that practical life. In the streets prejudiced and bigoted speakers spewed forth their invectives, inciting pogroms, while in litigation or on embassies dishonesty and fraud, men and their well-being, stood at the bar of justice. Advocates, whichever side they espoused, sought to lift out these issues in sharp relief for their listeners. Finally, both in its theory and practice oratory influenced the street corners, embassies, and courtrooms over the 700 years here under discussion. While we usually have no clue where the rhetors and advocates

---

[103] P. Oxy. 2690.

[104] Schmidt, *loc. cit.*, p. 30.

[105] P. Oxy. 2340.

[106] Corax seems to have had a five-part *partitio*: prooemium, narration, arguments, digression, and epilogue. Sometimes lawyers in the country at large combined arguments and proofs into one step. Schmidt, "Einfluss," pp. 4 f.

[107] P. Mich. Inv. 2964 (verso). See the discussion of the second century court proceedings here described in O.M. Pearl, "Excerpts from the Minutes of Judicial Proceedings," *Zeitschrift für Papyrologie und Epigraphik*, VI (1970), 271-77.

[108] P. Oxy. 33.

[109] See Schmidt, *loc. cit.*, pp. 74 ff. for summary statements of pleading in Egypt.

learned their theory, we can nonetheless detect such knowledge in the speeches.

Some of the speaking, as Philo's stinging indictment of both Flaccus and Gaius Caligula or Appian's scornful speech before the emperor (P. Oxy. 33) suggests, must have startled all who heard them. Angry men, bred in a restive city and fearless in their character, emerge in numerous deliberative and legal documents of Greco-Roman Alexandria. The excitement of their rhetoric came not from their cultivated artistic ability but from the boldness and vehemence with which they presented their evidence, arguments, and theses. Only men foredoomed to death or at least convinced that the truth lay on their side could have dared such presentations. One does not find this in the more objective exercises ($\mu\epsilon\lambda\acute{\epsilon}\tau\alpha\iota$) of the classroom. But if these spokesmen failed for the moment, they nonetheless succeeded in providing for us indicators to the trenchant character of men who may have been unjustly accused or treated.

CHAPTER IV

SPOKESMEN FOR TRUTH (CONTINUED)
CHRISTIAN PREACHERS :

No city, apart from Jerusalem, so affected the development of Christianity as did Alexandria.[1] Here the early preachers had to contend with lawlessness, riots, idolatry, gnosticism, and heresies of nearly every sort, most of which originated in Egypt by the second century and from thence their spokesmen communicated them to other churches abroad.[2] But given the heterogeneous population of Alexandria and the fact that every great religion has its aberrations, this is not surprising. Unfortunately, we have little account of the spoken word in these debates, though particular sermons, by Origen, for example, do supply hints of the theological turmoil of the city. And for good reason: he was at the center of it.

From the time of the Founder of the Christian religion to the present, the Faith was always one of propagation, not only because believers were commanded to "Go!", to preach, or because of the conviction that truth lay on their side, but because out of the abundance of the heart the mouth spoke. On the other hand, we have no evidence that either pagans or Jews, counterparts of the Christians, in Alexandria engaged in any preaching to outsiders during this time, unlike St. Paul in Asia or Europe. Both non-Christian groups seemed content to augment their numbers by births into the family, although in Jesus' time Palestinian Jews proselytized and at great effort.[3]

But the twelve apostles whom Jesus chose (a second Matthew

---

[1] J[ohn] M. Creed, "Egypt and the Christian Church," p. 300.

[2] John L. von Mosheim, *Historical Commentaries on the State of Christianity during the First 325 Years from the Christian Era* (New York, 1851), I, 369, trans. Robert S. Vidal and James Murdock; and Abel F. Villemain, *Tableau de L'Éloquence Chrétienne au IVe Siècle* (Paris, 1851), p. 87.

[3] *Matthew* xxiii. 15.

replacing Judas Iscariot) took the Good News to the far-flung regions, and so completely fulfilled their task that St. Paul could declare a generation after the foundation of the Jerusalem church in about A.D. 30 that the Gospel had been preached throughout the known world.[4] Origen, the famous Alexandrian theologian and preacher, echoed the thought two centuries later that Christians had sought to carry the message throughout the world, even to individual country homes ($\dot{\epsilon}\pi\alpha\acute{v}\lambda\epsilon\iota s$).[5] Eusebius in the fourth century accounted for the wide dissemination of the Gospel on the grounds that (as he believed) the world had been divided among the early apostles, each responsible for various parts of it—a statement which makes sense in view of the travels of St. Paul, and the probable ones of Thomas, Bartholomew, and others.

THE EARLY CHURCH

How did news of the Christian faith find its way to Egypt? Four avenues seem likely, the first three suggested by the historical accounts in the *Acts of the Apostles*.[6] On the Day of Pentecost, A.D. 29, about 120 followers of Jesus experienced an extraordinary power enabling them not only to understand unknown tongues, but themselves to speak in them. At this time Jewish pilgrims and proselytes from throughout the Mediterranean world (including Egypt) were in Jerusalem for the Jewish holiday of Pentecost, heard of the phenomenon, investigated it, and were amazed to hear the disciples speak in a wide variety of foreign languages, each auditor understanding the message in his native tongue ($\check{\epsilon}\kappa\alpha\sigma\tau os\ \tau\hat{\eta}\ \dot{\iota}\delta\acute{\iota}\alpha\ \delta\iota\alpha\lambda\acute{\epsilon}\kappa\tau\omega\ \dot{\eta}\mu\hat{\omega}\nu\ \dot{\epsilon}\nu\ \hat{\eta}\ \dot{\epsilon}\gamma\epsilon\nu\nu\acute{\eta}\theta\eta\mu\epsilon\nu$).[7] These Jews returned to Egypt, either to reside in Alexandria or pass through it, and told others of what happened. Their contagious experience and enthusiasm would have caught fire in the local synagogues.

The second likely vehicle was the Ethiopian eunuch, Finance

---

[4] $\dot{\epsilon}\nu\ \pi\alpha\nu\tau\grave{\iota}\ \tau\hat{\omega}\ \kappa\acute{o}\sigma\mu\omega$ *Colossians* i. 6. See also *Romans* x. 18.

[5] "Contra Celsus," III. 9, *Writings of Origen*, II (Edinburgh, 1877), trans. Frederick Crombie.

[6] Luke, the author of *Acts*, is almost universally regarded as accurate and careful in his writing, both in this book and in the Gospel which bears his name. I see no grounds for doubting the historicity of these events, though the conclusions I draw from them cannot be proved now by available evidence.

[7] *Acts* ii. 8.

Minister of Candace, Queen of Ethiopia. While certainly not a Jew by race, he nonetheless visited Jerusalem to worship on an unknown occasion, perhaps as a proselyte from a pagan background. Enroute home, he was reading in his chariot from the book of Isaiah, at which point the Apostle Philip, one of the original Twelve, came along and, invited to join the pilgrim in his chariot, climbed aboard and began explaining to him what it was he was reading. The man believed and "went on his way rejoicing."[8] In returning to Ethiopia the Minister would almost surely have passed through Alexandria, very likely taking the opportunity to speak formally and informally both within and without the local synagogues.

The third and even more compelling messenger was the gifted Apollos, native of Alexandria, who appeared in Ephesus *circa* A.D. 52. Luke tells us that he was eloquent and well-versed in the Old Testament scriptures (ἀνὴρ λόγιος ... δυνατὸς ὢ ἐν ταῖς γραφαῖς), that he spoke boldly in the synagogue (παρρησιάζεσθαι ἐν τῇ συναγωγῇ), and mightily confuted the Jews (εὐτόνως ... τοῖς Ἰουδαίοις διακατη-λέγχετο δημοσία).[9] He must have had some considerable practice in his hometown prior to journeying to Ephesus, and perhaps had studied rhetoric there. After receiving fuller instructions from the husband-wife team of Priscilla and Aquila because of his incomplete knowledge of the new sect and its expressions of faith, Apollos probably returned not long afterwards to his hometown and there preached. That he spoke publicly roundabout following the Ephesus experience we know from Paul who chided the Corinthians for their partisanship, some claiming to belong to the Apollos camp—suggesting his persuasive ability—while others preferred Paul.[10] He seems to have combined Hellenism with Judaism, much as Philo did, though he saw a fulfillment not shared by that Jewish philosopher.[11]

The fourth messenger to bring the Gospel to Alexandria may have been Mark, another of the early Apostles.[12] He arrived in

---

[8] *Acts* viii. 26 ff.

[9] *Acts* xviii. 24-28.

[10] *I Corinthians* iii. 1-6.

[11] A[rchibald] T. Robertson, "Apollos the Gifted," *Biblical Review*, VI (1921), 380-83, and 387-88, and James V. Bartlet, "Apostolic Age," p. 136, Vol I in *Ten Epochs of Church History* (New York, 1899), ed. John Fulton.

[12] Whether or not Mark, the probable founder of the Alexandrian church, should be identified with John Mark, the co-worker with St. Paul is not an entirely settled point. See John M. Neale, "Patriarchate of Alexandria," pp. 4-5.

Alexandria, that part of the world having been allocated to him (if we may believe Eusebius), where his first convert was one Annianus (or Hananias), a cobbler by trade. He preached in the city, greatly irritating the idolatrous Greek residents as he boldly attacked their gods. Later he left, traveled to Jerusalem, then Rome, and finally returned to Egypt *circa* A.D. 49, where he remained until his death at the hands of Greeks and Egyptians in A.D. 62 on the annual feast honoring the local god Serapis.[13]

But Mark's role in early Alexandrian church history is not a settled point for at least three reasons. First, Eusebius, the first known authority to credit Mark with establishing the church in Alexandria, states simply, "They say that ... Mark was the first that was sent to Egypt, and that he proclaimed the Gospel which he had written, and first established churches in Alexandria."[14] But why does Eusebius use "they say" ($\phi\alpha\sigma\grave{\iota}\nu$)? He must have relied on tradition even in his time, and not solid evidence. Yet there surely were some grounds for the belief to gain a foothold in the minds of the people. But the Markan tradition appears unknown to either Clement or his pupil Origen in the late second/early third century perhaps because Alexandria itself was indifferent to historical matters. Second, Alexandria never claimed Mark as its patron saint, a step one would expect, in view of his relationship with St. Paul, if in fact he pioneered its work. This contrasts with John at Ephesus and Peter at Rome. Third, our initial concrete information of the Alexandrian church stems from the late second century. We might assume that if the church grew from Mark the Apostle's work, its pride would have dictated research to establish and perpetuate the fact, much as has happened with the Mar Thoma church in India, notwithstanding Alexandrian indifference to historical matters.

In responding to this two points should be made. An important ecclesiastical see like Alexandria would not have allowed the persistence of a report such as Eusebius knew, especially when it concerned a relatively obscure apostle like Mark, unless it contained some

---

[13] Georgy S. Bey, "Education in Egypt during the Christian Period and amongst the Copts," *Bulletin de la Société d'Archéologie* (Copte), IX (1943), 104, and de Zogheb, *Études sur L'Ancienne Alexandrie*, pp. 199-100.

[14] Eusebius, *Historia Ecclesiastica*, II. 16, in *Nicene and Post-Nicene Fathers*, 2nd ser., I (New York, 1925), eds. Henry Wace and Philip Schaff; but see the Greek text.

basis in fact.[15] It would have wished for itself all the honor due it, especially in connection with apostolic founding. Second, perhaps Mark was not the first bearer of Good News—more likely the Jews from Pentecost or the Ethiopian eunuch were the real pioneers—but rather the one who came and stayed for a considerable length of time, hence genuinely establishing and pastoring the new flock. It resulted then in confusion: some holding Mark should be credited with the work, while others clung to either an unnamed Jew, Apollos, or even the foreigner from Ethiopia. Hence Eusebius' statement reflects this uncertainty.

EARLY PREACHING

Other reasons lead us to believe the Gospel came early to Alexandria and hence preaching followed in its train. The apocryphal *Epistle of Barnabas* borrowed from the martyr Stephen who was stoned in Jerusalem sometime around the mid-first century (*Acts of the Apostles*, vii). Since the *Epistle* was probably written in Alexandria and sometime in the earliest years of the second century, the *Acts of the Apostles* with its summary of Stephen's speech must have been standard literature among the Christians there in the late first century.[16] Moreover, the *Epistle* also relies on the *Didache*, the *Teaching of the Twelve*, which can be placed no later than A.D. 100 and which likely originated also from Alexandria.[17] Good literature traveled rapidly in the ancient world, as we know from P. Iand. 90 which stems from the first century B.C./A.D. and contains a part of Cicero's second oration against Verres (70 B.C.), and which was copied from an earlier document. Further, Christian literature circulated in the Mediterranean world prior to the canonical biblical ones,[18] for we know that letters to Christians in various churches moved with remarkable rapidity in the ancient world. The "Shepherd of Hermas" was known in Alexandria in the same century it was composed, and the epistles of Ignatius of Antioch were quickly

---

[15] C[olin] H. Roberts, "Christian Book and the Greek Papyri," *Journal of Theological Studies*, L (1949), 161.

[16] Philip Schaff, *Teaching of the Twelve Apostles* (New York, 1889), p. 119.

[17] Roswell D. Hitchcock and Francis Brown, *Teaching of the Twelve Apostles* (New York, 1885), pp. xc-ci.

[18] Cf. *II Thessalonians* ii. 2.

collected and dispatched to Philippi, and Origen knew of them. Irenaeus, writing *circa* A.D. 190, was read in Alexandria within ten years or so of his composing. It is likely, then, that the New Testament Gospels and Epistles—all completed prior to the close of the first century[19]—were known in Alexandria by A.D. 100.[20]

The means by which Mark established the church in the seaport city cannot at this point in history of scholarship be pinpointed. He doubtless preached, as did other early Christians, first in the Jewish synagogues,[21] until he was either thrown out, or felt so uncomfortable as to leave voluntarily. Thereupon Gentiles would have joined the small group, as we know happened in Asia Minor and Palestine.[22]

If time and social permutations have obscured the early beginnings of a western city like Rome or an eastern city like Antioch (Syria),[23] much more should we expect the transcultural changes in Alexandria— of language, religion, and education—to hide from modern eyes its early events involving humane concerns. We must expect confusion and incomplete records. Harnack has declared that "the worst gap in our knowledge of early church history is our almost total ignorance of the history of Christianity in Alexandria and Egypt (in the wider as well as the narrower sense of the term) up till A.D. 180."[24] But by the time we first learn of it the church is sufficiently strong so that persecution has not strangled its life. Thus, the strength of the Alexandrian community of believers strongly implies the Gospel must have been proclaimed by a growing throng of Christian laymen and clergy alike. The number of the faithful had grown too rapidly

---

[19] The dates of all the New Testament books are not settled, but recent scholarship, as contrasted with that of the nineteenth century, pushes the dates to earlier decades than was formerly thought possible.

[20] Adolf von Harnack, *Mission and Expansion of Christianity in the First Three Centuries* (New York, 1908), I, 374, trans. James Moffatt.

[21] *Acts* xiii. 14, xiv. 1, xvii. 1, 2, and xviii. 4.

[22] *Acts* x, *passim*.

[23] R.W. Pounder, *Saint Paul and His Cities*, p. 72, and William M. Ramsay, *St. Paul the Traveler* (London, 1927), p. 40.

[24] Harnack, *Mission and Expansion of Christianity*, II, 158-59. De Lacy O'Leary (*Saints of Egypt* [London, 1937], p. 2) has echoed this statement with: "we simply have no reliable information" until the episcopate of Demetrius (189-231) when the church appears as a flourishing entity with a catechetical school. See also Kenneth S. La Tourette, *History of the Expansion of Christianity* (New York, 1937), I, 69.

for a few teachers/preachers to account for it unless they were extraordinarily persuasive, an unlikely possibility in view of the available evidence.

The imperfect picture of the early years of the church complicates the study of its religious discourse. A single papyrus, P. Lond. 1912, of the first century hints of the effectiveness of preaching in Alexandria and throughout the ancient world.[25] In this Claudian letter to the Alexandrians the emperor specifically enjoins the Jews from continuing to foment unrest, introducing a common plague (κοινὴν νόσον) for the whole world, as well as to so presumptuously send their own embassies to argue civic affairs. At least one scholar suggests that Claudius' real concern is to thwart the upheaval the Christian faith was causing among the Jews themselves, much as had happened elsewhere in the Roman Empire.[26] If such is the case, Jews would be prohibited from inviting to Egypt outsiders from Syria, Palestine, or elsewhere for fear of unsettling Alexandria with that unrest which infested the synagogues. Since Christians and Jews were not readily distinguishable in the early years of the first century, this letter could well have referred to Christian missionaries.

Now it is true that the Christian missionaries had made a significant impact on the Mediterranean world, particularly in Greece and farther to the west, and this alarmed all the emperors from the first into the fourth century. Indeed, at Philippi, Thessalonica, Ephesus, and elsewhere preachers ran into riotous opposition, being accused of having turned the world upside down (οἱ τὴν οἰκουμένην ἀναστατώσαντες οὗτοι, Acts xvii. 6), and identifying the plague with Christianity capitalizes on that rapid and disruptive expansion. Yet it claims too much for P. Lond. 1912. The social convulsions growing out of deep-seated hatred between Jew and Greek were much more profound that Christian preaching in synagogues had produced. The feeling originated, as we have seen, from the very nature of the people themselves, and long antedated the advent of Christianity.

The Alexandrian church, differing as it did in clientele and mentality from the churches at Rome and Corinth, to whom important apostolic letters were written, doubtless relied strongly on propagation by

---

[25] Paul noted that some regarded preaching as so much foolishness. *I Corinthians* i. 18.

[26] F[rederick] F. Bruce, "Christianity under Claudius," *Bulletin of the John Rylands Library* (*Manchester*), XLIV (1962), 312-13, and *CPJ*, II, 153 ff.

word of mouth, but we do not know for certain the contents of any of their first century sermons. They must have dealt, however, with topics similar to those we find elsewhere in the first three centuries: the gospel of love (*John* xiii.34), the life, death, and resurrection of Jesus (I *Corinthians* xv.3f), his calling men to repentance (*Mark* i.14f), and his fulfillment of what the Prophets had foretold (*Luke* iv.16ff).[27] The emphasis on love (respect, concern) was more than sentimentality or even a difference of language, for "the Christians really considered themselves brothers and sisters, and their actions corresponded to this belief."[28] Genuine love affected their regard for each other, raising the social status of many (including slaves) from convention to that of sacredness and morality.[29] This would indeed produce the change about which Claudius may have written.

Rampant polytheism—every Egyptian home contained an idol representing the household god—offered particular challenges to preaching done largely by laymen. Unlettered preachers account in part for the dearth of sermon materials which have survived: many were not worth saving. Yet they clearly had a significant effect on listeners, as did the early Apostles elsewhere in the Empire. In Alexandria, says Harnack, more than in any other city, "the church understood how to present Christianity in forms which were suited to the varied grades of human culture, and this feature undoubtedly proved an extraordinary aid to the propaganda of the religion," though later the large numbers of uneducated members would prove embarrassing to the church's existence and spiritual growth.[30] Preachers, whether in the Delta or Athens, used three means to assail idolatry:

1. they attacked the gods' abominable vices;
2. they sought to exhibit the folly and absurdity of what was taught about the gods; and
3. they tried to expose the origin of polytheistic nonsense.[31]

Keeping oneself free from all contamination of polytheism was his

---

[27] Hugh T. Kerr, *Preaching in the Early Church* (New York, 1942), pp. 31-40, and Harnack, *Mission and Expansion of Christianity*, I, 87-88.

[28] Harnack, *Mission and Expansion of Christianity*, I, 149.

[29] *Ibid.*, and Paul's letter to Philemon, *passim*.

[30] Harnack, *Mission and Expansion of Christianity*, II, 175 and I, 219 ff. See also John A. Broadus, *Lectures on the History of Preaching* (New York, 1876), pp. 48 ff.

[31] Harnack, *Mission and Expansion of Christianity*, I, 291.

supreme duty once he pledged his allegiance to the Christian God. It took precedence over all other matters.[32] While later teaching played an important part, especially in establishing Christians more in their faith, preaching remained for an indeterminable period of time the chief means of propagating the Gospel to unbelievers, as St. Paul had earlier observed.[33]

Another indication that the preaching of Alexandria probably followed these lines is the fact that Stephen (*Acts* vii) influenced the early second century *Epistle of Barnabas*, as earlier pointed out. A Hellenistic Jew of the Diaspora, he ran head-on into conservative Judaism, was tried, and condemned for his radical views. Barnabas, like Stephen, deigned to take the torch from Jewish hands and place it in the vanguard of the Christian church. Luke's summary of Stephen's speech (*Acts* vii) mentions some of the topics found in the later *Epistle*,[34] suggesting Barnabas' later use of the martyr's last speech.

But religious persecution of Christians hindered preaching during the first four centuries of the Empire, just as it did the livelihood of Jews. Yet the two groups reacted differently to the oppression, not only because the savagery normally sprang from different sources, but also because of a different attitude toward life. Greeks and Egyptians typically fought with the Jews, as in the pogroms of A.D. 38 and 115-17, while the imperial government normally was the worst enemy of the Christians, as seen in the Decian and Diocletian outrages of the third century. Judaism, no longer a theocracy, and having largely abandoned its earlier view of separatism held through Old Testament times, saw oppression as depriving them of rights lawfully theirs. It, therefore, reacted strongly to oppression. In the second century it felt at one with the political ideals of the city (though hardly satisfied with how these ideals often worked out in practice) and accomodated itself—within limits—to that system. At the same

---

[32] *Ibid.*, I, 292.

[33] Paul's statement in *I Corinthians* i. 21 sets the tone for the first century propagation of the Gospel: it was God's pleasure through the foolishness of preaching ($\mu\omega\rho\acute{\iota}\alpha\varsigma$ $\tauο\hat{\upsilon}$ $\kappa\eta\rho\acute{\upsilon}\gamma\mu\alpha\tauο\varsigma$) to save them that believe. For an indication of apostolic sermons in Western Asia and Greece in the first century see *Acts of the Apostles, passim*, though assuredly the accounts there are at best summaries of the preachers' rhetorical efforts, as Luke the scribe admits (*Acts* ii. 40).

[34] L[eslie] W. Barnard, "Saint Stephen and Early Alexandrian Christianity," *New Testament Studies*, VII (1960-61), 31-45.

time it decried the humiliating poll-tax, and continued its upward struggle for full Alexandrian citizenship.[35]

Christians, on the other hand, enjoying the exhilaration and liberty new converts normally experience, saw themselves as primarily citizens of another world, hence strangers and pilgrims here. They were not so concerned as the Jews with personal freedom or with rights they might otherwise have claimed.[36] We have no evidence, then, that Christians ever revolted against persecution in Alexandria. Some, and Origen and Peter were among them, did flee when oppression became severe, but they never initiated rebellion. Their physical and passive resistance to evil does not suggest they welcomed oppression, beheadings, and burnings at the stake, but that they determined by their lives or deaths to honor their God.[37] However loyal they were to the emperor, respectful of laws, and devoted to the common good, their monotheism, emphasis on self-control—a quality of life largely unknown to Alexandrians—and high ethical standards kept them under constant suspicion by both local and national authorities[38] from the time of Nero until shortly before Constantine's Edict of Toleration (313).

Official bigotry and obduracy grew more severe in the third and early fourth centuries. The persecution under Severus in the opening years of the third century indicates a church at least important and strong enough in numbers to be noticed, and doubtless it grew as time elapsed. Around 202 the emperor forbade under heavy penalty anyone's converting from another religion to either Christianity or Judaism. But after the initial trauma and enforcement of this edict, Alexandrian Christians realized fifty years of tranquility[39] and probably renewed their public preaching. The mid-third century bloodbath under Decius prompted Dionysius of Alexandria to recall Jehovah's great plague on the country 1500 years earlier when every

---

[35] Tcherikover and Fuks, *CPJ*, I, 36 and 63-64; BGU 1140; Davis, *Race Relations*, pp. 116-17.

[36] When St. Paul, on appeal of his trial before Porcius Festus, demands to be heard by the Emperor himself he does so not primarily because of personal rights that he has as a Roman citizen, but for the larger issue of freedom of speech (παρρησία), allowing the Gospel to be preached more widely. See *Acts* xxv. 11 f.

[37] Lebreton and Zeiller, *History of the Primitive Church*, II, 1225-26.

[38] *Ibid.*, II, 1218.

[39] *SHA*, "Septimius Severus," xvii. 1, and E[dward] R. Hardy, Jr., "Patriarchate of Alexandria: A Study in National Christianity," *Church History*, XV (1946), 82.

Egyptian household mourned the loss of one member. Later (303-04) Diocletian renewed the violence with the Edict of Nicomedia (303) which demanded the razing of all churches, destruction of Christian literature, imprisonment of all Christian priests, and death for all who refused to sacrifice to the Roman gods. Any Christian holding public office or honor was driven out, and subsequently denied all legal recourse. The purge almost eliminated the Christian community and shamed some Egyptians so profoundly that they risked their own lives and property to hide their persecuted friends.[40]

Such restrictions certainly affected preaching, but extant documents do not indicate to what degree. Probably by sometime in the late first century preaching had largely ceased in the open-air if it ever occurred there at all, and was found mostly in homes, in a less formal style. The Christian religion, by the third century was becoming more institutionalized with a professional clergy so that when churches were destroyed and their preachers imprisoned, the spoken word surely suffered. With the Christian scriptures largely decimated, laymen were increasingly pressed into service. At the same time, persecution encouraged only the bravest to make the decisive step of faith, leaving aside the more timid and uncertain bystander. Thus, while the reigns of terror depleted the ranks of the faithful, they doubtless provided the community with a nucleus strong in heart and spirit.

The community of Alexandrian worshippers was large though scattered among many churches, if we include the fringe groups which strayed off onto theological tangents. Not only was the local bishopric second only to Rome's, but church attendance became faddish thus appreciably increasing the fringe numbers. "Fashionable people in Alexandria, Antioch, and hundreds of smaller towns, began to speak ... almost as enthusiastically about the favorite preacher of the hour, as they spoke of the favorite horse in the races ...,"[41] and probably with the same kind of insight. With the rise of literacy (discussed in the next chapter) in the second and

---

[40] Dionysius of Alexandria, "To the Alexandrians" [Epistle XII], trans. Stewart D.F. Salmond, *Ante-Nicene Fathers*, VI, and Eusebius, *H.E.*, VI, 41. The latter provides a fuller account of the Decian persecution. A more complete account of Dionysius and his *Epistles* (in Greek text) may be found in Charles L. Feltoe, "Letters and other Remains of Dionysius of Alexandria," *Cambridge Patristic Texts* (Cambridge, 1904), ed. A[rthur] J. Mason.

[41] Broadus, *Lectures on the History of Preaching*, pp. 60-61.

third centuries the number of Christians from among the literati and nobility swelled so that the demand for better educated and more eloquent preachers increased during that time. It is not coincidental that Origen's preaching career fell into this period.

Early preaching was done then mostly by laymen in Alexandria and in the ancient world generally. Whether Greek or Jew they had responded more readily than rabbis to the Christian message, and in the very nature of things were more numerous than the rabbi-teacher. Further, new converts were eager to participate in fulfilling the Great Commission to "Go!" and proclaim a new life which brought hope and freedom to others. Too, laymen had not institutionalized themselves, hence on the one hand they felt a greater sense of freedom to speak openly and unabashedly, but on the other, shackled by Judaic tradition, they harbored strong feelings against women preachers, as had St. Paul himself.[42] One therefore finds no mention of women in the lay movement. By the late second or early third century lay-preaching was so widespread that the Alexandrian bishop, Demetrius, forbad laymen from preaching in the presence of bishops, seeing it as an affront to their office.[43]

But if pulpit work or open-air speaking was done by laymen, why do we find no *ars praedicandi* to help the preachers in their ministry? If commanded to "Go!" to the uttermost parts of the world, one would expect Greek Christians to devise original ways of doing so. That they seemingly did not can be attributed to two factors. In the first place, Alexandria was a center of analysis and criticism, not one of originality. Though a Greek outpost and loyal in their allegiance, particularly in education, the believers resembled Romans in copying and adapting what others had developed. But further, Clement and Origen feared the artistic approach to spoken discourse, as indeed they might when they observed what went on around them in the sophistic schools, on the street corners, and the like. They preferred to grasp thoroughly ideas, then let God provide the necessary artistry *ex tempore*.

Where then did this preaching, unlearned as it was at times, take place? It must have started in the synagogues, but shortly moved

---

[42] *I Timothy* ii. 11 ff, and Joseph Bingham, *Antiquities of the Christian Church* (London, 1878), II, 712.

[43] Alexander of Cappadocia, "Epistles," IV, in *Ante-Nicene Fathers*, VI, 154, trans. Stewart D.F. Salmond.

into private homes or into the open air.[44] The fact, however, that Christians did not confine their proclamation to particular buildings but felt at liberty to speak wherever or whenever the opportunity arose, gave offense to the Jews who found it intolerable to engage in any kind of religious worship except in a prescribed place, normally a synagogue.[45]

But the early Christians found private homes advantageous for several reasons. First, an omnipresent God was any place where two or three of them gathered together, just as Jesus had promised.[46] They were not obliged to travel to special buildings, the desert, seashore, or other natural places. Then, because temples closely approximated their heathen counterparts, Christians preferred nontraditional places of worship in order to avoid any semblance of perpetuating erring practices. Third, the debasement of Jewish synagogues by mobs, and on occasion by the imperial government, gave Christians pause before erecting their own buildings, since a recognized place of worship could serve as a focal point in riots. When persecution of Jews resulted in sacking their temples, Christians learned the need of adapting to private homes and to disperse themselves throughout the city. Finally, the Christians simply lacked money to build larger meeting places. The sect had made its greatest impact on the lowly and unlettered, that segment of the population with limited means. Moreover, what money the group did have they spent on what they felt was more important than bricks and mortar. Had not the churches of Jerusalem and Philippi early established precedents of helping the poor?[47] When, however, their numbers outgrew a home's largest room which at best was small compared with Greek and Egyptian temples, it became necessary to

---

[44] Karl F.W. Paniel, *Pragmatische Geschichte der Christlichen Beredsamkeit und der Homiletik von den ersten Zeiten des Christenthums bis auf unsre Zeit* (Leipzig, 1839) p. 93, disputes this, arguing that the preachers bypassed the synagogues. But because of the close connection between Judaism and Christianity, because Jesus, Paul, Peter, and others felt completely at home in the synagogues for the first forty years or so of the first century, and because this was the natural starting place for any Christian preacher, native or not, Paniel simply lacked basis for his statement.

[45] Philo (*In Flaccum*, 48 f) felt Jews could not pay homage to God if their formal houses of worship were destroyed.

[46] *Matthew* xviii. 20 and *Acts* vii. 48.

[47] *Acts* vi. 1 ff, and *Philippians* iv. 10-18.

either divide or to secure larger and more easily recognized quarters—with the problems this would entail.

The decorum of the preaching service varied from place to place, but probably found women separated from men, and audiences standing while the preachers sat (following the Hebrew custom), though they might rise in times of emotional fervor. On the other hand, if and when preachers spoke in the open air, they undoubtedly followed the Greek custom of standing. Sermons would not have been read or memorized, yet they had prior preparation, as we know from Origen.[48]

Preaching figured prominently in the lives of Alexandrian believers. On some occasions, as when at least two bishops were present, two or more sermons were heard at the same service. Ofttimes, especially during Lent, preachers spoke daily—in nearby Cappadocia and on Cypress sometimes twice a day but multiple sermons were uncommon in Alexandria and the chora. Origen commonly preached on Wednesday and Friday, and occasionally daily.[49] The reader of Scriptures in some parts of the Orient, perhaps also in Alexandria, would stand in a high place to be seen and heard by all and in order to quiet the audience would sometimes call out "thus saith the Lord" ($\tau\acute{\alpha}\delta\epsilon$ $\lambda\acute{\epsilon}\gamma\epsilon\iota$ $\acute{o}$ $\kappa\acute{\nu}\rho\iota o\varsigma$).[50] Then at different points in the service several presbyters (elders) exhorted the people to holy living The religious discourse at such meetings was usually of four types: exposition of Scripture, with the assumption listeners would apply biblical principles to their lives; panegyrics on saints and martyrs of earlier years; topical sermons at special times of the year or on festive occasions; and sermons on special doctrinal topics to illustrate truth against heresy and to show the right way to live.[51] Contemporary primary sources illustrate some but not all of these types.

In the second century A.D., more than the first, we are hard pressed to produce solid evidence for preaching, though P. Oxy 656 contains a fragment of a Septuagint version of *Genesis*, and John's

---

[48] Paniel, *Pragmatische Geschichte der Christlichen Beredsamkeit*, pp. 93 ff, and Edwin C. Dargan, *History of Preaching* (New York, 1905), I, 37 ff.

[49] R.P. Lawson, *Origen: Song of Songs—Commentary and Homilies* (Westminster, Md., 1957), p. 16.

[50] Bingham, *Antiquities*, II, 693-95 and 698-99.

[51] Bingham, *Antiquities*, II, 713 ff; and James Donaldson, "Constitutions of the Holy Apostles," II. vii. 57, *Ante-Nicene Fathers*, VII (Buffalo, 1886), eds. Alexander Roberts and James Donaldson.

Gospel is known in the Delta at least by A.D. 135.[52] As elsewhere, the Scriptures (Old and New) must have been read aloud in Koine Greek rather than in Hebrew or Aramaic, for most Jews had long since forgotten the ancient Hebrew tongue, and Greeks never learned it. But Harnack correctly states, "we know next to nothing of any details concerning the missionaries (apostles) and their labours during the second century; their very names are lost, with the exception of Pantaenus, the Alexandrian catechetical teacher and his mission to 'India.' "[53] Now Pantaenus probably went not to India but rather to Arabia in the second century where he found Bartholomew had left an edition of Matthew's Gospel for the Jewish residents. Jerome notes that Bartholomew stopped in Arabia to preach to the Jews, and perhaps this is where Pantaenus went a century and a half later. In all probability mission-preaching in Alexandria, like that of St. Paul in Asia Minor and Greece, had died out by the close of the second century, being replaced by the catechetical school and worship within a more structured group.[54]

Many Alexandrian sermons in the Roman era were polemic in nature, doubtless because they were preached in combat—spiritual and intellectual—with Arians, Nestorians, Monophysites, and other philosophically oriented sects. The intellectual and social climate, always unsettled, lent itself to disputation and persuasion on many fronts, as we know from the numerous church councils held in the city. Here, as elsewhere, some listeners were convinced while others scoffed.[55] The many educated converts who were won over provided the gnostics with serious rivalry in the intellectual arena during the first two centuries.[56] Significant also for the growth of the Alexandrian church was the fact that Christian preaching did not adopt the colours and subtleties of the rhetorical instruction found in North Africa and Asia, or at least not until considerably after apostolic times.

[52] H.C. Snape, "Fourth Gospel, Ephesus, and Alexandria," *Harvard Theological Review*, XLVII (1954), 8.

[53] Harnack, *Mission and Expansion of Christianity*, I, 350-51. Jerome (*Letters to Magnus*, 4) also believed that Pantaenus, a convert from Stoicism, had traveled to India to preach to the Brahmins and philosophers.

[54] Harnack, *Mission and Expansion of Christianity*, I, 86.

[55] Matter, *Histoire de L'École d'Alexandrie*, 2nd ed., III, 84.

[56] Harnack, *Mission and Expansion of Christianity*, II, 42.

Yet one type of rhetorical vehicle was popularized in Alexandria and merits examination for its qualities and use.

ORIGEN AND THE HOMILY

The homily (ὁμιλία) as a speech form came into its own in the third to fifth centuries in the Byzantine church, but the idea originated centuries earlier. Aeschylus spoke of it (*Thebes*, 599) in the sense of intercourse with or company of people, and Jews had used it in a didactic and explanatory sense of understanding Scriptures. It remained for later and Christian writers and speakers, Clement and Origen among them, to extend its meaning to express what takes place in a meeting between a preacher and his congregation when they are studying Holy Writ.[57] It became an important vehicle not only in Clement's "Hypotyposis", and in the Alexandrian Catechetical School, but in the religious discourse of Origen himself.

In his hands it became an important means of explaining the meaning of biblical passages. Distinguished from the logos (λόγος) or *sermo* which was more in the classical Greek sense of public discourse, the homily was conversational in tone, often lacked a central thesis, and provided a kind of running commentary—verse by verse—of a chapter. It compared one idea with another in the Bible and used allegory and other figures freely—at times too freely, by modern standards.[58]

The homily continued into medieval times and even into the twentieth century, but it reached its zenith in popularity and utility in the third to fifth centuries. P. Oxy 1601 and 1602, dating from this period, are but two of several examples. In each of them the speaker explains the text, then exhorts believers to be chary of Satan ("your adversary the Devil walketh about seeking to devour [you] ..."

---

[57] Dargan, *History of Preaching*, I, 49. Clement also preached, but his public sermons have not come down to us—unlike the literary product of his namesake of Rome with whom the former is often confused. We shall return to Clement of Alexandria in the next chapter when discussing education.

[58] William F. Arndt and F. Wilbur Gingrich, *Greek-English Lexicon of the New Testament and other Early Christian Literature* (University of Chicago, 1957), v. ὁμιλία; G.W.H. Lampe, *Patristic Greek Lexicon* (Oxford, 1961), v. ὁμιλία; (no editor), *New Catholic Encyclopedia* (New York, 1967), VII, v. "homily;" and James Hastings (ed.), *Encyclopedia of Religion and Ethics*, X (New York, 1955), v. "Preaching."

1601) and to follow Christ ("Remain [steadfast] ..., receive ... Christ Jesus ..., accept the word ... 1602).

When the modern Western reader peruses the homilies of the ancient world he is struck with two vastly different rhetorical products. On the one hand when he reads those of St. John Chrysostom of Antioch or Origen of Alexandria he is struck with solid and mature thought, with preachers whose reflective processes moved ahead of most of their contemporaries, whether secular or sacred. He finds exegesis which, while occasionally a little contrived and fanciful by modern standards, nonetheless has well stood the test of time, and can yet edify the serious reader. One would expect in an age when theological thought was much less crystallized than in the twentieth century that listeners would have greatly profited by such lectures and sermons which, like Demosthenic speeches, smelled of the lamp of diligent work.

On the other hand, the invertebrate products of preachers, like some of those of Athanasius, lacked real substance on occasion and appear today as sweet and insipid. They merit reading only as curious museum pieces. That Alexandrians could and would listen to them testifies to their superficial character and low taste.

As suggested earlier Origen (c. 184-c. 254) was the most important Alexandrian preacher utilizing the homily. This third century teacher/ preacher not only commanded the highest respect of any pulpiteer, and headed the famous catechetical school (before he was 20 years old), but also constituted the transition from the traditional sermon to the homily. Modern critics have denied him a place among the ranks of great preachers,[59] but near-contemporary evidence suggests the contrary. While he cannot be placed qualitively in the same rhetorical class as the Attic Ten, he had a large and celebrated following. Eusebius tells us that many and distinguished philosophers came to hear him, and Jerome opines that he was a man of incomparable eloquence and knowledge so that when he opened his mouth he dumbfounded others.[60] A careful scholar, he cared little for

---

[59] John Ker, *Lectures on the History of Preaching*, 2nd ed. (London, 1888), p. 63, Edwin C. Dargan, *History of Preaching*, I, 54, and Matter, *Histoire de L'École d'Alexandrie*, III, 85.

[60] μάλιστα ἐπιφανῶν οὐκ ὀλίγοι. *H.E.*, VI. xviii. 1 ff. Conceivably this statement could refer to Origen's teaching in the School. Jerome, *Epistles*, xxxiii. 4: *sed quia gloriam eloquentiae ejus, et scientiae ferre non poterant, et illo dicente, omnes multi putabantur.*

Greek rhetoric as taught in the West or practiced in the sophistic schools of Alexandria and Antioch; it was too self-centered and contrived, magnifying men and manner at the expense of mind and matter. If later generations could in retrospect discern profitable features in the rhetorical training of the day, Origen's proximity to the phenomena and his religious zeal hindered his perception of such positive values. Yet, his simplicity of exposition did not prevent occasional loftiness in style nor his seeing allegorical interpretations in it, for whether by grammatico-historical, moral, or spiritual (allegorical) analysis, Scripture had much to teach one who would listen and ponder.[61]

Origen's homilies—some preserved in Greek, others in Latin translation by Rufinus and Jerome—cover both the Old and New Testaments. Of the 206 Migne published in his *Patrologia Graeca* we have texts of them from the Pentateuch (*Genesis, Exodus, Leviticus,* and *Numbers*), the historical books (*Joshua, Judges, I* and *II Samuel*), the Prophets (*Isaiah, Jeremiah,* and *Ezekiel*), as well as the poetic book of the *Canticles*. In the New Testament he wrote on *Matthew, Luke, John,* and some of Paul's *Epistles*. We do not have the original or intermediate source of many of the extant texts which have come to us from the desks of Rufinus and Jerome, but the present ones likely represent at least the substance and probably much of the style of the original homilies. Early in his preaching career he wrote out his homilies, but later in life his extemporaneous delivery called upon the wide and intensive reading of earlier years. Shorthand reporters (ταχυγράφοι) listening to him recorded his speeches, providing the basis for the later translations into Latin which have survived. The tautology which we sometimes find may stem from scribal errors or (more probably) from the speaker's emphasis of selected portions,[62] as he would have learned from earlier Athenian

---

[61] Dargan, *History of Preaching*, I, 51. Origen was not, of course, the first preacher to treat Scripture allegorically. Not only had Philo two centuries before done so, but even the pagan Egyptian priests in the *Book of the Dead* in the second millenium B.C. so treated it. Broadus, *Lectures on the History of Preaching*, p. 54, and R[ichard] B. Tollington, *Selections from the Commentaries and Homilies of Origen* (London, 1929), p. xxxv.

[62] Origen disclaimed any flourishes of style, or perhaps simply lacked the ability. His homilies are at once clear, simple, plain in style, and sometimes dull. His father, Leonides, was probably a rhetorician, though one does not find in the son's works the attention to style he would expect in the era of the Second Sophistic. Philip Schaff, "Ante-Nicene Christianity," *History of the Christian*

speeches. But repetition in the texts does occur from time to time.

In his thirteen homilies on *Exodus* he typically begins with a proposition or statement, proceeds through verse by verse exposition and exegesis—a vague resemblance of classical narration ($\delta\iota\acute{\eta}\gamma\eta\sigma\iota\varsigma$, *narratio*)—then ends with the benediction from *I Peter* iv.ll, and a final "Amen."[63] In III (*Exodus* iv) on the excuse of Moses that he was not eloquent before Pharoah, Origen replies that all men on occasion lack eloquence and stand mute. God it is who must open their mouths for good causes, while Satan prompts them to buffoonery, obscenities, and useless talk. In VIII (*Exodus* xx) on the First Commandment of the Decalogue we predictably find him acknowledging in a polytheistic society that there are many gods to seduce the faithful from the worship of Jehovah. "To thee also who through Jesus Christ art come out of Egypt and hast been led forth from the house of bondage, it is said, 'Thou shalt have none other gods before me.' " Deliverance was not only for the ancient House of Israel, but for all men: Egypt was not only Israel's prison, but allegorically was contemporary man's as well. Jerusalem and Judea represented the houses of liberty for those leaving their former life and looking for true freedom.

Between A.D. 244 and 249 at an undetermined place Origen preached his 28 homilies on the book of *Numbers* in which he depicted the journey of the ancient Jews as a type of the spiritual odyssey of the Christian.[64] In XX (*Numbers,* xxv), a comparatively long homily taking perhaps a half-hour in delivery, he begins with a prefatory statement recounting the historical seduction of Israel by Moab, then shows the moral sense that luxury can lead to sin. Yet if one arms himself (following Paul in *Ephesians* vi. 14-17) he will withstand the moral battle and finally be united with God. Should he choose otherwise his destiny lies with Satan; there is no middle ground. This speech, like many that he gave, shows the typical three interpretations he normally found in Scripture: grammatico-historical, moral, and spiritual. In XII (*Numbers* xxi. 16) the three

---

Church (New York, 1901), II, 786-88, and Paniel, *Pragmatische Geschichte der Christlichen Beredsamkeit*, pp. 175-79.

[63] In considering the *Exodus* homilies I have used chiefly P. Fortier and H. de Lubac, "Origène: Homélies sur L'Exode," *Sources Chrétiennes*, 16 (Paris, 1947).

[64] For the discussion of the *Numbers* homilies I have used André Méhat, "Origène: Homélies sur les Nombres," *Sources Chrétiennes*, 29 (Paris, 1951).

are not quite so clear, but we see at least two when he holds that while the Israelites had a literal well Christians have a spiritual one, the Word of God, which brings refreshment from Father, Son, and Holy Spirit.

But sometimes he carried his allegories too far, as in XXVII of the *Numbers* collection. In speaking of the Israelites camping at Thara (Terah; *Numbers* xxxii. 26-27) he understood Thara to mean a mental stupor (*contemplatio stuporis*) into which one might fall because of some great thing (*alicuius magnae rei*) happening to him. But reading the biblical text itself does not support this interpretation. The city was simply one of several places where the Israelites camped. Either he had access to data not mentioned in the original account or he read into the verse what he wished to find. At any rate, the allegory strains the narrative.

The twenty-six *Joshua* homilies came near the end of Origen's preaching career (A.D. 249-50) and while they probably were preached not in Alexandria, but in Caesarea, they merit passing mention because of the speaker himself.[65] He sees many adumbrations for the contemporary Christian: at the Jordan River the Kingdom for the Christian begins and a new conqueror rules; Jericho is the city of evil which falls under the onslaught of the Word of God and the Apostle's doctrines; Rahab prefigures the Gentiles who hear the Good News and believe; and the Canaanites are the demonic powers which war against the soul. Homily II (*Joshua* i. 2) shows not simply the death of Moses and the rising of Joshua, but for contemporary men, the death of the Mosaic Law and the new regime of the Gentiles. Jesus (Joshua; the Hebrew language does not distinguish the two) has supplanted Moses.[66] When one sees, the preacher went on in era of persecution, that Jesus Christ has been crucified, the church grows 30-60-100-fold. When he sees the gathering together of the saints, and the people of God observing the Sabbath, not by abstaining from ordinary affairs (*con versatione communi*), but from acts of sin—when this and more comes about—then know that Jesus, Son of God, holds the leadership.

Luke appears to have been a favorite book of Origen, if we can

---

[65] I have used Annie Jaubert, "Origène: Homélies sur Josué," *Sources Chrétiennes*, 71 (Paris, 1960), for the discussion of the *Joshua* homilies.

[66] *Iesus post Moysen suscepit et obtinuit principatum.* Rufinus translation.

judge by the thirty-nine homilies devoted to it.[67] They date from A.D. 233-34, but as with most of the other rhetorical works, we find few hints of the occasion. Some of them, III, IX, XV, and XXIV could not have consumed more than 3-5 minutes, if our texts approach completeness. And those numbered XIV, XXI, XXII, and XXIV were probably directed to his catechumens, for he treats explicitly baptism as a necessary preparation for receiving the sacrament of the Lord's Table, while XVIII (*Luke* ii. 40-49) depicts Jesus' parents searching for him at the age of twelve and finding him "not simply in the temple, but sitting in the midst of the doctors." Origen probably had his young students in mind when he said, "Y[ou], therefore, seek Him in the temple of God; seek Him in the Church; seek Him among the teachers who are in the temple, and who depart not from it. If you so seek Him, you will find Him." And in XXXIII in veiled language he invites his listeners to follow the example of Naaman the leper to be cleansed by washing in the Jordan (baptism) and become clean.

Origen's method of preaching was basically a verse by verse exegesis and exposition of Scripture, and probably every verse of every chapter of a selected book. However, in the Lukan homilies which Jerome has preserved for us the first 33 cover for the most part the initial five chapters of the book (chiefly i.1 - iv. 27), but the final six treat only five of the remaining 20 chapters. In view of his normally thorough and systematic approach to his topic, he very likely examined the other chapters as well, but those works have not survived. Because of these qualities his expository homilies far outnumber those of a hortatory nature, and thus they have been copied and recopied until today they constitute an important part of the Origean corpus.

At the close of all 39 he prefaces the last statement in each with some phrase referring to Jesus and then concludes with the brief benediction from *I Peter* iv.11, "to whom belong the glory and dominion for ever and ever. Amen." (*cui est gloria et imperium in saecula saeculorum. Amen*). The same conclusion occurs in those of *Exodus* and *Numbers* as well, suggesting both a (now) conven-

---

[67] In discussing the Lukan homilies I have used Max Rauer, "Homilien zu Luka" in *Origenes Werke*, IX (Berlin, 1959), M.F. Toal, trans., *Sunday Sermons of the Great Fathers* (Chicago, 1957), I, and Henri Crouzel, François Fournier, and Pierre Perichon, "Origène: Homélies sur S. Luc," *Sources Chrétiennes*, 87 (Paris, 1962).

tionalized liturgical form as well as a basic desire to glorify his Lord. In the Lukan homilies, unlike in his others, there is little introduction, and never any attempt to capture effectively the attention of the audience. He seldom includes a final summary or call to action; this he seems to accomplish in the benediction. While one can theorize that the expositions were intended for a small coterie of disciples and hence no such effort was needed, the supposition remains that they were seemingly composed for the community at large. Probably he was simply following (or entrenching) the custom of making no initial adaptation to either audience or occasion.

Yet Origen concerned himself with his immediate audience, this is abundantly clear. In the first place, he spoke in Greek, not in the native Egyptian tongue of the chora and found in parts of the city. He did so because, as a Hellenistic scholar, he was not only raised in a Greek-speaking family, but was Greek in virtually every-thing but religion. He therefore spoke to those he most wished to reach. This means that few Egyptians would have found their way into either his classroom or his congregation. It is possible, of course, that he employed interpreters, much as Scythopolis used Procopius in Palestine to interpret into Aramaic,[68] and as the Alexandrian courts came to do for native Egyptians, but not only have we no evidence to support such a theory for his speaking but it is highly unlikely.

Then too we note his overriding concern with the here and now much in keeping with the general disposition of the Alexandrians.[69] While this strikes one as odd in view of his own disciplined study and mastery of earlier works, it shows that he simply accommodated himself to the realities of the speaking situation. One finds little in his preaching to urge his listeners to search out the truth by study and reflection. He often spoke briefly though sometimes his analysis would extend to a half-hour (as in his treatment of *I Samuel* i & ii). The homilies rather play on the restlessness of his listeners and their preoccupation with the present. He was, in a word, relevant.

Since one purpose of the Origean homilies was to teach biblical content and explain Scripture, the speaker drew heavily—almost

---

[68] Fergus Millar, "Paul of Samosata, Zenobia and Aurelian: The Church, Local Culture and Political Allegiance in Third-Century Syria," *Journal of Roman Studies*, LXI (1971), 7.

[69] "L'exégèse d'Origène est donc orientée par les préoccupations fondamentales du moment." Jaubert, "Origène," p. 13.

exclusively—from other parts of the Bible. In his second homily on *Canticles* (i. 12b - ii. 14) he cites the Scriptures 77 times: 35 from the Old Testament (eight from the *Psalms*) and 42 from the New (*Matthew*, 16 times). And in his lengthy exposition of *I Samuel* i and ii he alludes to the Old Testament 83 times (of which 43 come from the books of *Kings*) and 70 times to the New (of which Paul's *Epistles* to the Corinthians are cited 25 times). In XIV (*Luke*) he quotes or refers to Paul's writings nine times from a total of 16 references to the New Testament. This high regard for Paul probably stems from the latter's perception of many allegories and types in the Old Testament, an insight which particularly pleased Origen who also felt that the Scriptures had more to offer than mere history. So Origen's keen memory, thorough grasp of sacred writing, love of allegory (especially found in Paul), and intellectual acumen served him and his audiences well.

Origen's theory of preaching was basically simple. As previously suggested, to him Scripture had three meanings: the grammatico-historical (which established the context), the moral (which applied the verse to the present day) and the spiritual or allegorical (which lifted one to higher heights). He believed that the preacher must know both the Scriptures and the hearts of men, and that he must become as a child to other children, much as God became a child in Jesus, in order to win them for the Kingdom. Thus Origen sought to preach plainly, directly, and often briefly,[70] to allow maximum understanding. One finds in him a "subdued fire that reveals the tale of mental suffering and exhausting toil. Hence that austere solemnity, that absolute sincerity, that breadth and dignity of mind, which grasp and detain the reader with the same spell that was cast upon Gregory."[71] But in arresting his audience he did so not by reference to his own personal experiences or even to those of others around him but by the internal and inherent power of the ideas he developed. If Gregory of Nyssa saw the allegorical inter-pretation as merely one of several techniques useful to the preacher, Origen conceived of it as the very basis for his preaching.[72] Listeners

---

[70] Eusebius, *H.E.*, VI, xxxvi, Bingham, *Antiquities of the Christian Church*, II, 717, Paniel, *Pragmatische Geschichte der Christlichen Beredsamkeit*, pp. 175-83, and Dargan, *History of Preaching*, I, 52.

[71] Bigg, *Church's Task under the Roman Empire*, p. 168.

[72] C.W. Macleod, "Allegory and Mysticism in Origen and Gregory of Nyssa," *Journal of Theological Studies*, N.S. XXII (1972), 371.

were intellectually challenged, morally exhorted, and spiritually uplifted with this type of preaching, though twentieth century congregations, accustomed to the Greek *sermo*, would find much of it inadequate.

While Origen made no initial efforts to adapt to his audience, various clues in his sermons suggest that he either tried to recapture waning attention of his listeners, once he had begun, or his amanuenses took more than normal care in their shorthand accounts. In Homily VI (*Luke*) he says that God has given to this our gathering and assembly (*huic coetui nostro atque conventui*) a share of His power, while in VIII (*Exodus*) he declares that Scripture itself, "if you will listen with attention and patience [*si intente et patiente auditis*], will be able to instruct us."[73] Elsewhere on the *Canticles* he exhorts, "you members of the church, speak to the daughters of Jerusalem" [*Et tu, ecclesiastice, ad filias Hierusalem converte sermonem*].[74] One might construe such statements as general exhortations to anyone reading Scripture or worshipping, nonetheless they may have obliquely called back the audience's ebbing attention to the issues at hand. In any event, one must look closely for such adaptation; it is not nearly so obvious as in the more classically oriented sermons summarized in the *Acts of the Apostles*.

We see another side of Origen's rhetorical ability. In the minutes of a recently discovered work, *A Conversation of Origen with Heracleides*, which highlights the trial of Bishop Heracleides probably between A.D. 244 and 249 and perhaps in the bishop's own Alexandrian church,[75] the defendant's orthodoxy had been called into question. Origen, experienced in theological issues and the one under whose preaching Heracleides was converted, was asked to take an active role in the examination of the prelate. The dialogue centered around the beliefs of Heracleides with specific questions like, if Jesus Christ was God, did He really die on the cross? Or, what is the nature of the soul? The account of the trial—some of it is

---

[73] Conceivably this could refer to their reading and heeding habits.

[74] So Jerome.

[75] The largely complete Greek text (based on P Cairo Inv 88745) with French translation was first published by Jean Scherer (1949) and may be found in his "Entretien d'Origène avec Héraclide" (Paris, 1960), *Sources Chrétiennes* 77. An English translation is available in John E.L. Oulton and Henry Chadwick, "Alexandrian Christianity," *Library of Christian Classics* (Philadelphia, 1954), II, 430 ff.

verbatim, as shown by the quotations following the frequent use of "——————— (name) said ($\epsilon \hat{\iota}\pi\epsilon\nu$)—shows Origen in command of the situation at every point. He questions, makes short speeches on theological points such as the essence of the soul, and, as in the homilies, copiously supports his statements with Scriptural references. His sifting and challenging forces the bishop, not his match, to admit two gods in the Christian faith. But Origen's monotheism would not let him rest with that. Quickly drawing the analogy of Adam and Eve becoming one flesh, though not one spirit or soul, and of the righteous man as wedded with Christ, yet distinct from Him, he sought to draw the parallel in the Trinity. But his analogies broke down, and each side was left with two gods, however objectionable it seemed to Christian doctrine.

The audience at the Heracleides trial seems to have drawn both clergy and laymen—perhaps even some non-Christian laymen, for Origen feared he was casting his pearls before swine (xii. 22ff and xv. 7ff). Additional evidence for this stems from the fact that after he was queried on the nature of the soul he hesitated to answer because he feared he might confuse the uninstructed laymen present. The altercation, though confusing to the untutored, must have been charged with excitement and feeling as this highly gifted theologian sought to frame the acceptability of, or their opposites to, specific doctrines.

We do not know the outcome of the trial, whether or not the bishop was acquitted of heresy, but we do see Origen as an advocate thoroughly schooled in his subject, gentle, but with questions which lead to problematic answers. In the courtroom or the classroom he was considerate, kind, and erudite.

Origen's heart and mind moved too rapidly for the church in Alexandria. Demetrius, the local bishop, not only banished him for certain irregular beliefs regarding the Trinity and for his unorthodox ordination in Jerusalem (when Origen was in exile), but even had him excommunicated on grounds curious by some twentieth century theological standards. As Neale points out, in an age when doctrine was not clearly settled, Origen mixed what today would be called heresy with orthodoxy concerning the Father, Son, and Holy Spirit. When he and others were hammering out beliefs on the anvil of experience and reflection it was difficult to keep paradoxical matters in nice balance.[76]

[76] Neale, "Patriarchate of Alexandria," pp. 28-35.

OTHER PREACHERS

Following the death of Origen the quality of preaching dipped as less able men about whom we know little assumed pastoral responsibilities in Alexandria. Anatolius of Laodicea (fl. third century) with a sound background from the study of rhetoric, physics, astronomy, and philosophy early served for awhile in the Alexandrian senate and was highly esteemed by his fellow residents. But he left the city in 262 and with a penchant for theological matters became bishop of Laodicea where for the most part he established his reputation.[77]

Dionysius, Bishop of Alexandria (247-64), was probably a professor of rhetoric before his conversion, and later headed the Catechetical School. He had studied pagan authors, but repudiated much of their philosophy, and later as a Christian, fled Alexandria under Decian's intense persecution of the mid-third century.[78] If the extant fragments accurately portray his preaching, they suggest a verse by verse exegesis of both the Old and New Testaments, something in the Origean tradition.

Pierus (fl. 275) distinguished himself as a preacher, teacher, and ascete. His skill in rhetoric and dialectic won a large following for him and prompted Jerome later to call him "Origen the Younger,"[79] a reputation surely based on more than the twelve treatises (sermons?) which he seems to have written, but which have not survived. His death is hidden in obscurity, but he was probably martyred sometime after 309, for we can date his biography of Pamphilius of Caesarea in about that year.[80]

We know little of Peter (fl. third century) who fled the city *circa* 250 under the Decian persecution perhaps not so much for his own safety but so the oppressed church would not lose its leader.[81] One of his sermons (of unknown date) exhaustively treats the possible situations Christians would encounter under persecution, and who

---

[77] Eusebius, *H.E.* VII. xxxii. 6-13.

[78] See his fragments in English translation in *Ante-Nicene Fathers*, (Buffalo, 1886), VI, 111-20, eds. Alexander Roberts and James Donaldson, and Lebreton and Zeiller, *History of the Primitive Church*, II, 1017-18.

[79] *Ut Origenes junior vocaretur. De Viris Inlustribus*, 76.

[80] Eusebius, *H.E.*, VII. xxxii. 26-27, and L[ewis] B. Radford, *Three Teachers of Alexandria: Theognostus, Pierus, and Peter* (Cambridge, 1908), 44-48.

[81] Radford, *Three Teachers*, pp. 58-59.

later examine their relationship to the local church. The sermon's fifteen canons would help believers determine whether or not to readmit to their fellowships those who had (1) recanted their faith; (2) feigned madness to avoid persecution; (3) offered sacrifices at the command of their masters; (4) bribed officials to bypass them; and (5) forsook all their property and fled.[82] In an age of frequent and intense persecution clear guidelines were needed, and this Peter who himself fled sought to provide.

These and countless others played their part in the 19 church councils in ancient Alexandria, but virtually no accounts of the debates have survived.[83] The final agreements and confessions emanating from these third and fourth century meetings tell us little of the oral arguments which attacked or defended the various articles of faith, though the doctrines indicate an oral discourse heated and erudite in character as men from far and near argued with their counterparts.

The philosophizing tendency of Alexandria, with its indebtedness to Greek thought and Asian mysticism, and its intellectual superficiality, encouraged the growth of sects and speculations generally. Arius brought his ideas from Asia Minor and argued that the Son was subordinate to the Father. He was tried and condemned by the Synod of Alexandria in 320, and at the Council of Nicea five years later. But before he and his disciples were driven from the city by Bishop Alexander,[84] they preached in several churches of the city. No texts have survived of these sermonic works, but clearly they and their written counterparts were sufficiently disruptive not only to condemn Arius, but also lead to the prelate's prohibiting local priests from preaching to the impressionable Alexandrians, though bishops could.[85] This restriction sprang probably from the fear that the orthodoxy of the less educated preachers could not

---

[82] Peter of Alexandria, "Canonical Epistle," James B.H. Hawkins, trans., *Ante-Nicene Fathers*, VI, 269-79. The editors of the latter work have published for us the commentaries by Balsamon and John Zonaras which provided basis for reconstructing the substance of Peter's sermon.

[83] Councils were held in 231, 235, 258, 305, 306, 308, 315, 319 (or 320), 321, 324, 326, 328, 340, 352, 362, 363, 371, and 399.

[84] Charles J. Hefele, *History of the Christian Councils* (Edinburgh, 1894 ff), I, 239-40, and 247-48.

[85] *Catholic Encyclopedia* (New York, 1910), VII, 443-444, and Bingham, *Antiquities of the Christian Church*, II, 710-11.

always be trusted because of their limited study. Bishops, on the other hand, were less susceptible to heretical views and to social pressures.

A century after Origen and in the wake of the Edict of Milan preaching reached another high point. It came into its own at about the same time in all parts of the Empire: Egypt, Asia Minor, Greece, and the western regions of Gaul,[86] and continued to have a significant impact on the social order. Its influence and artistic achievements would prompt Fénelon more than a thousand years later to look back and observe that "the good way of speaking" was maintained longer in the East than in Rome and the West,[87] while another French scholar could say in the nineteenth century that by Constantine's era style was elevated and compassionate, doing great justice to the faith of the Fathers.[88]

But this could be said of too few. As in earlier periods so in the fourth century presbyters (elders), especially those in smaller churches with no resident bishop, primarily shouldered the responsibility of teaching and preaching. Lacking the discipline and system of an Origen or Athanasius, they wandered in their public discourses so that probably the Alexandrian church, like its counterparts in Asia Minor, was obliged to place a time limit on sermons. How long such a restriction continued in either place we do not know, but as early as the third century homiletical texts suggest varying lengths up to thirty minutes, depending on the number of speakers at each service and on the occasion.[89] And by the fourth century the practice seems fixed.

ATHANASIUS

If the preaching of a Dionysius, Pierus, or Peter only tantalizes us with numerous unanswered questions—and it does—we can say

---

[86] Villemain, *Tableau de L'Éloquence Chrétienne au IVe Siècle*, pp. 81 ff.

[87] "Dans l'orient, la bonne manière de parler et d'écrire se soutint davantage...." Archbishop-Duke de Cambrai, *Oeuvres de M. François de Salignac de la Mothe Fénelon* (Paris, 1787), III, 304. See the English translation by Wilbur S. Howell, *Dialogues of Eloquences* (Princeton, 1951), p. 147.

[88] "[L]'éloquence des docteurs d'Alexandrie est, dans les siècles primitifs de l'Église, la plus magnifique expression de la foi chrétienne et de la science grecque." Matter, *Histoire de L'École d'Alexandrie*, III, 83.

[89] Dargan, *History of Preaching*, I, 69.

more about Athanasius, some of whose homiletical works have survived.

This Alexandrian bishop was the most important of the fourth century preachers and picked up the torch laid down by Origen and others. Athanasius (c. 296-373) was consecrated to his office before he was thirty, and took part in the Council of Nicea in 325. A guide to the young and gentle to the weak—a man of true pastoral quality— he was nevertheless a vigorous man of common sense and a lion to the subversive.[90] He was a ready debater, disdaining contrived artistic elements in his preaching, and relying more on philosophic and argumentative reasons than stylistic flourishes, especially in his younger years. At times his sermons constituted a veritable *tour de force*. His professional life epitomized the anti-Arian struggle, as can be seen in his substantial work, *De Incarnatione Verbi Dei*, written before he was thirty years old. His sermon, "Christ the Eternal God,"[91] is a solidly argued case against the Arians, but totally devoid of illustrations to vivify his contentions. Whether the bare skeleton was intended merely as an outline for later extemporizing or simply that he, like Origen, saw little need for rhetorical adaptation, we do not know. In any event, the biblical references which occur serve more for argument than for illustration. In general the sermon commands higher praise than some of his later homilies.

At his best the bishop was excellent in content and style. His "Homily on the Laborers in the Vineyard," based on *Matthew* xx. 1-16, probably dates from his early ministry and provides considerable food for thought. He begins by reading the text, as in the "Homily on Mercy and Judgment,"[92] then explains that each character is not simply for that parable alone, but has his counterpart for listening now. God is the Master; the laborers which were early hired by the keeper are Moses, Aaron, and Joshua; those appointed at the third hour were the Judges of Israel; those hired at the sixth hour were Samuel, David, and all the other prophets; those secured at the eleventh hour were the Christian Apostles; and the Vineyard Keeper, of course, is Christ. He inserts a lengthy discursus on Judas—

---

[90] Frederic W. Farrar, *Lives of the Fathers* (London, 1907), I, 499 f.

[91] Henry C. Fish, *History and Repository of Pulpit Eloquence* (New York, 1857), I, 54 f. See also Matter, *Histoire de L'École d'Alexandrie*, III, 87.

[92] Both the Coptic text and English translation may be found in E.A. Wallis Budge, *Coptic Homilies in the Dialect of Upper Egypt* (London, 1910). This work is based on P Brit Orient Inv 5001.

a type of those who complain because the late workers get as much as the early ones—but later returns to the text and rounds out the thought. The final appeal calls for the unconverted man to place his faith in the church which is borne along by the Father, Son, and clergy.

Stylistically he often excelled. In "Laborers" he contrasts Judas with other imaginary characters. Using the Greek figure of epanaphora he declares

Better Cain who killed a man, than Judas who killed God.
Better Saul who hated a man, than Judas who hated God.
Better the hardheartedness of Pharaoh towards the people, than the hardheartedness of Judas towards God ...
Better Achan who stole the accursed thing, than Judas who stole the gifts of charity."

He employs apostrophe—"Oh Judas, what did you do? ... You wasted your life and lost this great honor, the glory of apostleship."— and in "Christ the Eternal God" he juxtaposed rhetorical questions one after the other.

What advancement, then, was it to the Immortal, to have assumed the mortal? Or what promotion is it to the Everlasting to have put on the temporal? What reward can be great to the Everlasting God and King, in the bosom of the Father? See ye not, that this, too, was done and written because of us and for us, that us [sic] who are mortal and temporal, the Lord, become man, might make immortal, and bring into the everlasting kingdom of heaven?

By contrast, his "Mercy and Judgment" depresses one because of its lack of substantive materials, its contrived nature and rambling organization, and the low level to which it is geared. The central thesis is clear enough: it is right for Christians to mingle mercy with judgment, for did not Hosea enjoin, "keep mercy and judgment and draw nigh to God"? But the internal organization breaks down so that one has the sense of moving from one superficial point to another with neither organization, real insight, nor adaption to occasion or audience. The reader is left wondering when and under what circumstances the homily was given, and how it spoke to the needs of the faithful. The sense is panegyric, the sentiment more pronounced—almost sweet—and the thought considerably less rigorous, at times practically empty. One finds among these later efforts of Athanasius, in contradistinction to Origen's works, too few homilies that would tease him to read them a second time. One can only conjecture what could have prompted fourth century Alexandrian audiences to listen with any degree of care, and concludes that if it were not for the listeners' superficial, non-reflective character they would not have done so. Yet Athanasius set forth a central thesis, unlike one finds in many of Origen's works, and a theme which transcended the simple exhortation to live a virtuous life.

Athanasius' "On the Soul and Body" is not much better.[93] He does not begin with a text, and the organization, almost totally lacking, gives no clue to his theme or his audience. Yet he seems to call his flock to a serious consideration of death, for it is that which imprisons the soul and leads to its eternal torture and forlornness apart from God. Perhaps the occasion was the continued persecution of Christians which would force them to weigh seriously the price of discipleship, or perhaps he sought to unravel mysteries of the inner nature of man. Unfortunately, we do not know.

If the arguments and ideas in Athanasius and other Alexandrian preachers were often unprovocative or non-existent, it was in part due to the purpose of the homily: exhortative and illuminative, and not argumentative. At the same time many of them were copiously documented with biblical references of allusions. In his "Mercy and Judgment" the twenty-one biblical allusions include eleven from the Old and ten from the New Testament but his "Homily on the Soul and Body," has few from either section. But the modern reader peruses most of Athanasius' homilies only as relics of another era to discover what they may have provided for his listeners; he does not read them for nourishment of the soul, as he might Origen's or Chrysostom's works.

His ebullient and impetuous rule in Alexandria garnered for Athanasius many enemies who succeeded in exiling him five times while he held the bishopric. His repeated and effective attacks on the insidious potential of Arianism[94] made him ultimately a marked man. On one occasion when he was under heavy attack one Antony, a desert hermit, came to Alexandria to support Athanasius against

---

[93] Budge, *op. cit.*

[94] Zogheb can call him "un des plus grands hommes de l'Église." *Études sur L'Ancienne Alexandrie*, p. 218. For additional information see Lietzmann, "From Constantine to Julian," *History of the Early Church*, III, 192, and 247-51, Sozomen, *Ecclesiastical History*, II. xvii (London, 1855), trans. Edward Walford, and William Smith and Henry Wace, *Dictionary of Christian Biography* (Boston, 1877), "Athanasius."

Arian supporters. People flocked to hear the hermit, listening "with beating hearts to his rude, firey, uncultured eloquence."[95] But the bishop's own impatience with subverters and his violent attacks on outspoken detractors led to Julian's banning him altogether from Alexandria, *circa* 362. He, more than any other of the Alexandrian clergy of his early days, had a *force irrésistible* in the pulpit which both frightened and angered the emperor, but unfortunately few of these sermons have survived.

Homiletical style in Alexandrian works offered no striking contrasts to those of Gregory Thaumaturgus or John Chrysostom heard elsewhere in the Empire. If the thrust of the Delta's homily lacked punch, it did so not because of the language employed or the lack of figures and ornaments, but because of the weakness in thought of some (Athanasius, for example) or the rambling organization of others (like Origen). But stylistic figures were there. Direct address—"Oh my beloved," "Oh my brethren!" "Oh my beloved brethren," or in the case of Origen, "You catechumens"— could be found frequently.[96] Rhetorical questions occurred in Alexander's "Homily on the Incarnation of our Lord": When does one enjoy life? When he's in his mother's womb? Nay! When he's nursing at her breast? Nay! When in the vigor of early manhood? Nay! When old? Nay! Apostrophe, addressing someone absent as if he were present, finds a place in Athanasius' "Laborers:" "Oh Judas, what did you do? ... You wasted your life and lost this great honor, the glory of apostleship." Or again ("Soul and Body"), "Oh thou death, that carries off people of every age and condition—the children, the old men, the youth, and the man of mature growth." Yet the homilists seemed reluctant to thunder forth with striking use of the second person plural, unlike what Jesus, Peter, or Paul did earlier. Perhaps this resulted from the speakers' preaching mostly to sympathetic listeners, while earlier Apostles often spoke to antagonistic audiences—or at least the meagre evidence might lead us to this conclusion. At any rate, when one does find it, as he does occasionally in Origen,[97] it does not cut with the edge of the *sermo* in classical style.

---

[95] Farrar, *Lives of the Fathers*, I, 500.

[96] Theophilus, "Homily on the Virgin," Athanasius, "Homily on the Soul and Body," and his "Homily on Mercy and Judgment," and R.P. Lawson, *Origen: The Song of Songs.*

[97] Homily XVII (*Luke*): "You were a heathen ... you were a sinner."

In characterizing Alexandrian preaching one sees several qualities over the spread of centuries. First, unlike the the classic speech of the secular world, the typical homily carried no adaptation to either audience or occasion. The reader today has considerable difficulty in determining when and to whom the speeches were given because of this very lack of adjustment. Second, homilies often rambled in organization. If Origen worked seriatim verse by verse through a particular passage, Athanasius and others would not necessarily. Many of the typical homilies of the Empire defy any sort of systematic organizational analysis whatsoever. The modern reader senses either an undisciplined mind in the speaker and audience or perhaps incomplete texts—or both. Third, and related to the preceding deficiency, is the absence of a thesis, particularly in Origen's works. Yet other preachers centered on a particular idea, sometimes virtually stating their central point, but having done so they subsequently had difficulty keeping their speech marching toward a goal with the proper beat and emphasis. Fourth, seldom can one find any call for study and reflection of a particular point, no encouragement to examine the text for oneself, or to seek divine guidance in privacy elsewhere. Normally the speaker dwells on the here and now, much as did the panegyric orators of the First and Second Sophistic. Such an approach, while not ultimately building strong religious believers, was geared to the Alexandrian temperament. Finally, rhetorical style and delivery was normally conversational, as each was calculated to sustain listeners on basically an elementary level. Origen's occasional lofty style was the exception more than the rule, for Theophilus, Athanasius, and often Origen himself preached on a low key. Seldom does one find rhetorical practice of the quality of some of the early preachers in Asia Minor and Europe,[98] all of which implies that those Alexandrians reached by preaching were for the most part shallow in their thinking.

What results, temporary or lasting, came from the preaching in Alexandria during the first four centuries of the Empire? At least three consequences can be found. First, pulpit oratory clearly gave new hope to people otherwise on the fringes of civilization and Greek culture. It placed a value on their lives which they could not find in Greco-Roman polytheism. If pagans held them expendable, Christians saw them as creatures of a God who cared. Second,

---

[98] *Acts, passim.*

it weakened the Hellenism of the gymnasium,[99] for Christianity emphasized personal redemption as more important than physical fitness and Greek literature. Its concern for a body of theological and metaphysical truth rather than a strong and graceful physique undermined the gymnasium as the seed-bed of Hellenism, for the school completely passes from the scene by the late fourth century.[100] Finally, it enervated sophistic training in the city, for unlike school exercises whose topics within the cloistered walls of the classroom were often removed from the contemporary scene, preaching sought to move men to a better life here and hereafter, as well as putting them into a proper relationship with their Creator. Sophistic training, as we shall see in the next chapter, largely saw rhetoric as a means of self-aggrandizement rather than a vehicle, a discipline, for changing the contemporary scene. Yet few if any Alexandrian "sermons" carried the impact, the wallop, found in earlier models by Peter and Paul in first century Palestine, Asia Minor, or farther to the west, and accordingly the efforts are the poorer for the omission.

Despite these local and positive effects, we find no evidence that the Alexandrian church, unlike its counterpart at Jerusalem, sent out any missionaries to other lands—Pantaenus excepted. It seemed content to reach its own neighbors, refute current heresies, and corporately worship. Perhaps the constant attacks from every side sapped all the Christians' energies, making it difficult to move out. On the other hand, had they taken more seriously the Great Commission[101] they might have been less concerned with heresies simply because time and strength would have been channelled in other directions. It is however more than passing strange that when an outsider, in the very nature of things, had come to Alexandria with the Good News, the local Christians in turn would not have felt a constraining inward force to reciprocate to other people. Perhaps they did, but if so the ancient sources have left no record of it.

In fine, available evidence, while not permitting us to complete the rhetorical mosaic as we should like, leads us to conclude that

---

[99] H. Idris Bell, "Hellenic Culture in Egypt," *JEA*, VIII (1922), 152-53. In the following chapter we shall discuss the gymnasium in greater detail.

[100] Davis, *Race Relations*, p. 65. Matter (*Histoire de L'École d'Alexandrie*, III, 82) says, "Là [i.e., Alexandria] où la parole était donnée à Origène, à Clément d'Alexandrie, à S. Athanase, à S. Cyrille, à tant d'autres moins illustres mais aussi graves, il n'y avait plus de place pour des sophistes."

[101] *Matthew* xxviii. 19-20.

Christian preaching fared in Alexandria much the same way it did elsewhere: some preaching was substantial, while other kinds were mediocre at best. Yet the organized church flourished and produced individuals who in turn fed it as good shepherds. We can find serious short-comings in the Delta's preaching, but the fact remains that the church still grew and in many respects prospered in very difficult political times. Perhaps more we should not expect.

CHAPTER V

GRECO-ROMAN EDUCATION

When one moves from the study of Alexandrian practitioners of truth to their rhetorical theory—and practice has always preceded theory—he is struck by similarities and differences in what he finds farther to the west. Similarities there were because since its foundation the city had been a Greek outpost of civilization and emersed itself in things Greek. But differences obtained simply due to ethnic variety and geographic distance from Athens and Greek culture.

"The first thing that any handful of Greeks did upon 'settling' in a barbarian country was to establish a gymnasium," remarks Moses Hadas.[1] And so it was in Egypt. These institutions were scattered throughout: in Alexandria, Naucratis, Ptolemais, Arsinoe, and elsewhere—even in small villages—and normally were privately endowed, unlike those financed by the state in Athens. Strabo notes that Alexandria's gymnasium was located in the center of the city, extended over 600 feet in length, and was the most beautiful of all the buildings in the city.[2] Appearing in Egypt at least by the third century B.C.,[3] the gymnasium sought not only to prepare young

[1] Moses Hadas, "Hellenistic Litterature," *Dumbarton Oaks Papers*, (Washington, D.C.) No. 17 (1963), p. 34, and H. Idris Bell, "Roman Egypt from Augustus to Diocletian," *Ch. d'Ég.*, XIII (1938), 351 where the same point is made.

[2] Strabo, *Geography*, XVII. 1. 10. Cf. also *PW*, VII, 2005, and Gratien Le Pere, "Expédition Français d'Égypte" in Zogheb, *Études sur L'Ancienne Alexandrie*, p. 27n.

[3] Bell, "Roman Egypt from Augustus to Diocletian," p. 351; Ulrich Wilcken, "Papyrus-Urkunden," *Archiv*, VI (1920), 389; and Thomas A. Brady, "Reception of the Egyptian Cults by the Greeks (330-30 B.C.)," *University of Missouri Studies*, X (1935), 26-27; and Brady, "Gymnasium in Ptolemaic Egypt," *Philological Studies in Honor of Walter Miller* (University of Missouri Studies), XI [1936] No. 3, p. 10. An inscription possibly of the third century B.C. with its πρῶτος φίλος (first friend), may refer to the initial benefactor of a gymnasium in Ombos (Upper

men for later political life—another indication that Alexandria likely had a senate in Ptolemaic Egypt—but also to establish Greekhood in an alien culture.[4] This goal it would achieve by teaching classical Greek literature, as well as all the professional courses one could expect to find in higher education.[5] The institution was better known in Roman than Greek Alexandria, and probably increased in importance from Ptolemaic to Roman times.[6]

What part did the gymnasium and schools generally have in the teaching and practice of rhetoric? Did they operate in much the same way as their counterparts in Greece and Rome? Did they use the same textbooks, theories, approaches to practice, or do we find greater originality? Were the schools open to any who might wish to attend, or only to selected ones, as in Rome? What, if any, disciplinary methods were used? These and similar questions need answers as we examine the rhetorical-educational system of Alexandria.

Yet when we move beyond broad outlines of education to its

Egypt). See Ludwig Mitteis and Ulrich Wilcken, *Grundzüge und Chrestomathie der Papyruskunde* (Leipzig, 1912), I, Pt. 1, 138.

[4] Hadas, "Hellenistic Literature," p. 34.

[5] Jean Delorme, *Gymnasion: Étude sur les Monuments Consacrés a l'Éducation en Grèce* (Paris, 1960), pp. 316-17. Delorme's monograph is the best available study of the gymnasium, but minimizes the one in Alexandria. I am at a total loss to understand Martin P. Nilsson's note (*Hellenistischen Schule* [Munich, 1955], p. 95) that the Egyptian gymnasium neglected literary instruction. I see no evidence to support such a position; all the data suggest the gymnasium performed in much the same way it did at Athens and elsewhere, as noted in the text.

[6] I shall deliberately omit any systematic discussion of the gymnasiarchy, that prestigious but financially onerous office held by leading citizens of the city. The twentieth century has no equivalent of it, for it combined the kind of responsibilities we find in the Chairman of the Board of Trustees of a college or university, and those in its Superintendent of Buildings and Grounds. Gymnasiarchs were normally leading citizens, often (though not always) wealthy, and were obliged to provide body oil, lighting, maintenance of the baths, and other day-to-day items. They occasionally went on embassies, as we find in the case of Isidorus and Lampon. Helpful insights can be found in P. Oxy. 1416; Pierre Jouguet, "Vie Municipale," pp. 322 ff; Brady, "Gymnasium in Ptolemaic Egypt," pp. 9-20; B[ernhard] A. van Groningen, "Pap. Oxy 1416 and the History of the Gymnasiarchy," *Actes du Vᵉ Congrès International de Papyrologie* (Brussels, 1938), pp. 505-11; and E[efje] P. Wegener," βουλή and the Nomination to the ἀρχαί in the μητροπόλεις of Roman Egypt," *Mnem.*, 4th ser., I (1948), 308.

details in Alexandria we are hard pressed, simply because our present records provide incomplete data. Neither in Alexandria nor in Egypt at large could one find compulsory education for the native Egyptian children, though private schools and tutors there were for those financially able to afford them. In any case, these would likely have proceeded no farther than the elementary level.

ELEMENTARY AND SECONDARY EDUCATION

For Greek children education came in essentially three stages: the elementary school (διδασχαλεῖα), the secondary school or gymnasium (γυμνάσιον), and for some the epheboi (ἔφηβοι).[7] In the elementary school where students were prepared for later rhetorical training, papyri and ostraca tell us that the pupils began with writing, then took notes of texts from dictation or from a model. When instruction turned to the classics and moved across a broad spectrum of literature, criticism, and history, as in the Roman Empire, moralistic maxims were used much like the McGuffy Readers were in nineteenth century America. Following the writing and reading aloud exercises came grammatical and stylistic ones in which the young scholar learned finesse and ability in using his native language.[8]

It was however in the later education of the private rhetorical schools and the gymnasium that most rhetorical training could be found. In the latter intellectual regimen accompanied physical exercises to produce the whole man,[9] while the rhetorical schools seem to have copied rather closely the procedures in Rome and Antioch. Direct evidence does not spell out in detail rhetoric's clear role

---

[7] Taubenschlag, *Law of Greco-Roman Egypt*, II, 58-60, and Mitteis and Wilcken, *Grundzüge und Chrestomathie*, I, Pt. 1, 136 ff. I am omitting further reference to ephebic training, even though this essentially military and physical training institution apparently included in some unknown way rhetorical instruction. Most of our information is based on Athens and not elsewhere. But see Albert Dumont, *Essai sur L'Éphebie Attique* (Paris, 1876), 2 vols, especially Chapter 6 of Vol. 1, "Études Littéraires."

[8] Mitteis and Wilcken, *Grundzüge und Chrestomathie*, I, Pt. 1, pp. 137-38, and J. Grafton Milne, "Relics of Greco-Egyptian Schools," *JHS*, XXVIII (1908), 121-32. For the grammarian's task see Gaston Boissier's "Instruction Publique dans l'Empire Romain," *Fin du Paganisme* (Paris, 1909), I, 145-218.

[9] Delorme, *Gymnasion*, p. 466.

in these institutions—what books were used at each level, precisely how the subject was taught, or the background of the teachers—but several indirect items suggest likely methodology. Both institutions sought to perpetuate Greek thought and culture which included not only Homer (the most popular of any of the Greek authors) but also selected Attic orators. They hoped to maintain the enthronement and reign of Athenian culture in an alien land. Sophists and teachers achieved this goal by preserving the purity of the Attic tongue in a people far removed from the homeland and by constant heralding back to the great writers of the past. In due course however koine made serious inroads into the everyday speech of the people, as both papyri and the Septuagint fully attest. Further, we have no reason to believe that Greek immigrant families radically changed their educational views from what they had practiced in the homeland where we know rhetoric found an important place in the gymnasium.[10] What Isocrates had said of Athenians was largely true of Alexandrians as well: "that the name of Greek should be thought no longer a matter of race but a matter of intelligence; and should be given to the participators in our culture rather than to the sharers of our common origin."[11] This in fact proved true, except for the native Egyptians who with rare exception remained on the fringes of society. Finally, the large number of rhetorical papyri found in Egypt prove the significant role the spoken word in theory and practice had in Greco-Roman education, though we can not always ascertain if the recovered fragments originated from the gymnasium or private schools. We may surmize, however, that rhetoric was taught in the Ptolemaic gymnasium.[12]

In the early Roman period the character of the gymnasium changed. It became a state institution under governmental subsidization and

---

[10] "About this [gymnastic] training we know very little, but what we know indicates that it was exactly the same as that of which we have evidence in many documents of Hellenistic times found in the ancient Greek cities of Greece and especially in Asia Minor." Rostovtzeff, *Social and Economic History of the Hellenistic World*, II, 1058-59.

[11] *Panegyricus*, 50, cited in Richard Jebb, *Attic Orators* (London, 1893), II, 16.

[12] Mitteis and Wilcken, *Grundzüge und Chrestomathie*, I, Pt. 1, 138, though they note that there is no direct evidence ("keine direkten Belege") for it; and H.I. Bell, "Hellenic Culture in Egypt," *JEA*, VIII (1922), 150; and É[mile] Amelineau, *Résumé de L'Histoire de L'Égypte*, p. 167. Amelineau declares that Ptolemy I wished to transplant to Alexandria "tout ce que la Grèce contenait de gens illustres ou simplement remarquables dans les lettres et dans les sciences." *Ibid.*

control—unlike the elementary schools—although private gifts continued to support it.[13] The school, never for the masses whether Greek or native, always appealed to the middle and upper classes, that is, those who could financially afford the tuition, as well as to those families from whom public servants would come.[14] Under Augustus and his immediate successors, Alexandria became for a time the chief seat of polite learning in the Empire, as rhetoric combined with philology and literary criticism. "In accordance with the demands of the age, rhetoric and philosophy, which had previously been of minor consequence, became the chief subjects of study, and with the coming of large numbers of students from over the seas she developed into a large center of instruction, more like Athens (which was now in temporary eclipse) than the earlier Alexandria."[15] And so rhetorical training flourished in the city.

The Western portion of the Empire laid the groundwork for what sprang up in the East. Under the Romans the private rhetorical schools became increasingly committed in their workshops to declamatory education (described more fully below) with its *suasoriae* and *controversiae*. The former, as in Rome, looked to the past for its deliberative subject matter, while the latter examined contemporary but politically nonsensitive problems for its judicial topics. In no case did teachers or administrators attempt to re-write the traditionally oriented curriculum they inherited. Three years was the normal length in the late Empire, though one wishing to become a professor might stay longer in the schools. Students, mostly in their early teens, sat for no examinations and took no degrees, since public declamations attested to their talent.[16]

This kind of rhetoric in the Empire was heavily geared to the law courts and for three reasons. First, as previously noted, political oratory had fallen on evil days with Rome's concern for peace. Thus young men did not find it advantageous to contemplate a politico-oratorical life matching that of Demosthenes or Cicero. What was once thought to be the highest the state could offer now had largely vanished. Then, the wide demand for lawyers prompted students and their parents to view with covetous eyes this vocation

---

[13] A[rnold] H.M. Jones, *Later Roman Empire*, 284-602 (Oxford, 1962), II, 998.

[14] Taubenschlag, *Law of Greco-Roman Egypt*, II, 33-34, and 60-62, and Nilsson, *Hellenistischen Schule*, p. 85.

[15] William Boyd, *History of Western Education*, 5th ed. (London, 1950), p. 79.

[16] Jones, *Later Roman Empire*, II, 998-99.

with its prestige and substantial income. A legal education and career was a second-choice for many, but a significant one nonetheless. Finally, the Romans were more practically oriented than Greeks, and the practice of law in every age has been a practically-oriented profession.

The pragmatic bent of the rhetoricians produced a rhetorical instruction which, simply and opportuney, followed lines of expediency. Since the mid-fourth century *Rhetoric* of Aristotle and the *ad Alexandrum* on down to the anonymous *ad Herennium* and Cicero's *de Inventione* and *De Oratore*, theorists had set forth the five parts of the speech situation, though sometimes more implicitly than explicitly. But in the Empire, while the *ad Herennium* and Ciceronian works enjoyed wide popularity elsewhere, we have no evidence that any Latin rhetorical author was widely used in Alexandria. No papyri of any of their works have been found, nor does one find concrete evidence that their theories figured directly into oral discourse—declamation excepted, as we shall see. It is safe to say that any Latin rhetorical theory taught by Alexandrian teachers and learned by their students took on a Greek dress even if its undergarments came from a Roman drawing board. One sees in Aristotle and in the *ad Alexandrum* principles which Latin writers later developed more fully: the five parts of speaking, the three kinds of orations and their ends and adaptation, all of which the Romans spun off more completely.[17] It is significant that one papyrus of the *ad Alexandrum*, P. Hibeh 26, dating from the third century B.C. has come to light, but it shall be treated later. These principles along with amplified discussion and opportunity for classroom criticism and practice constituted the standard schoolroom fare. Students examined written speech models and their historical background, determined how arguments had been conceived, organized, and delivered,[18] and composed their own original efforts not only as models for their peers to judge, but also for invited audiences to hear.

If the gymnasium and rhetorical schools emphasized style and delivery—and the latter did—they did so in part from a natural

---

[17] M[ax] L.W. Laistner, *Christianity and Pagan Culture in the Later Roman Empire* (Ithaca, 1951), pp. 11-12. For an able review of rhetoric's part in Greco-Roman education in the West, see Donald L. Clark, *Rhetoric in Greco-Roman Education* (New York, 1957), pp. 59 ff. and 181-205.

[18] John W.H. Walden, *Universities of Ancient Greece* (New York, 1912), pp. 204 ff.

flamboyance typical of Alexandrians, as well as from the realization that judges were not conciliated by cold arguments alone but also from a spirited delivery. Moreover, the repeated use of legal subjects in declamations, while not the only source of topics, shows the close relationship with the legal profession many students highly coveted. Whereas in Rome students could attend the forum to listen to the masters, "thus learning war upon the field of battle" much better, thought Tacitus, in Alexandria such practical education was impossible except perhaps in early Ptolemaic Egypt and after the second century of the Empire.[19]

Starting with theory, since it was easier than practice, the teacher introduced his students to elementary exercises ($\pi\rho\omicron\gamma\acute{\upsilon}\mu\nu\alpha\sigma\mu\alpha$) which gave simple but graduated patterns to follow in proceeding from the easy to the difficult. The exercises started with telling fables and tales, continued through commonplaces (coloring the accepted facts of the story), and concluded with impersonations and encomia on people or places. These made up the sort of training Theon describes in his *Progymnasmata*, discussed later.

Following the elementary exercises, the student selected non-controversial matters such as imaginary monologues which might legitimately have characterized Alexander when he decided to sail to the East, or which a contemporary of Demosthenes might have uttered when praising the Athenian's foreign policy. These latter were the *suasoriae*, the first part of the declamation.[20] Such declamatory exercises had sprung up in the Golden Age of Greece— whether in the workshops of Aeschines or Demetrius of Phaleron, the ancients could not agree—were used extensively in Cicero's day and found their way abroad soon after they were introduced in Athens. But we find no evidence that Alexandrian students translated speeches or theoretical texts from Greek to Latin, or vice versa, as adjuncts to this or other parts of their education, as Pliny urged for the Western schools.[21] But they clearly did use Greek themes.

[19] Gaston Boissier, "Schools of Declamation at Rome," *Tacitus and other Roman Studies* (New York, 1906), p. 165, trans, W[illiam] G. Hutchison.

[20] Boissier, *Fin du Paganisme*, I, 158-59. An English translation of the *suasoriae* used elsewhere in the Empire may be found in William A. Edward, *Suasoriae of Seneca the Elder* (Cambridge, 1928). The controversiae of Seneca have never been translated in their entirety into English, but selected ones appear in Parks, "Roman Rhetorical Schools," *passim*.

[21] *Epistles*, VII. ix.

The second part of the declamation, the *controversiae*, permitted the young man before an audience of students and towns-people to choose historical personages or contemporary situations, take one of two sides of the arguments, and contend for it.[22] He examined the problems of divorce, adultery, poisoning, intrigue, prostitution— all common topics of any age. In order to determine the facts of the case the lad sought to answer three questions: (1) was it a question of fact (*an sit?*): did X kill Y? (2) was it rather one of definition (*quid sit?*): X may have killed Y, but maybe in a fit of anger, and not with prior malice; and (3) was it a matter of interpretation (*quale sit?*): he did it, but the act prevented many others from being injured.[23] They were serious efforts at rhetorical criticism, for they demanded analytical abilities and called upon the school lad to adopt the most defensible position.

PAPYROLOGICAL CLUES TO EDUCATION

Alexandrian youth treated the exercises ($\mu\epsilon\lambda\acute{\epsilon}\tau\alpha\iota$) and declamations in about the same way as did their cousins in the West, so the papyri now prove. P. Hib. 15, dating from sometime between 280-240 B.C., is one such *suasoria* by an Athenian general and geared to a Greek audience. It calls for action on an unknown occasion involving Alexander the Great, and says in part,

> But now I foresee the future, and urge you to take action and not to neglect the good fortune which ... I entreat that we, men of Athens, may not proceed to action with inadequate numbers and without the aid of your power, nor yourselves be forced to the alternative of either obeying the order of others, or with an inferior force risking an engagement.

The lively and clear style of P. Berl. 9781 of the third century B.C. from Hermopolis suggests also a school exercise because of its decorative writing and anonymity. The speech, like nearly every literary papyrus ever found, is only a copy of either the original or another someplace in the lineage, and defends Demosthenes in his Leptines harangue. It bears many similarities to his style, and

---

[22] Parks, "Roman Rhetorical Schools" presents a clear picture of the conduct and substance of the Western rhetorical schools.

[23] Clark, *Rhetoric in Greco-Roman Education*, p. 235.

attacks the four defenders (σύνδικοι) whom Demosthenes berates at
the end of his own speech.[24]

Declamatory papyri of Greco-Roman Egypt often betray their
classroom purpose by general statements, lack of proper names and
audience adaptation, as well as scribal corrections on the fragment
itself. One or more of these characteristics occur in several documents
of the Roman period. P. Oxy. 216 of the first century B.C./A.D.
probably originated from an Alexandrian school and appears to
follow the line of a *suasoria*. An Athenian orator, exercized over a
threatening letter from a foreign potentate—either Philip of Macedon
or Alexander (before the latter became emperor)— says in part:

[Are] we at a threat in a single letter to exchange freedom for slavery?
Whither has it vanished, that pride of empire for which we fought? I am
considering whether my reasoning is at fault ... Have the walls of the
city fallen? What Athenian has been taken prisoner? Where either on
land or sea have we failed in battle? ... We know how to be steadfast
in times of peril, we never desert the banner of freedom ... Let the threats
in his letters deceive barbarians; but the city of Athens is wont to give
commands, not to receive them.[25]

In the early first century one fragment, P. Lond. 256 (verso) contains
what appear to be parts of three speeches whose extracts permit a
reconstruction something like the following: A has given B a talent
of money which B hides in a cache known to both. Later A comes,
digs it up, and makes off with the undisclosed amount. B discovers
what has happened, pursues him, takes back the money, accusing
A of theft. Both charge the other with dishonesty. The fact that
this work contains no contemporary names—specific names were
first introduced in the West in the first century A.D.—that the author
passes from direct to indirect style on several occasions,[26] and treats
the topics artificially, suggest this speech is not for the courtroom,
but rather is a controversia for the classroom building.

---

[24] Karl Kunst, "Rhetorische Papyri," *Berliner Klassikertexte aus den Staat-
lichen Museen zu Berlin* (Berlin, 1923), VII, 1-4; *Archiv*, VII (1924), 227; and
John U. Powell, and Eric A. Barber, *New Chapters in the History of Greek
Literature*, 2nd ser. (Oxford, 1929), pp. 120-21.

[25] See Powell and Barber, *New Chapters*, 2nd ser., p. 119.

[26] Frederic G. Kenyon, "Fragments d'Exercices de Rhétorique Conservés
sur Papyrus," in *Mélanges Henri Weil* (Paris, 1898), 243-48. At p. 248 Sir Frederic
says, "Il est donc hors de doute que nous avons sous les yeus le canevas d'un
exercice de rhétorique, la matière d'une *declamatio*. ..." also Kennedy, *Art of
Persuasion in Greece* (Princeton, 1963), p. 51.

Three other papyri of the first century also show declamatory education. P. Lond. 138, probably the author's original, for there are many corrections written on it, contains parts of two, maybe three, speeches of a forensic variety. Again the absence of current names suggests it came from the classroom. P. Vindob. 26747 and 29747, two tattered portions of a papyrus roll from Dimeh, form part of a progymnasma or perhaps declamatory fragment. Several orthographic mistakes, its labored penmanship, and other matters suggest an elementary school product.[27]

We have further evidence of declamations from the Roman era. P. Yale Inv. 1729 of the first century contains the accusation by a speaker of an admiral ($\sigma\tau\rho\alpha\tau\eta\gamma\delta\varsigma$). According to the ten portions of this papyrus the orator depicts the negligence of a commander who fails to pick up or care for his wounded men following a severe engagement, either the Battle of Arginusae (406 B.C.) or one very similar to it.[28] The style seems more vigorous than the declamations of Libanius, Himerius, and others, and contains a ring of authority about it, unlike those normally originating from school declaimers. Haebelin and Egger agree on these latter matters, yet the former could not explain the lack of proper names.[29] Even declamations normally carried those. Despite this the presence of numerous corrections and abbreviations point to the classroom work of a schoolboy. At the same time the practiced hand is not that of a neophyte, and the use only of the recto and not also the verso hints that the writer was possibly a man of some means.[30] Nonetheless, the decision that it is a school product, perhaps a "rough draft of a model speech on an historical theme which was composed for eventual use as a rhetorical exemplum,"[31] is followed here in the absence of contrary

[27] "Griechische Literarische Papyri I," *Mitteilungen aus der Papyrussammlung der Nationalbibliothek in Wien* (Papyrus Erzherzog Rainer), Ser. III, 49-50 (Vienna, 1932), eds. Hans Gerstinger, *et. al.*, and *Archiv*, XIV (1941), 136-37.

[28] Émile Egger (*Mémoires d'Histoire Ancienne et de Philologie* [Paris, 1863], especially "Fragment Oratoire Inédit," pp. 175-96) was the first to give serious attention to it. In the historic confrontation at Arginusae ten generals were placed on trial, and six later executed.

[29] C[arl] Haeberlin, "Griechische Papyri," *Zentralblatt für Bibliothekswesen*, XIV (1897), 344.

[30] See Deborah H. Samuel, "Rhetorical Papyrus in the Yale Collection," Ph.D Diss. (Yale, 1964), for a complete discussion, supplemented by the Egger study above.

[31] Samuel, "Rhetorical Papyrus," p. 153.

evidence. But all we can glean from it for our purposes is the theme which the young orator may have used.

Additional declamatory topics we see in the second century A.D. P. Lond. 139 notes an Athenian's refusal to acknowledge Philip of Macedon's authority after the murder of a young king,[32] while P. Oxy. 1799's empty generalities vindicate, probably before an Athenian academic assembly, Demosthenes' foreign policy in regard to Philip, following the Battle of Chaeronea.[33] Of the same period but of a different genre is P. Lit. Lond. 193 whose speech by an "Atticising Sophist" in the first part praises modesty, while the second portion lauds a bird, its singing, feathers, strut, and fighting ability,[34] the sort of panegyric display common in the rhetorical schools.

From the late second/early third century P. Harr. 2 contains a probably rhetorical exercise in which a student seeks to define negation (ἀπόφασις) and affirmation (κατάφασις), while P. Hamb. 167 is a relatively rare Latin declamation, treating in dialogue form its subjects of sickness, death, travel, and flight. At times in ungrammatical form, it in general resembles the *controversiae* of Seneca. P. Oxy. 858 probably originated in an Alexandrian school of rhetoric of the same period, but with a setting of 339-38 B.C. It criticizes Demosthenes for his public behavior when news of the capture of Elatea reached Athens. "How can I listen to Demosthenes," the orator asks, "[he] who has no breastplate, no spear, no sword, not even one inherited from his father?" The three topics of P. Oxy 2400 show the continued influence of Greece on Egypt and its rhetorical education. Perhaps representing the stock offerings of an itinerant sophist,[35] each topic is set forth in a grammatical sentence:

[32] *Archiv*, X (1932), 221.

[33] *Archiv*, VII (1924), 228, and Powell and Barber, *New Chapters*, 2nd ser., pp. 72-73 and 121. Perhaps P. Hamb. 133 (late first/early second century), as a forensic speech against one Zoilus who has killed the small child of a freedman belonging to a well known Dionysius, may also have been prepared for the classroom.

[34] Powell and Barber, *New Chapters*, 2nd ser., pp. 123-24, and John Powell, *New Chapters*, 3rd ser. (Oxford, 1933), pp. 251-53.

[35] Loebel, Roberts, Turner, and Barnes (*Oxyrhynchus Papyri*, XXIV, 107-09) see it as more likely the reverse: that is, a sophist's standard bill of fare, rather than a classroom effort, but only because they believed there was little ground (up to 1957) for holding that declamation was taught in Egypt. I believe we no

first the name of an historical or literary person, then notation of the action he took. When the declamation is forensic, the verb is accusatory in nature; when epideictic, the verb is more general. The topics include: (1) the accusation of Cleon for his notorious proposal of 428 B.C. to massacre the male population of Mytilene; (2) a prosecution or defense of Euripides on a charge of impiety for casting Heracles as mad in a play at the Dionysia; and (3) common situations involving Alexander the Great as, after his sacking Thebes, he offers their land to the Athenians to till. In addition to suggesting the influence of Athenian life in Egypt, the fragment also indicates the fidelity to which schoolmasters adhered to Greek education.

Other primary evidence also supplies information on declamatory efforts. P. Ryl. 59, a third-century writing exercise of Demosthenes' *De Corona*, shows the first several words of that oration πρῶτον μὲν ὦ ἄρδρες Ἀθηναῖοι τοῖς θεοῖς εὔχομαι written six times, hinting of either a school exercise or perhaps a budding calligrapher practicing a court hand.[36] From the late third/early fourth century P. Vindob 29789 suggests a progymnastic collection, but not from the hand of a school lad. Simulating the work of Aphthonius, it contains three exercises: two expressions of character (ἠθοποιία) and one encomium. In one of the character sketches, the speaker wishes he were dead, so horrendous is the unnamed situation.[37]

As with other rhetorical evidence from Greco-Roman Egypt, so with the school exercises, we lack sufficient data to complete the desired picture of the progymnasmata and declamations in the gymnasium and rhetorical schools at large. Those we have cited contain praise and blame of people and animals, many grammatical errors or corrections, lack of current names and audience adaptation, and often an artificial or contrived discussion of the topic at hand. Unfortunately the evidence does not permit us to see any changes

---

longer need be so cautious.

One must recall that papyri are not what they purport to be, for what appears as a Demosthenic or Isocratean speech may well be the student's grammatical or rhetorical version for classroom use of what the orator said. The actual text of the papyrus, then, springs from a written assignment, while the genre he reports is oral. P. Berl. 13405 copies (thus scribal) a declamation (rhetorical) of one Lesbonax of perhaps the second century. But all papyri with such dual functions are here treated as rhetorical evidence.

[36] As Professor Turner pointed out to me in a letter.

[37] *Archiv*, X (1932), 222-23.

or trends from Ptolemaic Egypt to Roman Egypt. Nor do we know from the papyri or even secondary sources whether *suasoriae* or *controversiae* were used more. If the former in fact outnumbered the latter one might conclude, albeit tenuously, that there was comparatively little advanced education at which level *controversiae* were used. But not only is the argument of *ex silentio* always risky, but one discovers no trends in those papyri discovered and published. Probably the practice differed little from that in the West.

In either period, however, one finds no thought given to declaiming on contemporary political or social events even on the "safe" side of topics—such as the commonization of Attic Greek into the koine, or the contributions of the gymnasium to the perpetuation of Greek life. Furthermore, professional timidity of teachers and students kept them from deliberating on more controversial matters outside the classroom, though non-academic orators boldly accused the emperor to his face. Given the limited freedom necessitated by a politically insecure government, one would not expect to find full-scale debates on, for example, the new Jewish sect of Christianity which sprang up in Palestine and quickly spread throughout the Mediterranean world, or the professional incompetence of the prefect. But why brash Alexandrians so prone to press the law to its limits in other contexts would not pick the government's side in a *controversia* is difficult to understand. Why the classroom was more conservative than was Philo before Gaius in A.D. 38-39 one can explain only on grounds of coercion by the government and fear by the students. Nowhere do we find anything within the walls of the academy which approaches the bravery of some of the speakers in the *Acta Alexandrinorum*. No Alexandrian scholar ran the risk of his counterparts in practical life before the emperor. So the emperors permitted the rhetorical schools and their declamatory exercises not only because they were integral parts of classical education and did no harm, but also because they provided a pseudo safety valve for those who felt oppressed by the government.

What effect had the declamations on the rhetoric of Alexandria and Egypt generally? As with the second Sophistic movement elsewhere in the Empire, it had entries in both red and black ink in its ledger. On the negative side the close adherence to the past, unconcern about audience analysis or living issues, its emphasis on memory and stylistic flourishes, and its playing to shallow Alexandrian character, drove it more and more from reality. The absence of a boule for centuries where public discourse of a different sort could be heard drove Alexandrians to seek entertainment in the rhetorical schools. Indeed, this entertaining characteristic in many papyri immediately indicates the nature of the literary fragment. Whereas in Cicero's day the declamation had been an educational training tool largely practiced in private, in the Empire it became a vehicle not only for the school lad but also for the adult declaimer to publicly display. So not even the "safe" topics which later were argued in the boule found any place in the classroom. Entertainment superseded relevance. When persecution broke out repeatedly in the third and fourth centuries we have no record of any itinerant or resident sophist or school boy handling the crises of liberty, famine, plague, or children suffering. Nor after the Edict of Milan (313) do we find anyone speaking on controversial matters of the day. In the great issues of life the teachers and students exerted small leadership, no imagination, and only limited political or social influence on the Alexandrian scene. Their training largely steered a careful course between the Scylla of topics too controversial and the Charybdis of total abandonment. Yet this middle course was not satisfactory. Rhetorical instruction, particularly that of declamation, its teachers and students, retreated behind a Maginot Line of exercises which as a group was not sufficiently important for anyone to anthologize, unlike what the Elder Seneca did farther to the west.

On the positive side declamation and rhetorical training helped preserve a semblance of eloquence which otherwise would have died out. Classroom studies, concerned as they were with developing vocal stability and flexibility in the speaker, gave defensible instruction in analysis of arguments, organization of ideas, style, and delivery—though admittedly some of it was exaggerated. Often subjects in the forensic speeches drew upon the least publicized parts of antiquity—romance, marriage, divorce—affording us cultural insights not otherwise possible. And these topics proved important throughout the courtrooms of the Empire, and not just in Athens and Rome. Since, however, Alexandrians normally magnified matters and sometimes even incorrectly construed history, one must treat cautiously information from the exercises.[38] At the same time the presence

---

[38] Boissier, "Schools of Declamation at Rome," pp. 185-88. The young orator's reference in P. Oxy. 858 to speakers being fixed by the boule betrays his ignorance of Attic law.

of other teachers and the public at large would serve to restrain reckless statements. Finally, declamations kept alive the classical heritage and literature of the Greek world in the Alexandrian atmosphere because education was not conceived of in throw-away packages. It was almost sacred. So, papyri found thus far provide a broad base upon which to fill gaps in our knowledge, particularly for rhetorical themes, as well as make certain generalizations about rhetorical training in the city.[39] In all, Alexandrians seemed quite content with declamatory training and never suggested it should be replaced with something else. Why should it? Did it not prepare their sons for a coveted and practical legal career?

Another teaching device, written speech models, was used within and without the classroom apparently much more widely than declamations, or at least our evidence for them is more extensive. In transplanting Greek culture to the Eastern Mediterranean, immigrants found no better way to teach Greek history and literature than to examine with great care the literary efforts of their forebears. Indeed, had not the great Library been established to perform that task, and in a highly sophisticated way? We are not surprised then to find, particularly with the emergence of the Alexandrian Canon by at least the second century A.D.,[40] numerous texts of speeches which the students had copied and studied in their education. Doubtless some of these were part of the libraries of private homes financially able to employ copyists or to purchase the work, but probably most originated in the classroom—a fact we know for certain with many of those found at Oxyrhynchus.[41] At the same time, however, we find no indication that students ever translated the models from Greek to Latin, or vice versa, and probably because

[39] But we should recall that some extant papyri were never a part of any classroom work; they were the private property of Egyptian and Alexandrian residents. Other fragments originated only from the classroom, or perhaps after classroom use.

[40] Julius Brzoska, *De Canone Decem Oratorum Atticorum Quaestiones* (Breslau, 1883), p. 55. As treated elsewhere in this study of Alexandrian rhetoric, some hold to Pergamum as the proper site, and *circa* A.D. 125. The matter is unsettled.

[41] Frederic G. Kenyon, "Library of a Greek at Oxyrhynchus," *JEA*, VIII (1922), 133.

the city remained so thoroughly a Hellenic and Hellenistic outpost.

So Ptolemaic Alexandrians, unlike their later progeny in the Empire, did not study all the Attic Ten—or if they did we have no evidence of it—though they surely knew of them. Dinarchus, Antiphon, Isaeus, Isocrates, and Lycurgus seem totally foreign to the Delta during the period of the Greek kings. Oxyrhynchus, with its thousands of papyri from a schoolhouse rubbish heap, should reveal some fragments if in fact the orators were known, but they have not yet come to light. Since we know more about this city than any other town of corresponding size in the Empire,[42] we can presume certain educational parallels in Alexandria.

The literary ties between Oxyrhynchus and Alexandria were close, not only because of the constant intercourse between them and the ease of Oxyrhynchus residents borrowing books from Alexandria,[43] but also because some of the Oxyrhynchites were professors at the Museum. Further, some of the rhetorical texts circulated beyond Alexandria, as we know from P. Ant. 27 which contains a fragment of a Demosthenic speech once written in Alexandria. Such importations to Oxyrhynchus may have resulted from a greater confidence in the accuracy of the Alexandrian manuscripts at the Library, or they could have resulted from the wider availability and economy of texts in the Delta city. But whatever their source, many papyri do furnish us with a broad spectrum of models for several centuries.

As improved techniques of identification and combining of various papyrological fragments into larger wholes have ascertained more orators and authors, we have a clearer idea of how prominently rhetoric figured in education. The following table, based on Pack's *Greek and Latin Literary Texts from Greco-Roman Egypt* (2nd ed.),[44] but updated here, tabulates known papyri from Egypt, and provides

---

[42] MacLenna, *Oxyrhynchus*, p. 9. For the city's place in the early Empire, see also Eric G. Turner, "Roman Oxyrhynchus," *JEA*, XXXVIII (1952), 78-93. In the third century it had twenty pagan temples, two Christian churches, and a Jewish synagogue. To belong to its gymnasium one must prove from both sides of the family that he sprang from stock accepted by a list drawn up in A.D. 4-5.

For an early but still valuable discussion of the significance of papyri see H.I. Bell, "Historical Value of Papyri," *JEA*, VI (1920), 234-46.

[43] Turner, "Roman Oxyrhynchus," p. 92, and Musurillo, *Acts of the Pagan Martyrs*, p. 273n. See also P. Oxy 2192 which clearly links the classical scholarship of the two cities.

[44] (Ann Arbor, 1965).

evidence of wide-spread use of and interest in speech models or treatises, and of theorists and orators who though they never visited Alexandrian schools or theatres, still were known in Egypt through Greek literary training.

RHETORICAL PAPYRI FROM EGYPT BY PERIOD

Author	Unknown period	B.C.			A.D.					Total*
		3	2	1	1	2	3	4	5+	
Aeschines	4				1	7	11			23
Antiphon						3				3
Aristotle										0
Anaximenes			1			1			1	3
Demosthenes	3		1	1	4	41	30			80
Dinarchus						1	2			3
Dion Chrysostom								1		1
Harpocration						2				2
Homer				1	2	7	(hundreds)			—
Hyperides			1	1	3	2				7
Isaeus					1	1				2
Isocrates	1				2	18	10	11	1	43
Lycurgus						1	1			2
Lysias			1		1	7	2			11
Plato (*Gorg.*, *Phdr.*)						6	5			11
Adespota (anon.)	2	8	2	2	5	20	26	7	2	74
Cicero				1	(6 of 5th/6th cent.)					

*Because of inability to definitely establish the period of some papyri they are assigned to the later of two periods when doubt exists.

The above chart contrasts pleasantly with the table published by Willis some years earlier[45] when he could report the following for the orators: Aeschines-14, Antiphon-1, Demosthenes-76, Dion Chrysostom-1, Hyperides-4, Isaeus-2, Isocrates-39, Lycurgus-2, and Lysias-6. Expectedly, Demosthenes in both reports emerged as the most celebrated orator, but his relative popularity is not so assertive in Pack's second edition as in Willis' account, simply because later findings have shown increased glory the others enjoyed. Similarly,

[45] William H. Willis, "Greek Literary Papyri from Egypt and the Classical Canon," *Harvard Library Bulletin*, XII (1958), 5-34.

when the next compilation comes from the press, quite a different relative standing may emerge, but it is safe to predict that Demosthenes will remain the most universally admired of all the orators.

What speeches were the most widely studied, copied, and housed in libraries? Those for which we have positive identification provide the following breakdown (sometimes not totaling the same figure as in the above chart because two or more speeches may be found on the same papyrus):

Aeschines: "Against Timarchus"-10
              "Against Ctesiphon"-9
Antiphon: "Concerning Truth"-3
Demosthenes: "On the Crown"-20
              "On the False Embassy"-11
              "Against Timocratus"-7
              "Against Midias"-6
              "Philippics"-6
              "Against Aristarchus"-5
              "Against Leptines"-4
              "Olynthiacs"-4
              "On the Peace"-3
              "Against Aristogeiton"-3
              "Against Boeotus"-3[46]
Dinarchus: "Against Philocles"-2
Dion Chrysostom, Oration XIV-1
Hyperides: "In Defense of Euxenippus,"-1
              "For Lycophron"-1
              "Against Demosthenes"-1
              "Against Philippides"-1
              "Against Athenogenes"-1
              "Against Demeas"-1
              "Funeral Oration"-1
              "For Chaerephilus"-1[47]

[46] Several other Demosthenic speeches occur once or twice. For a complete rundown on the twenty-eight speeches of the famous orator, and their frequency and provenance, see P[ieter] J. Sijpesteijn, "Parchemins et les Papyrus de Demosthene," *Ch. d'Ég.*, XXXVIII (1963), 297-305.

[47] See P. Oxy. 2464 for the Demeas speech and Harpocration's *Lexicon of the Ten Orators* ("*ΛΟΥΣΙΕΥΣ*," Oxford, 1853). Pollux, *Onomasticon*, X. 15 (W[ilhelm] Dindorf, Leipzig, 1854) also mentions the πρὸς Δημέαν speech. P. Oxy. 2686, a second century A.D. fragment, probably of one of Hyperides, mentions

Isaeus:	"On the Heredity of Nicostratus"-1
	"Against Elpagoras and Demophanes"-1
Isocrates:	"To Demonicus"-14
	"To Nicocles"-7
	"Panegyricus"-7
	"On the Peace"-5
	"Busiris"-1
Lycrugus:	"Against Leocrates"-1
	"Against the Accusation of Menesaechmus"-1[48]
Lysias:	"On Behalf of Eryximachus"-1
	"Against Theozotides"-1[49]
	"Against Eratosthenes"-1[50]
	"Against Hippotherses"-1
	"Against Theomnestus-1
Cicero:	"Against Verres"-3[51]

Significantly, of all the Roman orators in antiquity Cicero is virtually the only Latin speaker to find his way into Greco-Roman education in Egypt. One of the three manuscripts of "Against Verres," P. Iand. 90, represents the oldest existing document of any speech of Cicero (first century B.C./A.D.), showing our continued indebtedness to papyrological discoveries.

Several further points command attention in the rhetorical papyri. In view of the practical orientation of Roman education, one should be undismayed that relatively few theoretical treatises have come to light, as contrasted with the hundreds of model speeches. As the previous chart indicates, no copy of Aristotle's *Rhetoric* has been found, though several other of his works—*Topics, Ethics,* and *Categories*—have been uncovered. At the same time, P. Hibeh 26, containing 180 lines of the *Rhetorica ad Alexandrum* and dating from the early third century B.C., suggests some concern with Greek

---

one Chaerephilus, thus suggesting one of two speeches Hyperides wrote for Chaerephilus, the salt fish dealer. Christianvs Jensen's study (*Hyperides Orationes Sex Cum Ceterarvm Fragmentis* [Teubner, 1963], Frag. 183) mentions one speech for Chaerephilus (ὑπὲρ χαιρεφίλου περὶ τοῦ ταρίχους).

[48] Both speeches are noted by Suidas, *Lexicon* (Halis, 1853; ed. Godofredus Bernhardy).

[49] Both of these speeches were previously lost. For a discussion of the Eryximachus speech see P. Ryl. 489.

[50] Pack incorrectly lists this as "Pro Eratosthenes."

[51] Several of Cicero's speeches occur once or twice.

rhetorical theory, but how widely its principles figured in practice is not clear. This contrast in popularity between models and theory perhaps grew out of Alexandria's superficial approach to classroom rhetoric, for its enjoyment for haggling could be better nourished by models than theoretical treatises. Then, the chart does not show the nearly 700 papyri of Homer, including commentaries, glossaries, and scholia on the *Iliad*, *Odyssey*, and *Homerica* generally. He was known at least by the second century B.C., and became the most popular of all the Greek poets or orators throughout the Greco-Roman period. Further, all the manuscripts found anywhere of Hyperides are papyri discovered in Egypt, so that as a literary figure he is entirely the child of that country.[52] But more important, fragments of three of his lost speeches, "Against Philippides," "Against Athenogenes," and "On Behalf of Euxenippus" have been found, bringing him back into proper focus. So also with Lysias, for P. Oxy. 1606 represents at least four lost orations of his: "On Behalf of Eryximachus," "Against Theozotides," "Against Hippotherses," and "Against Theomnestus"—the last one not to be confused with two other private speeches against Theomnestus. (A discussion of this work follows below.) Fourth, Andocides, one of the Ten in the "Alexandrian" Canon, finds no place among the literary papyri, and probably was never used in the Alexandrian classroom. The answer is not easy to uncover. We find no inherent reason why his "Mysteries" or "Peace" orations could not have served admirably in school declaiming or in preparing embassies for their hearings before the emperor. "On the Peace" was especially adaptable with its use of practicality, honor, expedience, and justice themes common to all public discourse. We may not learn for decades whether or not his speeches had a part in training young speakers, but probably they did not. Finally, Dinarchus' relative obscurity probably results from the fact that his imitation of Demosthenes or his plagiarism of others had little to commend it when students could study the original speeches of Demosthenes. As Seneca the Elder reminds us, the imitation always falls short of the real (*semper citra veritatem est similitudo*).[53] The original and authentic had more to commend them than did the copy.

---

[52] Powell and Barber, *New Chapters*, 1st ser. (Oxford, 1921), p. 155.

[53] *Controversiae*, I. Pref. 6, and Jebb, *Attic Orators*, II, 373 f.

Mention should be made of the important find in P. Oxy. 1606 containing portions from the second/third century A.D. of four previously lost speeches of Lysias. The first of these private orations, "Against Hippotherses," is couched in grand style and carries a part of Lysias' speech (circa 403/02 B.C.) when he sought to have his land restored after the Thirty Tyrants had siezed it. One Hippotherses who purchased the tract from the Tyrants now refuses to give it up. Since the law required the return of such land to the former owner, Lysias goes before the court seeking relief. He praises (in the third person) his own patriotism, generosity, good character, and suffering under the recent oppression, and deplores the fact that one returning from exile under the Tyrants should "be deprived of [his] property as if [he] were the wrongdoer." On the other hand, Hippotherses is a coward, unpatriotic, treasonous, and undeserving of the decision.

The second of the four—the last two are unknown, though still from Lysias' corpus—"Against Theomnestus," shows a nameless plaintiff at an unknown time claiming to have loaned thirty minae to Theomnestus who could in turn pay off a debt to one Theozotides. The transaction took place with no witnesses, and now the defendant denies in fact the loan. But Theozotides, the third party, seems to have been paid, so the plaintiff (through the mouth of Lysias) argues that if he did not make the loan, Theomnestus must plea one of two ways: either he received the money from someone else, or he was able to pay Theozotides from his own resources. He then promises to show, by means of evidence, that the defendant did not borrow from anyone else; but the papyrus breaks off before we can determine the second horn of the dilemma. Presumably he would have indicated that the defendant was unable to liquidate the debt from his own substance, hence with the strong presumption remaining that he borrowed from the plaintiff, but of this one can only speculate.

In addition to the known rhetorical fragments numerous other items of unknown authorship have been found in Egypt. Dozens of fragments of speeches, eight bits of rhetorical theory, two rhetorical catechisms, and one lection (the latter citing speeches of Aeschines, Demosthenes, Hyperides, and Dinarchus) have also been discovered.[54]

---

[54] Pack, *Greek and Latin Literary Texts*, 2nd ed., pp. 116, 123-24, and 131-34.

We know some of the papyri, P. Ryl. 59 may be one example, were used in classroom training because here and there a word or phrase may be written repeatedly to imprint an idea on a young mind, or perhaps afford practice for others wanting to learn to write well for official purposes. Moreover, not infrequently the original writing is corrected by a second hand, as in P. Lond. 138, indicating the teacher's perusal of the student's work, or labored penmanship or spelling errors, as in P. Vindob 26747 and 29747, betray their origin. When Oldfather remarked that we cannot doubt but that "it was the schools that were responsible for the preservation of so many literary papyri as we have,"[55] he apparently meant to give a large share—though perhaps not most—of the credit to that institution for its consistent use and reproduction of literary works which have come down to us. Assuredly without these works, as, for example, those from the school mounds of Oxyrhynchus, we should be much the poorer.[56]

The large number of findings of the second and third centuries of the previous chart comes not merely from chance excavation, as might be suspected. More importantly, education significantly accelerated so that not only did the number of literates exceed the illiterates, but one found a higher ratio of the former to the latter than at any previous time in Greco-Roman history.[57] Further, with the reading public greatly enlarged at this time and the resulting multiplication of copies from a kind of *insanabile scribendi cacoethes*, literary papyri became cheaper and more readily available, thus also accounting for greater discrepancies in textual particulars.

Perhaps it was coincidental, but after the *Constitutio Antoniniana* of Caracalla in 212 made virtually all inhabitants citizens (*cives*), eliminating much of the push for admission to the gymnasium (which heretofore had figured importantly in one's becoming an Alexandrian citizen), that institution begans to fade from the scene. The emperor's abolishment for the most part of first and second class citizenship and the consequent lowering of standards for admission to the gymnasium may well have hastened its demise, for by the late fourth century it has dropped from sight. Just as likely

---

[55] Charles H. Oldfather, "Greek Literary Texts from Greco-Roman Egypt," *University of Wisconsin Studies in the Social Sciences and History*, IX (Madison, Wisconsin, 1923), p. 67.

[56] Mitteis and Wilcken, *Grundzüge und Chrestomathie*, I, Pt. 1, 138.

[57] Roberts, "Literature and Society in the Papyri," p. 273.

was the impact the Christian religion, now a legitimate form of worship, had since it deemphasized the gymnasium's stress on the physical body and Greek literature, and refuted the polytheistic basis of the institution. In any event, by the end of the fourth century the gymnasium, library, and other educational-cultural institutions of Ptolemaic and Roman Egypt have disappeared, never to arise again. Surely the marked decline in literary papyri including those of Attic speeches is related to the demise of the gymnasium, perhaps to the Library, and to the political situation in general.[58]

SOPHISTS

Not only did the pupils study models and perform in their classrooms, but as elsewhere in the Empire, resident and itinerant sophists also orated for the public, though not as freely and extensively as in Antioch and Rome. Philo tells us that in his day Alexandria's lecture halls and theatres were crowded almost daily with auditors of discourses on virtue and other topics. But he also notes that their thirst for morality and knowledge was superficial, since their minds wandered to commerce, family, civic affairs, pleasures, and the like. Listeners—students and adults—attended, but were present in body only.[59] While this exaggerates the situation, sophists did provide the live professional models the students needed, faced as they were for over two hundred years with the absence of a senate.[60] One interesting rhetorical example, P. Hib. 13 (third century B.C.) suggests what must have been true in Alexandria as well, because of her obsessive interest in music. This copy of an earlier diatribe probably by Hippias of Elis, the contemporary of Socrates, shows the speaker attacking music theorists and contending that selected musical rhythms do not affect one's moral character. "[C]ertain persons ... assert that some [musical] times make us temperate, others wise, others just, others brave, others cowardly, being unaware that enharmonic melody would no more make its votaries brave

---

[58] *Ibid.*, p. 275.

[59] Cited in Drummond, *Philo Judaeus*, I, 5.

[60] Matter (*Histoire de L'École d'Alexandrie*, III, 81) flatly stated that Alexandrians did not speak publicly as did their oratorical predecessors, the Attic Ten. While this is partly true, Matter lacked the papyrological evidence which now calls this categorical statement into question.

than chromatic will make them cowards." All the folk around Thermopylae use the diatonic system, yet they are braver than tragedians who regularly used the harmonic. "Therefore, enharmonic melody makes men brave no more than chromatic makes them cowardly."[61]

Two other professional speakers have left evidence of their work in the second century A.D. P. Milan 20 from Tebtunis portrays, presumably, a nameless schoolmaster who directed students in their rhetorical exercises and studies. Its character, however, is a little misleading, for it contains spelling errors and occasionally some confusion which, perhaps, come not from the illiteracy of the anonymous sophist, but from the mistakes of the transcribing student.[62]

Alexander of Seleucia, another sophist, traveled to Egypt (and probably Alexandria) where he lectured and declaimed as he did in Antioch, Tarsus, Rome, and Athens. He studied under and profited most from the work of the sophist Favorinus, but Philostratus who catalogued several topics of the *suasoria* on which he spoke at one time or another nicknamed him a "clay Plato" ($\pi\eta\lambda o\pi\lambda\acute{a}\tau\omega\nu a$), suggesting he was a kind of sham, at least in comparison to the earlier Athenian.[63] If he continued the trend of earlier sophists, he probably took time following his lectures to talk informally about his topics, answer questions put by both students and adults, and to draw some principles from them.[64]

The florid, asian style, so common in the oral discourse of sophists and their students, seems to have been introduced to Ptolemaic Alexandria by its reputed author, Hegesias of Magnesia,[65] but oddly enough we find no direct evidence that it was ever a controlling factor in the actual practice of speaking. The classroom and teachers preferred a Demosthenes, Lysias, and Hyperides to lesser Greeks whose style was more ornate.

But that the hegesian style probably crept into the city's early rhetoric is shown by several bits of evidence. In the first place, traveling sophists (described later) visited the Delta by at least the third century B.C., bringing with them the latest fads, as the Hippias

---

[61] See also Powell and Barber, *New Chapters*, 2nd ser., pp. 91-92.

[62] *Archiv*, XIII (1938), 116-17.

[63] Philostratus, *Lives of the Sophists*, 570-76.

[64] See Kennedy, *Art of Persuasion in Greece*, p. 168.

[65] *PW*, "Hegesias aus Magnesia." See also Strabo, *Geography*, XIV. 1. 41.

papyrus (P. Hib. 13) strongly implies. Alexandrians could hardly have resisted. Moreover, new ideas traveled rapidly to the literary centers of the ancient world, a fact noted in the earlier discussion for spreading the Christian message. Then, too, Clement in the *Stromata* deplored rhetoric's enslavement to pleasure, its rivers of silly words, its wrangling, and scorn of Truth,[66] all characteristic of the trend. On top of all this was the fact that the wide use of *meletai* and declamations in the second century schools lent themselves particularly to the asiatic style, much more so than if the education had followed that earlier prescribed by Isocrates whose theories and practice would not have accomodated declamatory education. So that style one saw in Antioch he perhaps found also in Alexandria.

THEORETICAL TREATISES

On the scholarly side of instruction the picture is generally faded and unattractive. No teacher with any creativity could long endure using entirely another author's works, not only because foreign treatises never quite meet all the needs of a local classroom, but also because each sophist would want to appear as his own authority. One would expect then to find textbooks of the art, joining together theory and practice. Moreover, the existence of the one demanded reflection and writing on the other. Several books of rhetorical theory used in Greco-Roman Alexandria have come to light.

Of major significance is a portion in dialogue form of the *Rhetorica ad Alexandrum* found in P. Hib. 26 taken from a mummy cartonage of the third century B.C. The period in which it was written and the fact it mentions no events after 343 B.C. lends further credence

---

[66] Clement, *Stromata*, I. iii, viii, and vi. An English translation by A. Cleveland Coxe may be found in "Fathers of the Second Century," Vol. II in *Ante-Nicene Fathers* (Buffalo, 1887), eds. Alexander Roberts and James Donaldson. A commentary on Clement's life and some critical evaluations of his work may be seen in Johann H. Kurtz, *Church History* (London, 1888), I, 153, William Smith and Henry Wace, *Dictionary of Christian Biography, Literature, Sects, and Doctrines* (Boston, 1877), I, 560 (though this sketch is now seriously dated), E[rnest] G. Sihler, "Clement of Alexandria," *Biblical Review*, III (1918), 564-95, and Schaff, "Ante-Nicene Christianity," Vol. II in *History of the Christian Church*, 8th ed., 782-84.

to the modern belief that Anaximenes of Lampsacus authored the *ad Alexandrum*.[67] We are unable, however, to pinpoint any direct use it had in the schools.

More sketchy and less certain is a theoretical fragment, P. Hamb. 131, of the same period which treats reasoning (ἐπίλογος), and the use of torture (βάσανοι) in eliciting evidence from slaves—subjects which both Aristotle and the *ad Alexandrum* treat.[68]

Again, two Alexandrian men named Demetrius wrote on rhetoric and about which works we know something. The first, a sophist of the second century B.C., wrote a rhetorical treatise at least part of which deals with homonyms, in keeping with the sophistic concern with style, but it has not survived.[69] The more famous of the two, the author of *On Style* (περὶ ἑρμηνείας) perhaps lived in Alexandria in the third century B.C.,[70] but since the evidence is at this point inconclusive and he has been treated thoroughly elsewhere, we shall pass over him here. In any case, we have no direct evidence of the latter's work in Alexandria.

But there is one bright ray of sunlight in an otherwise shadowy city, Aelius Theon. He wrote the most important work to originate in the city, the earliest surviving textbook for young boys enrolled in the elementary rhetorical schools.[71] His dates are unknown, though he probably lived contemporaneously with Quintilian who how-ever seems to have influenced the Alexandrian not at all. Theon held a loftier view of rhetoric's place in education and culture than did Quintilian, thus writing his *Progymnasmata* (προγυμνάσματα) not only for his students, but for teachers and the intellectual professions as well. His desire to uplift society around him not only won him literary friends but also provided rhetoric with a unified course of instruction more broadly based than that of his sophistic contemporaries.

[67] Bernard P. Grenfell, "Value of Papyri for the Textual Criticism of Extant Greek Authors," *JHS*, XXXIX (1919), 29, and Powell and Barber, *New Chapters*, 2nd ser., pp. 114-16.

[68] Pack, *Greek and Latin Literary Papyri*, 2nd ed., 2302. Aristotle (*Rhetoric*, 1376ᵇ31 ff) and the *Rhetorica ad Herennium* (II. 7. 10) treat torture, though Aristotle seems concerned with the torture of anyone, and not simply slaves.

[69] *PW*, "Demetrios" (96).

[70] G[eorges] M.A. Grube, *Greek Critic: Demetrius on Style* (Toronto, 1961), p. 56.

[71] Clark, *Rhetoric in Greco-Roman Education*, p. 179.

Theon's concern for upgrading rhetoric and mankind generally led him to bemoan students taking shortcuts and declining to submit themselves to the rigors of philosophy or filling their minds with inspiring thoughts. They were, as with most students in any age, more given to practice and action than to reflection and study. Advocating first the theory, then the practice, he wrote in the Introduction:

Nowadays most young men, far from taking up philosophy before they come to the study of eloquence, do not even touch the ordinary elementary branches, and, worst of all, they attempt to handle forensic and deliberative themes before they come through the necessary preliminary training.[72]

Moreover, just as a painter profits little by looking at the works of others unless he himself attempts to paint, so with the speaker: he will gain little from the efforts of the ancients in their writing or analysis unless he disciplines himself daily in practicing writing αὐτὸς ἕκαστος ταῖς καθ' ἑκάσλην ἡμέραν γραφαῖς ἐγγυμνάζηται).[73]

A formulary rhetoric teaching its theory by means of examples, the *Progymnasmata* takes up ten standard exercises which provide the rhetorical diet for the budding student: first, the maxim (χρεία) which he does not clearly define or explain but which could be illustrated by an anecdote; second, the myth (μῦθος) a false narrative presenting the semblance of truth (λόγος φευδὴς εἰκονίζων ἀλήθειαν);[74] it saw Aesop's fables in a different light than normally construed; third, the tale (διήγημα) which he does not distinguish from (διήγησις) narration, for he really means the same thing by them; fourth, commonplaces (τόποι) divided into simple and very simple, following the earlier treatment of the *ad Herennium* and Cicero's *de Inventione*; fifth, description (ἔκφρασις) emphasizes style and vocabulary; sixth, personification (προσωποποιία) places speeches

[72] *Progymnasmata*, 145; John W.H. Walden, *Universities of Ancient Greece*, (New York, 1912), pp. 200-01.

[73] *Progymnasmata* L[eonard] Spengel, *Rhetores Graeci* [Leipzig, 1885], I, 62), pointed out in Jebb, *Attic Orators*, I, p. 1 xxiii.

[74] The student was taught an appropriate style for fable. This differed from other kinds of discourse in its simplicity, naturalness, lack of artificiality, and clarity. Then he was instructed to tell the story in two different ways: (1) as if he had experienced, it, and was his own authority, and (2) as if another was the authority. Further, he was required to find as close a parallel in history as possible, and then to draw a moral from it. Later he learned how to expand or contract a fable by adding or deleting material. See the discussion in Walden, *Universities of Ancient Greece*, pp. 207 f.

into the mouths of others, as did Thucydides in his history of the Peloponnesian War; seventh, praise and blame (ἐγκώμιον καὶ ψόγος) are most appropriate for declamatory *suasoriae*; eighth, comparison (σύγκρισις) he discusses anew, though he included it earlier under topics and encomia; ninth, thesis (θέσις) divided, as under Cicero, into theoretical and practical (this view influenced later views of thesis); and finally, law or custom (νόμος) which would govern the speaker in what he might advocate. Indeed, the last four exercises were particularly suited to *suasoriae* deliberative oratory as the student reflected on the prospects for future action.

The skeletal *Progymnasmata* lacked the many examples the instructor would need to illustrate the principles, since it, like Aristotle's *Rhetoric*, was geared for the instructor's use in lecturing more than for the school lad to read by himself. Multi-faceted in its theoretical treatment, it sought to prepare its students for a noble profession which when rightly conceived dealt with more than simply talking with people. Rhetoric, when correctly understood, was more an attitude, a way of looking at life, a manner of treating people. Stoics and other rhetoricians differed from the author in his treatment of the discipline, but such detraction stirred him not.

Theon discouraged the teacher from negatively criticizing the student without also showing the neophyte how to improve—a hint that corporal punishment may have had a part in the discipline of some schools?—and urged that the mentor should allow the pupil to find new principles from old themes, thus releasing hidden talents. The models he recommended include first Demosthenes, then, Lysias and Aeschines, but seldom Isocrates (although Theon wrote a separate commentary on this Athenian teacher), Hyperides, Lycurgus, or Isaeus. In training students he advocated that since men are born with unequal abilities, teachers should "try to develop our naturally strong points and to make amends for our weak points, so that we may be able to handle, not large subjects only, like Aeschines, or small subjects only, like Lysias, but all sorts of subjects equally well, like Demosthenes."[75]

Neither Theon nor his *Progymnasmata* could claim the kind of originality or depth of understanding one finds in Aristotle's *Rhetoric*. Reichel points out agreements with Anaximenes, Isocrates, Cicero,

---

[75] Walden's translation of *Progymnasmata*, 171 (*Universities of Ancient Greece*, p. 205).

the *ad Herennium*, and Quintilian, although Theon may have looked to an intermediate source.[76] Even the title itself Anaximenes had used centuries earlier though in a different sense when he explained the use of the stylistic device of παραομοίωσις.[77] Nor did the idea of exercises originate with Theon, as both Aeschines and Demetrius of Phaleron had suggested their use in the late fourth century B.C. Moreover, his statement that χρηστόν ἦθος ἐργάζεται reminds one of Cato's dictum of *vir bonus dicendi peritus*.[78] The book's influence may well have moved beyond the Delta for PSI 85, a third century A.D. fragment of a rhetorical catechism in Oxyrhynchus, looks perhaps to Theon for its view of the maxim (χρεία).[79] Despite any lack of imagination the work constitutes the best theoretical treatise of any Alexandrian which has survived, and probably the best the Delta had to offer.

It may be true that Aristotle's *Rhetoric* was known in Alexandria[80]—though no papyri attest to this—and that, on the other hand, no peripaticist in Alexandria authored a techne of rhetoric.[81] Further, perhaps no rhetorical work as important as the *Rhetoric* was authored or even used there, but the general philosophical and cultural approach of Theon speaks well of Alexandrian scholarship, especially in view of the relatively sterile handbooks of the Byzantine period and later Middle Ages. Isocrates four hundred years earlier in classical Greece had sought to provide the rhetorical underpinnings

---

[76] Georg Reichel, *Quaestiones Progymnasmaticae* (Leipzig, 1909), p. 131. See also Aristotle's *Rhetoric* (1393ª24 - 1393ᵇ9) on the maxim and fable. For the Greek text (it has never been translated into English, although an Italian translation recently came forth) see Reichel, *loc. cit.*, pp. 20-114 or Leonard Spengel, *Rhetores Graeci*, I, 57-130. I have used chiefly the summary in *PW*, "Theon," 2nd ser.

[77] *Rhetorica ad Alexandrum*, 1436ª25.

[78] Professor Gerald Browne of Harvard University has pointed out to me that Theon details this further than Cato or Quintilian, noting that Theon's fuller phrase really says "exercise in the maxim (χρεία) produces not only a certain faculty in discourse but also a good character, since we base our exercises on the apophthegms of the wise." Cf. Spengel, *Rhetores Graeci*, I, 60.

[79] Herwald Schmidt, "Einfluss der Rhetorik auf das Recht der Papyri Ägyptens," Ph.D. Diss. (University of Erlangen, 1949), p. 7, and *Archiv*, vii (1924), 228-29.

[80] Karl O. Müller, *History of the Literature of Ancient Greece* (London, 1858), II, 275.

[81] Richard Volkmann, *Rhetorik der Griechen und Romer in systematischen Ubersicht* (Leipzig, 1885), 2nd, ed., p. 10.

for Greek culture and now Theon in the Roman era strove for much the same quality in Alexandria. If the earlier Greek reacted strongly against the superficiality of his Athenian colleagues, Theon now duplicated that same zeal in the Delta. Undoubtedly Isocrates' view of culture and rhetoric influenced Theon, for we know that the Alexandrian wrote a monograph on the Greek sophist, but the earlier Athenian does not come into his own among the papyri in Egypt until after Theon's death.

In addition to his *Progymnasmata* Theon also wrote two commentaries, one on Demosthenes (῾Υπόμνημα εἰς Δημοσθένην) who represented the grand style in speaking and whose popularity in Egypt we have already noticed, and the second on Isocrates (῾Υπόμνημα εἰς ᾽Ισοκράτην) who embodied the middle style. Too, he authored a work on rhetorical proof (῾Ρητορικὰς ὑποθέσεις), one on the structure of the oration (Ζητήματα περὶ συντάξεως λόγου), as well as several other works, so Suidas tells us.[82] None, however, has survived.

But rhetorical theory moved along other lines. In keeping with the concern of Alexandrians with legal pleading involving Greeks, Egyptians, and Jews, we should expect to find some theoretical treatment of court oratory. And we do. P. Lond. 256 from the first century A.D. contains practical instructions for the advocate, taken down perhaps in the classroom from the teacher's lectures and is very much like declamatory precepts. Including no proper names, it carries forth its theory by a catechetical format, as well as exposition by the teacher. In the case at point a man buries a talent of money in his friend's garden with the latter's consent. He returns by night and removes it without the property owner's knowledge. There are no witnesses. Is he guilty of theft?[83]

Another anonymous forensic treatise, P. Oxy. 410, written in the Doric dialect, dates from the second century A.D., but is based on a fourth century B.C. document. It resembles what we know

---

[82] Suidas, *Lexicon*, "Θέων," pp. 1152-53. Suidas' entries caution us from identifying Aelius Theon with Theon Valerius who wrote a commentary on Andocides, or with the fifth century sophist who lived in and taught rhetoric at Alexandria, or with Theon, the Alexandrian Stoic philosopher who wrote in the time of Augustus an *Art of Rhetoric* in three books, but which has not survived.

[83] Powell and Barber, *New Chapters*, 2nd ser., pp. 121-22, and Kenyon, "Fragments d'Exercices de Rhétorique Conservés sur Papyrus," pp. 243-48. This conceivably could be a *controversia*.

of the Sicilian *Rhetoric* of Corax and Tisias, and in content suggests Cicero's *Brutus* (46) and Hermogenes "Prolegomena."[84] Citing Aristotle's *Sophistici Elenchi* (183), it argues that Tisias was more important than his teacher Corax in developing the art of rhetoric, since he seems to have expanded Corax's technique which centered chiefly on probability. Since Tisias theorized on speaking in law courts, the present fragment possibly refers to legal discourse. We learn that (1) holding one's forces in reserve will give the impression of splendour (μεγαλοπρέπεια) which can be further indicated by the wide use of language and avoidance of abuse; (2) if the speaker blames the wicked, he will develop a reputation of being good, for most men hate evil; (3) in a speech to secure goodwill one should begin by feigning nothing as certain knowledge, "but [as] opinion and hearsay, whether from the jury or others. Such are the points in the exordium which are useful for giving an impression of fairness (ἐπιείκεια);" and (4) "one should take no pleasure in making indecorous and insolent statements [in his delivery], for that is mean and a sign of an intemperate disposition, while the avoidance of abuse is a mark of high-mindedness and an ornament of speech."[85] All of which is good doctrine for speakers.

Two other fragments, P. Oxy. 454 and 2087 of the second century need not detain us here. The first contains a familiar portion of Plato's *Gorgias* (507-08), and the second, a glossary of comparatively rare words drawing on Plato, Demosthenes, Aristotle, and Thucydides, is so severely limited in scope as to provide little of use. The latter carries some corrections in a second hand, suggesting either a teacher's perusal or a scholiast's reflections of a later time.

In the third century several items should be briefly mentioned. PSI 85, as previously noted, contains a rhetorical catechism in question and answer form, and in part resembles Theon's and Hermogenes' works.[86] P. Oxy. 2086 cites several rhetorical terms—

---

[84] See Christianus Walz, *Rhetores Graeci* (London, 1832 ff), IV. 12. The Hermogenes section of P. Oxy. 410 talks of producing an impression of fairness (ἐπιείκεια), and counsels on the judicious use of dissimulation (εἰρωνεία).

[85] W. Rhys Roberts, "New Rhetorical Fragment (Oxyrhynchus Papyri, Part III, pp. 27-30) in Relation to the Sicilian Rhetoric of Corax and Tisias," *Classical Review*, XVIII (1904), 18-21, and Powell and Barber, *New Chapters*, 2nd ser., pp. 116-117, and John G. Winter, *Life and Letters in the Papyri* (Ann Arbor, 1933), p. 257.

[86] *Archiv*, VII (1924), 228-29, and Pack, *Greek and Literary Texts*, 2nd ed., 2287.

proofs (ἀποδείξεως), deliberation (συμβουλευτικός), summarizing (κεφάλαιος), among others. It may refer to one of Demosthenes' (whose name is mentioned) "Philippics" or "Against Timocrates,"[87] but we can't be sure. Three fragments of Plato's *Phaedrus* dating from the late second/early third century are found in P. Ant. 77, P. Oxy. 1016 and 1017, so students learned some arguments against rhetoric.

More detailed in scope, P. Mich. 6 is an anonymous third century work, probably a rhetorical papyrus, dealing with myth (verso title: περὶ Μύθου), a division of progymnasmata. The style of the fragment is so abrupt—a fact uncommonly found in the Empire—as to suggest notes either of a student or professor, or at least an epitome of the subject.[88] The introductory statement of μυ[θ]ος εστι [λογο]ς εκ ψευδολογιας ... (no accents or markings) resembles Theon's introductory observation on myth: Μῦθός ἐστι λόγος ψευδὴς εἰκονίζων ἀλήθειαν .... (172). The verso defines a myth as "an untrue narrative having as the purpose of its composition the exhortation of one who is downcast in spirit to a praise-worthy life," and mentions various types of myths, including Aesopian, Egyptian, Cyprian, Libyan, and Sybaritic. Resemblance with Theon's *Progymnasmata* can also be seen when the anonymous author notes that the ingredients of myth consist of the obscure (ἀσαφής), the defective (ἐλλείπω), the exaggerated (πλεονάζω), the incredible (ἀπιθανος), the impossible (ἀδύνατος), the inexpedient (ἀσύμφορος), and the disgraceful (αἰσχρός).[89]

Rhetorical evidence from the fourth century is less abundant, but one work, P. Vindob 29834 from Dimeh in the Fayyûm, treats lecturing (πρᾶξις), especially that dealing with peace, in line with

---

Cf. the definition of chria (χρεία) with that of Theon, *Progymnasmata*, 9, 6, and Hermogenes (Spengel, *Rhetores Graeci*, II, 5).

[87] *Archiv*, X (1932), 220.

[88] J[ohn] G. Winter, "Some Literary Papyri in the University of Michigan Collection," *TAPA*, LIII (1922), 136-41.

[89] On the recto the papyrus reads: ... εκ του ασαφους, εκ του ελλιπους, εκ του πλεοναζοντος, εκ του απιθανου, εκ του αδυνατου, εκ του α[σ]υμφορου : ... ε[κ]του εσχρου ... (no markings) which compares favorably with Theon who held that ληπτέον δέ τά ἐπιχειρήματα ἐκ τόπων τῶνδε, ἐκ τοῦ ἀσαφοῦς, ἐκ τοῦ ἀπιθάνου, ἐκ τοῦ ἀπρεποῦς, ἐκ τοῦ ἐλλιποῦς, ἐκ τοῦ πλεονάζοντος, ἐκ τοῦ ασυνήθους, ἐκ τοῦ μαχομένου, ἐκ τῆς τάξεως, ἐκ τοῦ ἀσυμφόρου, ἐκ τοῦ ἀνομοίου, ἐκ τοῦ ψευδοῦς (179). See the whole article by Winter, *loc. cit.*, pp. 128-41.

principles of prudence, justice, and perception. The author could be Themistius, but the lofty situation—praise of an emperor, perhaps Julian—seems hardly appropriate to him, but rather more like Libanius.[90]

Another Alexandrian whose life is unknown but whose work has provided modern scholars with much information of ancient orators was Valerius Harpocration and his *Lexicon of Ten Orators* (Λέξεις τῶν δέχα ῥητόρων). A critic/historian more than a theorist, he was once thought to have lived in the fourth century,[91] but the discovery of P. Ryl. 532 limited him to no later than the third century, and finally P. Oxy. 2192 places him squarely in the second, in the reign of Marcus Aurelius. The latter fragment not only dates from this time but also mentions the fact that Harpocration is still alive.[92] The *Lexicon* lists in alphabetical order with some explanation the legal and political terms which occurred in the speeches of the Attic Ten. As an important source for many facets of ancient life and authors not otherwise available, it is the kind of literary effort made possible only by access to a large library such as Alexandria owned.[93]

THE CATECHETICAL SCHOOL

In addition to the oral discourse taught in the gymnasium, Museum, and private schools, its principles also found expression in another bright spot in the history of learning in Alexandria, a unique kind

---

[90] *Archiv*, XI (1935), 270-71. I shall omit from detailed consideration the interesting rhetorical catechism found in P. Vindob 754 (Boswinkel) of the sixth century because its date falls beyond the scope of this study. See, however, H. Oellacher's treatment, "Rhetorischer Katechismus in einem Wiener Papyrus," *Wiener Studien*, LV (1937), 68-78, and *Archiv*, XIII (1938), 117.

[91] And so I once held: see Donald C. Bryant, ed. *Ancient Greek and Roman Rhetoricians* (Columbia, Missouri, 1968), "Valerius Harpocration."

[92] On P. Ryl. 532 see also *Archiv*, XIV (1941), 136, and on P. Oxy. 2192 see also Turner, "Roman Oxyrhynchus," p. 92. Harpocration must not be confused with Aelius Harpocration who wrote an *Art of Rhetoric*, nor with Gaius Harpocration, a sophist who wrote on the oratory of Antiphon, Hyperides, and Lysias. See Suidas, Ἀρποκρατίων, *Lexicon*, pp. 336-37.

[93] Jean C.F. Hoefer, ed., *Nouvelle Biographie Générale* (Paris, 1858), XXIII, 440-41, and *PW*, "Harpokration" (5) contain about all the biographical information we have of the man. Mark Naoumides, "Papyrus of the Lexicon of Harpocration," *TAPA*, XCII (1961), 381-84 provides helpful paleographical data on P. Ryl, 532.

of institution, the well-known Christian Catechetical School. The academy sought to prepare new Christians for the life of faith and to establish more mature believers, leading some to go on to ordination. Its curriculum was sound, seemingly unstructured, and among its teachers and directors were some of the finest in the Eastern Mediterranean world.[94]

We cannot trace exactly the chronology of the School, for the first mention we find of it dates from the late second century when it is fully established and thriving. It must have existed, then, for decades, maybe a century prior to this, for the Christian Gospel spread rapidly in the first century necessitating some kind of systematic instruction.

The School, like its pagan counterparts, looked to oral instruction for several reasons. In the first place, since the curriculum and teachers attracted new converts some of whom were illiterate, books for them would have been excess baggage. Moreover, few books were available at the outset, and all were expensive to copy. Then, oral instruction had long been the accepted means of teaching in the Mediterranean world, as teachers in the School well knew. Why should they replace even for the literate students an honored and effective means with one unknown? Finally, oral instruction had played a part in the life of one who probably brought the Gospel to Alexandria, Apollos, whom Luke called an eloquent man,[95] for had not Aquila and Priscilla taken him aside to talk with him, and to amplify his knowledge?[96] Such reasons compelled Christian teachers to continue an educational process long maintained by their pagan counterparts.

Two director-instructors of the School merit special attention though neither posed in the formal sense as a public teacher of rhetoric. Clement of Alexandria—not to be confused with Clement of Rome—perhaps born in Athens, was converted under Pantaenus, the late second century missionary and Director of the School, and spent much of his life in Alexandria. His relatively affluent pagan home provided him with a foundation for a sound and encyclopedic education steeped in Greek learning. This he combined

[94] Lietzmann, "Founding of the Church Universal," pp. 296-97.

[95] *Acts* xviii. 24.

[96] Luke says he was instructed (κατηχημένος, from the verb κατηχέω) which was surely by word of mouth for the most part. Schaff, *History of the Christian Church*, II, 256.

with biblical verities in a way possible only for one who had access to an extensive library or with a prodigious training and memory.[97] He, like many of his successors, probably taught first at home rather than in halls, simply because this was the accepted way of doing it.

Without proposing to work as a professor of rhetoric, Clement nonetheless taught its principles to his catechumens, as we see from the *Paedagogus* and *Stromata* which grew out of his classroom work. He stressed, as one would expect in view of the Second Sophistic and his misgivings about it, content and style, treating the former positively and the latter negatively. His own mastery of Greek philosophy prior to his conversion prompted him to emphasize the need for thorough grounding in thought and ideas. Sound learning, as both he and Theon a century prior urged, liberated students from provincialism, but unlike his secular predecessor, he argued that it not only served as the handmaiden of theology, but also beckoned its disciples to ultimate truth. Indeed, so important was philosophy to man that perhaps God gave it so that he could better reflect upon his Creator. Accordingly, one should bring to bear all human knowledge of secular literature and incisive reasoning so he can better discern the true from the false, dialectic from rhetoric, responsible discourse from sophistic. And this is the more desirable because the ultimate goal for the Christian is not communal growth but personal development and a close relationship with the Father. The speaker, therefore, by his rhetoric has obligations to help individuals to achieve this end, and he delights to do so not only because of his high regard for them, but also because the Father loves them.[98]

Concerning ethical appeal, he counsels that men should have their heads shaved, unless they have naturally curly hair (!), but should leave their beards and mustaches as they better reveal one's

---

[97] The literature on Clement is extensive. See selected references in ftn. 66 above. English translations of the *Stromata* ($\Sigma\tau\rho\omega\mu\alpha\tau\epsilon\hat{\imath}\varsigma$) and the *Paedagogus* ($\Pi\alpha\iota\delta\alpha\gamma\omega\gamma\acute{o}\varsigma$), his two works bearing most closely on rhetoric, may be found in A. Cleveland Coxe, "Fathers of the Second Century," Vol. II of *Ante-Nicene Fathers*, eds. A. Roberts and J. Donaldson.

[98] *Stromata*, I. ii. v, vi, and ix, and T[errot] R. Glover, *Conflict of Religions in the Early Roman Empire* (London, 1909), 275. See "Clement of Alexandria" (Chapter IX) in *Conflict* for a fuller discussion of Clement's philosophy and thoughts, as well as the treatment of his individualism in David Paulsen, "Ethical Individualism in Clement of Alexandria," *Concordia Theological Monthly*, XLIII (1972), 3-20.

masculinity. He scorned the effeminacy advocated by some sophists, declaring that men should allow no blot on their manliness, movement, or habits.[99] Further, the believer's character should be of such high report that he will need to take no oath when pressed for the truth; he will always tell the truth.[100]

Reacting to the contemporary sophistic scene and undoubtedly to what he saw in Alexandria's lecture halls, he deplored complicating the speaker's message and displaying oneself at the expense of truth. In the *Paedagogus* he cites approvingly Jesus' statement that one is held accountable for every word he utters,[101] and believes that frivolous prating must be silenced for it produces disgust for the speaker and contaminates the soul.[102] In the *Stromata* he scornfully echoes his condemnation of the profane and vain babblings of some,[103] and lauds clarity and forcefulness. In preaching he cared not "by what term that which I wish to present is shown .... For I well know that to be saved, and to aid those who desire to be saved, is the best thing, and not to compose paltry sentences like gewgaws."[104] And further, "not only a simple mode of life, but also a style of speech devoid of superfluity and nicety, must be cultivated by the Christian who has adopted the true life ... since that style of speech is not elegant which can please rather than benefit the hearers."[105] If one is really concerned with truth and its application to man, he ought not to frame his language with art and care, but strive only to express the meaning as best he can.[106] Here he would depart from the stylistic vigilance of an Isocrates, Lysias, or Demosthenes.

Contemporary sophistic practioners Clement scorned because they were enslaved to pleasure, laughed at truth, sought the plaudits of men, ridiculed and attempted to confute Christian apologists, and babbled in their own jargon until they were rivers of silly words. Quoting *Isaiah* (xxix. 14) and St. Paul (*I Corinthians* i. 19) he predicted God would "destroy the wisdom of the wise, and bring to nothing

---

[99] *Paedagogus*, III. xi.

[100] *Stromata*, VII. viii.

[101] *Matthew* xii. 36.

[102] *Op. cit.*, II. 6, and *Ecclesiastes*, vi. 11.

[103] *Op. cit.*, I. x, and II *Timothy* ii. 14 ff.

[104] *Stromata*, I. x.

[105] *Ibid.*

[106] *Stromata* ii. i. He obviously does not mean this literally, for it ultimately leads to self-contradiction and utter inability to communicate effectively.

the understanding of the prudent."[107] He argued, like Plato (*Apology* 19B) and Isocrates ("Antidosis" 15), that sophistry made false ideas appear true, and reflected some Aristotelian thought when he held that the Stagirite conceived of sophistry as a dishonest art, since rhetoric begins with the probable, seeks to prove it, and finally aims at persuasion.[108]

On speech delivery he cited biblical precedents to encourage one to speak without embarrassment or hesitation, and to sum up his discourse in few words. The speaker must not talk too long, and should regulate the volume of delivery according to the situation, for "loudness of utterance is most insane," while an inaudible one is senseless and effeminate. He should modulate his voice in a variety of ways, for a wise man "keeps his utterance from loudness, from drawling, from rapidity, from prolixity."[109] The speaker should not be contentious, and in dialogue (as in the Socratic method of teaching) he should understand clearly the question before commenting.[110]

Other teachers of the Catechetical School probably also taught rhetoric, though to what degree, in what manner and whether directly or indirectly is not clear. While each is important to the history of learning, most will receive only passing mention here.

When the persecution by Severus in 202 forced Clement into exile, the School's leadership fell to his most brilliant pupil, the eighteen-year old Origen who also excelled as a preacher.[111] Born of Christian parents, *circa* 184, Origen was educated by his father Leonides (probably a rhetorician), and later by Clement and Ammonius Saccas, the Neoplatonist. After the martyrdom of his father, the young man helped support his family by teaching and copying manuscripts whence probably came his initial curiosity in textual criticism, an interest he developed with enviable skill later in life. Like Clement, he was a man of vast learning, including apparently knowledge of the Attic Ten, and shared his predecessor's belief that secular knowledge, especially philosophy, would aid in understanding the Christian scriptures.[112] But Eusebius also tells us that

---

[107] *Stromata* I. iii.

[108] *Stromata* I. viii.

[109] *Paedagogus*, II. vii.

[110] *Stromata* I. x.

[111] See Chapter IV for a discussion of his homilies.

[112] For sketches of Origen see Schaff, "Ante-Nicene Christianity," pp. 786-90, Eusebius, *H.E.*, vi. 2, 3, and *PW*, "Origenes." A helpful summary of Origen's

he instructed some students in geometry, arithmetic, and other preparatory studies (τἆλλα προπαιδεύματα), and the less learned in all the common school branches of knowledge (ἐγκύκλια γράμματα). This must have included rhetoric,[113] but his approach remains a mystery.

But of all the secular disciplines Greek philosophy most intrigued him. So thoroughly and effectively did he teach it that Eusebius tells us that many and distinguished philosophers from throughout the Mediterranean world came to hear him.[114] The highest praise, however, came from his pupil, Gregory Thaumaturgus, who, *circa* 238, in Palestinian Caesarea, perhaps in Origen's presence, gave a glowing panegyric of his former teacher—a speech which remains the best source for information on Origen's classroom.[115] Gregory praised his teacher for the wide range of instruction he gave his pupils (XIII), for setting before them the true and useful, especially in all that concerns true piety (XIV), and for aiding them in enjoying the sweets of the intellect (XV). Origen continued as head of the School until about 216 when Caracalla's persecution forced him from the city never again to resume his classroom duties there.

We learn too of Dionysius of Alexandria, probably a professor of rhetoric prior to his conversion and a former student of Origen, who also was banished for his faith;[116] of Pierus whose acumen and powerful preaching earned him the sobriquet "Origen the Younger;"[117] and of Didymus the Blind[118] who taught Jerome, Rufinus, Isidorus,

---

theology can be found in Lietzman, "Founding of the Church Universal," pp. 304-13, and in Lebreton and Zeiller, *History of the Primitive Church*, II, 952-80.

[113] *H.E.*, VI, 18: 3 & 4.

[114] μάλιστα ἐπιφανῶν οὐκ ὀλίγοι. *H.E.* VI. xviii. 1 ff.

[115] Gregory Thaumaturgus, "Oration and Panegyric Address to Origen," S[tewart] D.F. Salmond, trans., *Ante-Nicene Fathers*, VI, 21-39.
Gregory's statement of the latitude of Origen concerning the full sweep of knowledge (σὺν πάσῃ περιουσίᾳ εκπεριϊοῦσι πάντα καὶ διερευνωμένοις — XV) shows the liberality of this Alexandrian teacher in the liberal arts.

[116] Charles L. Feltoe, "Letters and Other Remains of Dionysius of Alexandria," p. 23, A[rthur] J. Mason, ed., and Lebreton and Zeiller, *History of the Primitive Church*, II, 1017-18.

[117] Jerome: *ut Origenes junior vocaretur* (*De Viris Inlustribus*, 76). See also Paniel, *Pragmatische Geschichte der Christlichen Beredsamkeit*, p. 214, and Photius, *Bibliotheca*, CXIX (Berlin, 1824).

[118] Not to be confused with the monk by the same name who lived at the same time. Cf. *PW*, "Didymos der Blinde."

and others and was the last of the eminent teachers of the School.[119] But unfortunately the literature is silent concerning how these men handled the rhetorical issues in the classrooms, the texts they used, or the models they found most appropriate. Yet rhetoric as a discipline they could hardly have avoided.

As with the gymnasium, we hear nothing of the Catechetical School after the fourth century. Why? At least three factors account for the School's demise after it helped establish the Alexandrian Church on a solid footing. Most important, Christianity had become the state religion under Constantine, thus acquiring freer air to breathe and more room in which to move. No longer would believers or others need to operate in private homes within an atmosphere of secrecy, potential arrest and oppression, though a more favorable climate did not appear simply with the emperor's affixing his signature to a document. It took time. Further, after the Council of Nicea (325) condemned certain heresies, extensive controversies subsided, leaving the erstwhile Jewish sect freer from heresy than at any time in the previous two centuries and hence it attracted fewer young apologists. While aberrations never disappear in any age, crystallization of issues significantly decreased the need for special instruction. Finally, with the Christian religion's becoming more fashionable, the number of faithful diminished who would take the necessary time and trouble for training. Alexandrians proved the dictum that political tolerance encourages indifference to matters of faith, and accordingly a religion often attracts elements of society not willing to pay the price of spiritual growth. While the contribution the School made in strengthening the faithful and refuting the heresies of the day will never be fully assayed, it did show its scholars and those of the ancient world that a chastened speculation and philosophic inquiry in times of great stress were compatible with Christian revelation.[120] The life of the school could not match that of the Platonic Academy, but its nearly 300 years far exceeded that of virtually every other ancient institution of learning both in length of days and quality of instruction. We should not expect more.

[119] Edward Ulback, "Didymus of Alexandria," *Bibliotheca Sacra*, XCVII (1940), 81-83.

[120] Frederic W. Farrar, *Early Days of Christianity* (New York, 1882), I, 280.

SECULAR TEACHERS

It remains to discuss the impact of the teachers of the rhetorical schools and where they as professional men fit into Alexandrian culture. We have no enthusiastic poet writing verse commemorating and cataloging the Alexandrian teachers as did Ausonius of those at Bordeaux, but we have seen that with the possible exception of Theon most of them taught the theories of the older Greek masters—including declamation—rather than giving thought to new concepts whether Greek or Roman. As with the Latin language and philosophy, Roman rhetoric never blossomed in the Alexandrian sunlight, devoted as the city was to its Greek heritage and intellectual mandate to perpetuate Greek paidea. Even the fragments we have in P. Oxy. 410 or PSI 85 suggest not so much new ideas and concepts as a different approach to teaching the subject, and in some respects the same must be said of Theon's *Progymnasmata*.

The fact that rhetorical training not only persisted but in the second and third centuries flourished indicates along with other evidence (cited below) that rhetoricians were held in some esteem. Moreover, OGI 709 of the second century implies that the Greeks in the Delta wished to erect an inscription on an Alexandrian altar honoring one of the city's rhetoricians,[121] providing him with the kind of acclaim we could expect was showered on Aristides after he visited there in the mid-second century. Philodemus' denial that teachers of the art were in good repute in early Ptolemaic days,[122] stemmed from his professional but negative bias toward rhetoric: he would have held the same view in any age and any locale if teachers included more than epideictic oratory in their art. But even if he was right in the early days, the picture had drastically changed by the second and third centuries (A.D.).

It is true, however, that we have the names of no instructors who during the first three centuries of the city can lay claim to a clear title of "rhetorical teacher." Sophists and unknown teachers there were, as we have seen, but our first name comes shortly before

---

[121] Wilhelm Dittenberger, *Orientis Graeci Inscriptiones Selectae* (Leipzig, 1905), II, 446-48.

[122] Philodemus, *De Rhetorica*, II, 105 (frag. XII) in Harry M. Hubbell, "Rhetorica of Philodemus," *Transactions of the Connecticut Academy of Arts and Sciences*, XXIII (1920).

the Roman victory at Actium and even this man made his reputation more in Rome than in Alexandria.

So Timagenes of the first century B.C. does not merit extended treatment. Born in Alexandria, son of the King's banker, he was taken prisoner by Aulus Gabinius (55 B.C.) in that tribune's Eastern campaign and transported to Rome where he was later released. Subsequently he set up his rhetorical school there, won the respect and friendship of Augustus because of his hard work, but later lost out when that emperor circumscribed free speech and closed Timagenes' school.[123]

Theodotus of Chios taught rhetoric in the same period as Timagenes, emigrated to Alexandria from his Aegean island home, and served as tutor and close confidant of Ptolemy XIII. When Pompey sought refuge in Egypt after the Battle of Pharsalia (48 B.C.), Theodotus urged that he be put to death, thus hoping to curry favor with Julius Caesar. It was his powerful speech and rhetorical art, says Ps-Plutarch, which persuaded the assembled group to make the fatal decision.[124] His counsel backfired, however, leading to his later crucifixion.

Didymus, a younger contemporary of Theodotus, lived in Alexandria in the early decades of the Empire and while he is remembered chiefly as a grammarian, he left a number of rhetorical works among his 3500 books—one ancient authority put the number at 4000!—and could understandably be called by Demetrius of Troezen the abusive name of book-forgetter ($\beta\iota\beta\lambda\iota o\lambda\acute{a}\theta as$),[125] because he could not recall all that he had written. His surname of $\chi a\lambda\kappa\acute{e}\nu\tau\epsilon\rho os$, implying a pitiless critic and an indefatigable worker, distinguished this erudite scholar from other grammarians of the same name.[126] Harpocration's second century Lexicon, our only source of Didymus' views on the broader themes of Attic rhetoric, verifies Didymus' commentary on Demosthenes and his work on Isaeus and Aeschines, but barely mentions his treatment of Isocrates, Lysias, and other Greek ora-

---

[123] William Smith, Dictionary of Greek and Roman Biography, III, 1131, Strabo, Geography, IV. 1. 13, PW, "Timagenes" (N.S.), Hoefer, Nouvelle Biographie Générale, "Timagène," and Suidas Lexicon, pp. 1124-25.

[124] δεινότητα λόγου καὶ ῥητορείαν ἐπιδεικνύμενος, Lives, "Pompey," LXXVII. 4.

[125] Athenaeus, Deipnosophistae, IV. 139c.

[126] If we assume fifty years of fruitful scholarship, this quantity of books averages out to about three books a fortnight!

tors.[127] However, he was the first of the ancients in the Roman Empire to write a special commentary on oratory which, due to his vast reading made possible at the Library, doubtless treated its subject in a full and effusive manner.

From the second century we have Agatharchides who began his career as a schoolmaster in Alexandria, and later came to be regarded as the oral interpreter, the reader-aloud, for Heracleides Lembos. He figured prominently in the lively ongoing debate between philosophers and rhetoricians,[128] and probably worked at the Museum where he had access to the archives and could compare Attic style with the Asian, for the latter he strongly attacked.

In the fourth century we know of Magnus of Nisibis, born in Antioch, *circa* 325, but who later emigrated to the Delta to work. Both a physician and a sophist—called by Eunapius a healing sophist ($\iota \alpha \tau \rho o \sigma o \phi \iota \sigma \tau \acute{\eta} s$) or by twentieth century critics, a psychosomaticist—he studied under Zeno of Cyprus, the founder of an iatrosophistic school of medicine, and, like his teacher, he used Aristotle's ideas on the body and its nature in his lectures. He was so persuasive that he talked others into better health! Many came from near and far either to admire his speaking or to learn some practical work,[129] so that his success and fame prompted Alexandria to build a special school in which he could lecture.

Yet the list is too brief; one is left wanting more, though he can confidently assert that teachers of rhetoric moved easily within the top echelons of government and society, and were widely sought after by students.

When we try to establish the remuneration paid the rhetoricians in the classroom we are hard pressed to come up with the specific figures for Alexandrians. We must reason largely by analogy and recall what was happening elsewhere, yet remembering that here, as in other matters, Alexandria may have been different. Under the Ptolemies we know nothing of their salary in the gymnasium, Museum, or private schools. Vespasian in his reign created an imperial chair for Quintilian,[130] but we learn of no specific chairs

---

[127] *PW*, "Didymos aus Alexandreia" (8) provides a full treatment of the man, along with Hoefer, *Nouvelle Biographie Générale*, "Didyme."

[128] *PW*, "Agatharchides."

[129] Eunapius, *Lives of the Sophists*, 497-98, and Wilmer C. Wright, trans. *Philostratus and Eunapius* (London, 1961), p. 321.

[130] For a fuller discussion of Vespasian's role in rhetorical practice and teaching,

of rhetoric in Alexandria until late in the Empire, and can only assume that if Rome, Athens, and eventually Constantinople had them, Alexandria may also.[131] We are left to wonder why Vespasian did not take the opportunity to honor Alexandria in view of the backing the city gave him in the critical days surrounding his elevation (A.D. 69) to the throne. But if he did we have no record of it.

At the same time he did provide that rhetoricians in Pergamum were exempt from billeting soldiers in their home and from paying taxes—so sacred and godly were they.[132] Likely the same privileges extended to other Eastern imperial cities as well.

During the third and fourth centuries evidence is more abundant. In the third century under Elegabalus provincial cities paid teachers of rhetoric from their local treasury,[133] but Elegabalus' successor, Alexander Severus, paid regular salaries from imperial funds to rhetoricians, grammarians, and physicians, and assigned lecture rooms to the teachers. Alexander also subsidized with food rations those students who were poor and born of free men, and in the provinces he granted many privileges to pleaders in courts,[134] as Emperor Pius had earlier done for selected rhetoricians in Asia.[135] In Diocletian's reign (284-305) teachers of rhetoric or geometry received the same salary, 200 denarii per student per month which was twice that paid to instructors of architecture. Still, the salary compared poorly with the fees of a lawyer: 1000 denarii per court case, but it was far above those of peasant farm hands who could count on 25 denarii per day. Thus a teacher of rhetoric with ten students received 2000 denarii per month compared to the farm hand's 600.[136] Later a rhetorician's salary increased to 250 denarii per student,

---

see my study, "Emperor Vespasian: Political Patron of Rhetoric," *Western Speech*, XXVII (1963), 158-64.

[131] Marrou (*Histoire de L'Éducation dans L'Antiquité*, 4th ed., p. 403) argues that endowed chairs obtained only in Rome ("elle concerne Rome seulement"), and not in the whole Empire. This may have held true for the first century A.D., but certainly not in the later Empire.

[132] Naphtali Lewis and Meyer Reinehold, *Roman Civilization* (NYC, 1955), II, 295.

[133] Hermann Göll, *Kulturbilder aus Hellas und Rom* (Leipzig and Berlin, 1880), I, 21.

[134] *SHA*, "Severus Alexander," XLIV.

[135] Theodor Mommsen, "Provinces of the Roman Empire," p. 393.

[136] Lewis and Reinehold, *Roman Civilization*, II, 468-70.

five times that of the elementary teacher's income.[137] Enforcement, however, proved too difficult, so the wage scale was ultimately retracted.

The Theodosian Code under Constantine noted many privileges either carried over from earlier times or inaugurated now for the first time for teachers of rhetoric. They were exempted from public obligations, could not be summoned to court or suffer indignities; if molested, the convicted offender would pay 100,000 nummi into the treasury; if a slave harmed them, the offender must be beaten by his own master in the presence of the injured one;[138] and they were not subject to military service or other compulsory public duties, nor required to quarter soldiers.[139] Local senates would nominate those wishing to teach—perhaps based on contests among various candidates, as happened in Athens—but the emperor himself made the final decision in such appointments.[140]

Gratian's concern for advancing education in the western portion of the Empire in the late fourth century permitted local municipalities the freedom of selecting their own rhetoricians while still paying their salary from the imperial treasury. Following the pattern of Constantine and Julian, he established (376) imperial chairs of Greek and Latin rhetoric in the largest and most populous cities in the West, but made no provisions for the small ones. In Trèves (France) he also raised to the highest point in history those who had the combined local-imperial appointment: 12 annonae yearly, with Latin and Greek grammarians receiving half that,[141] but there is some

---

[137] Marrou, *Histoire de L'Éducation dans L'Antiquité*, 4th ed., p. 380, and A[rnold] H.M. Jones, *Later Roman Empire*, II, 997.

[138] If the master consented to the slave's attack, he was obliged to pay 20,000 nummi and the slave held until the fine was paid.

[139] Thus not only relieving them of financial obligation, but providing more time for their professional literary duties.

[140] Clyde Pharr, *Theodosian Code and Novels and the Sirmondian Constitution* (Princeton, 1952), XIII. 3. 1 ff., and Walden, *Universities of Ancient Greece*, p. 141. The Pharr work compiles the laws for 125 years from 313-438 and provides much information concerning rhetorical teaching in the late Empire. Some of the same privileges continued into the fifth century in Constantinople and probably elsewhere in the Empire as well. See also Walden, *Universities of Ancient Greece*, pp. 149-71 ff.

[141] The value of the annona is uncertain, some seeing it as probably equal to a yearly ration of grain for one person, while others construe it as the sum a taxpayer paid in kind each year. But see Stanley F. Bonner, "Edict of Gratian

doubt that this extended throughout the East simply because he was not so interested in its culture and education, only in its produce. It seems probable that like Libanius, public teachers also received fees from their pupils which they were permitted to retain in addition to their state salary—much as attorneys who teach on law school faculties may do in the twentieth century. But teachers in private schools were forced to depend entirely on student-fees.[142] In the later Empire the four rhetorians in Alexandria provided by the Theodosian Code— Rome and Constantinople had five each, and smaller cities had three[143]—probably received both public and private support.

Before concluding this discussion of rhetorical education in general and of the teacher's place in Alexandrian society in particular we must examine a special problem which stemmed from the prior religious commitment of Christians who took seriously their faith. Suspicion by St. Paul and Clement of Alexandria of sophistic training discouraged some believers from taking up the profession of speech instruction with the result that one finds few Christian rhetoricians in the city during the first three centuries. By the opening of the fourth century and before the legitimizing of Christianity Arnobius could proudly note in the Empire at large many believers among the ranks of orators, grammarians, and philosophers.[144] But we have no specific knowledge that such is the case in Alexandria.

In the fourth century, the Apostate Julian, having turned his back on his earlier religious faith, could not leave the Christians alone. In 362 under the guise of what was best for the young people and the state, he banned Christians from the classroom on the grounds their faith-perspective undercut their effectiveness as teachers of Greek and Latin literature, based as it was on mythology and

on the Remuneration of Teachers," *AJP*, LXXXVI (1965), 137, Thomas O. Martin, "Aid to Education," *Seminar*, X (1952), 61, and Marrou, *Histoire de L'Education dans L'Antiquité*, 4th ed., p. 408.

[142] A[rnold] H.M. Jones, *Later Roman Empire*, II, 998 and 1001-02. Probably, due to a shortage of currency, teachers were often paid in kind, as Libanius was in Asia Minor, This is especially likely in view of Alexandria's large grain harvest (Bonner, "Edict of Gratian," 127 f). It would then be the teacher's responsibility to trade his quantities for whatever other products he might need.

[143] Martin, "Aid to Education," p. 65.

[144] Arnobius, "Adversus Gentes," II. 5, Hamilton Bryce and Hugh Campbell, trans., *Ante-Nicene Fathers*, VI.

polytheism. No Christian could be honest, he argued, if he taught one thing but secretly believed another; honesty and integrity were above all indispensable to a teacher of young people. Since all education, even grammatical exercises, was based on this mythological premise, his edict in effect placed Christians in the uncomfortable dilemma of either quitting the classroom or admitting to hypocrisy. Rhetoricians and grammarians of this persuasion abandoned the field, in spite of the opposition of men like Ammianus Marcellinus (XXII. 10. 7). While Prohaeresius, the famous sophist in Athens, was specifically excepted he nonetheless resigned his chair out of sympathy with his colleagues. However, when Valentinian, Julian's successor, came to power, he removed the limitation and placed the criteria on one's facts and not his faith,[145] permitting an indeterminate number to return. What Julian's prohibition did in Alexandria one can only conjecture, for we have no specific statements on the subject,[146] nor do we know how many Christian rhetoricians there were. But given the greater drive for unity in the Empire, it must have affected some teachers in the Delta city as it forced them to either remain in their positions and tacitly renounce their faith or step down as the law required.

In sum, the rhetorical training to the end of the fourth century A.D. proceeded along lines similar to those in the West with the progymnasma, declamations, and speech models (written and oral) consuming the major part of the student's training. These in turn were supplemented by theoretical treatises mostly imported, with the exception of Theon's *Progymnasmata* which though not highly original represented the best the Delta had. Rhetoricians at Alexandria fared well whether in the private schools or the gymnasium, though the former enjoyed greater popularity than those in the latter. Esteemed and rewarded for their professional ability, they

---

[145] See the numerous citations, but with comparatively little discussion on the subject in Julian's *Letters*, 422 f, Arnobius, "Adversus Gentes," II. 5, Augustine, *Confessions*, VIII. 5, Göll, *Kulturbilder aus Hellas und Rom*, I, 22, Laistner, *Christianity and Pagan Culture in the Later Roman Empire*, pp. 27-28, and Boissier, *Fin du Paganisme*, I, 203.

[146] One exception is Eusebius of Alexandria who had studied under Prohaeresius in Athens, and later went to Rome. But he was not teaching in Alexandria at the time of Julian's edict. Eunapius, *Lives of the Sophists*, 493, and *PW*, "Eusebios" (36).

CHAPTER VI

SUMMARY AND CONCLUSIONS

By the end of the fourth century significant rhetorical training and practice had died out in Alexandria, and the scene generally changed. No longer could one hear sophists lecture in her many halls, or eloquent preachers in plain or lofty style lifting worshippers to higher heights. The boule, established early in the third century, offered rhetorical possibilities, but its confinement to relatively unimportant municipal matters discouraged any elevated oratory. Latin, never popular in Ptolemaic or early Empire days of Alexandria, began to replace Greek both in education as well as in business and culture generally. Roman thought and practice slowly encroached on the ground once held firmly by Greek rhetorical theory and practice, so that by the third century we have the beginnings of Roman declamation. Yet neither Latin theory nor practice ever replaced Greek patterns to any significant degree. Not surprisingly, Cicero commanded greater popularity in the fifth and sixth centuries than in the earlier periods. Nevertheless Alexandria resisted the linguistic and cultural tide longer than cities elsewhere in the Empire, clinging as an important Greek outpost to Hellenic traditions.

Then, too, the Council of Nicea (325) had settled (within limits) certain theological issues, thus removing them from the arena of perennial public debate. Tribunals, by using agreed yardsticks, could simply label a man heretical if he did not measure up to the codified statements.

Also the educational institutions faded in the race for men's minds. The gymnasium, no longer a viable medium of Greek culture, succumbed to more indigenous institutions of learning, and its directorship became decreasingly important since it was viewed as an onerous and uncoveted responsibility, particularly in light of the institution's declining popularity. Roman indifference, even hostility, ultimately undermined the Library and Museum, as seen in Theodosius' orders for the destruction of the Serapeum which had long been closely associated with the Library. And the Catechetical School, for centuries an effective desk at which to teach and ground new converts in the elements and claims of the Christian faith, no longer filled the same need when Christianity was legitimized as in centuries before. So the School gave way to the cloisitered monastery whose location and intellectual atmosphere were largely removed from the affairs of life. Finally, with the assassination (415) of the philosopher Hypatia, the beautiful and talented daughter of the head of the Neoplatonic school, by "Christian" fanatics, Alexandria surrendered its claim as a center of thought and learning. Thus many symptoms across a wide front attest to the rhetorical-cultural eclipse of the city.

THE DEMISE OF RHETORIC

Why did the study and practice of oratory languish in Alexandria? The elder Seneca in the first century saw the decline of oral suasion in the West growing out of three conditions: (1) moral degeneracy due to luxury and a corresponding indolence. Young people had been given too many things by indulgent parents, hence they had little need to work for something better. (2) The Empire provided little incentive to master rhetorical prose either in theory or practice, for its repressions, particularly in deliberative and judicial oratory, suffocated the most serious and able students. And (3) the fateful and relentless march of history periodically stifles the rhetorical discourse of society, at first opening large areas for investigation and free expression, then under new rulers and changing conditions fencing off those same topics and muzzling their spokesmen.[1]

Taking these in a different order than Seneca mentions them, we can say that in part the same reasons hold for rhetoric's demise in Alexandria in the fourth century.

In the first place, Theon deplored the indolence of young men whose lethargy encouraged shortcuts to rhetorical maturity. Doubtless this stemmed in part from relative affluence, for poverty seems never to have troubled most Greeks in the Delta. Aristotle had

---

[1] Seneca, *Controversiae*, I, Pref. 7 f.

earlier claimed that poverty is the parent of revolution. If so, perhaps the converse is true: affluence and security will sire compliancy and little innovation. True, some civic leaders denied they could afford certain duties the boule wished to give them, but this was standard procedure. Perhaps, then, luxury and leisure did drive several nails into rhetoric's coffin just as they did in Rome.

Further in an era when the state was paramount and the collection of taxes and revenues doubly so, one does not expect to find great speaking, whether on the street corner or in the courtroom, if it compromised the government's press for gold. Money simply commanded greater attention and concern than did the rights of man. While equity and natural law clashed repeatedly with codified law in specific cases, these did not compare to senatorial debates of justice and injustice, expediency and inexpediency, or praise and blame which otherwise could affect millions of people.

Leaving for the moment Seneca's second reason for oratory's decline and moving to the third we might well demur at his accusation of the impersonal but relentless march of history. Perhaps Time in some way does influence socio-political conditions, and *maybe* history cyclicly returns to remold cultures, but for the most part it was the desires and greed of particular men which shaped the lives of the Alexandrians, for in the Delta there were little grounds for blaming impersonal elements, even *Pax Romana*. Particular people lived out the drama of life making demands at center-stage.

But Seneca's second cause merits the greatest consideration, that of governmental repressions. Many ancient monarchs could not tolerate free expression of ideas, such luxuries being extraneous to the peaceful running of government. Once the fishhook of commitment to freedom of speech lodged in a nation's throat the people and particularly their spokesmen would thrash about furiously like a powerful but helpless sailfish. This the emperors could not risk especially in riotous, tempestous Alexandria where for centuries the Ptolemies and later the Roman emperors ruled both it and the country at large as their private domain, and where its political life-blood was drained by the absence of an effectual senate.

This same muzzling stifled the classroom. Rhetoricians, unlike some Christian preachers of the first century, were intimidated and lacked the essential drive to be heard. They had neither a vision nor basic concern for the issues of religious bigotry, famine, or injustice in the marketplace. In an age of compliant scholars, one saw few outlaws among students and faculty.

Moreover, rhetoric found no place outside the classroom where it could put its theory and instruction systematically into practice. Teachers, pupils, and the Greeks at large apparently saw it as a pleasant tool for the few, an avenue by which the budding scholar could assume his role in Greek life, but as unsuitable for the many not so destined. While significant efforts were made to restore the boule long before it finally appeared in A.D. 202, we see no agitation to make it a meaningful political force in the Delta even after Severus reinstated it. Probably the residents feared he or his successors would again suppress it. Since eloquent men need to hear other eloquent men to maintain their eloquence, Alexandria fared poorly in practice. Though the senate was reactivated, rhetoric had too long sacrificed itself on the altar of expediency; its spokesmen were too timid to deliberate seriously matters of justice, honor, war and peace, and similar legislation. It could not live on as a live option in the minds of a people who saw its limited utility.

But two other factors were at work in Alexandria which Seneca could not see. In the first place, the land, so far as we know, could lay claim to no tradition of great speaking. Moses, to be sure, had begged to be excused because of his rhetorical ineptitude when Jehovah summoned him to plead Israel's case before the Pharoah[2]— suggesting some kind of oral standards—and Amenophis, perhaps an official of either that Pharoah or one close to him in time, had counselled his son on the prudence and decorum of court speech,[3] but neither of these gives any indication of significant deliberative or judicial oratory or its theory in pre-Ptolemaic Egypt like one finds in earlier Greece and Rome. Certainly when the question comes to judicial oratory this particularly held true. The oral species of prose sprang, so far as we know, from the Greek community after it emigrated to Egypt and not from the Egyptians.

Or to say it in different words, Egypt, prior to the settling of Alexandria, had no history of democratic institutions. Even after 330 B.C. what democracy there was could be found largely, perhaps only, in the Greek minority, as the native Egyptians and emigrant

---

[2] *Exodus* iii. 1-iv. 17.

[3] F. Ll. Griffith, "Teaching of Amenophis the Son of Kanakht. Papyrus B.M. 10474," *JEA*, XII (1926), 191-231.

Jews found on repeated occasions. True, the Sons of Israel had their gerousia, but it was no more than a parochial body governing their own people on religious matters. No clubs or organizations cultivated a basic desire to rule themselves by debating issues germane to their membership. The group closest to this kind of exchange was the knot of Museum scholars who, arguing largely among themselves, were so busy with their own narrow interests as to give little thought to developing democracy or extending its privileges to others.[4]

A second reason for the degeneracy of oratory but which Seneca did not consider was the fact that while rhetorical competence may "exist" it cannot thrive in a culture geared to an agrarian economy with little industry or business development. Man needs the complex problems of urban and international concerns before he carves out his niche in rhetorical history. From these social and political areas come the issues of war, peace, expansion, justice—all particularly important to the planting and flowering of eloquence. For centuries kings and emperors strapped Egypt to agriculture so that her rich valleys could supply grain to the Empire, thus stripping her of the necessary matrix for oratory.

But the demise of rhetorical training in Alexandria by the close of the fourth century A.D. did not leave the world nearly as impoverished as would have been the case if it had succumbed in Athens by the beginning of the fourth century B.C. Twentieth century theory and practice owe little to the Delta's textbooks, classroom efforts, courtroom discourse, or its secular discourse in general, but scholarship is immeasurably indebted to the nearby sands of Egypt for the hard evidence given us in papyri to show what was read and studied in its schools, preached from its pulpits, harangued from its street corners, and argued in its Roman boule. While Theon's *Progymnasmata* has survived, it has little colored modern rhetorical theory and practice, as witnessed in part by the fact that it has been translated in modern times only into Italian. If Origen's sermons reveal areas of controversy and lines of thought obtainable nowhere else, the classroom, judicial, and deliberative discourse provide few directions we could not discover farther to the West.

Yet we cannot expect originality of every teacher, practitioner,

---

[4] See Schmidt, "Der Einfluss der Rhetorik," p. 75 for similar statements in regard to the practice of court pleading in Egypt.

theorist, or even culture. To some is given the task to perpetuate, albeit well, the principles and practices of others. Such was the case for most rhetoricians and speakers in Alexandria. Though we may score them for what they did, we have little grounds for arguing that they did it poorly. Indeed, much evidence points to the contrary.

IN RETROSPECT

Thus, with the exception of legal pleading, one could no longer find after the close of the fourth century any systematic attempt to prepare young people for a public life based on rhetoric as conceived by the Greeks. Those interested turned to other matters in which the formal spoken word played a less significant role. Had students, teachers, and sophists in the discipline exercized their originality and talents on many of the pressing issues of the day—political, religious, cultural—the profession and discipline not only would have continued in a viable form, but played a more prominent role in the practical affairs of the people. While here and there we find a Philo and Origen who minister in various ways to the contemporary needs of the people, many other Alexandrians either did not perceive such privations, or declined to address themselves to them. Too long had theory and practice willingly resided in the sheltered classroom and conventional lecture hall to assume any other function in contemporary life. Ethos, ideas, and arguments lay sacrificed on the altar of popular acclaim and show. Formal speech, content with a respectable place in the curriculum and with emphasizing Greek thought and culture of the past, closed its eyes to religious bigotry, famine, injustice, and mass genocide its students could see on every hand. Where it was anchored to the past, and had no present role, it could expect no future, for no discipline or profession can long endure in such a sterile atmosphere.

Though geared to the past, neither the Alexandrian classroom, courtroom, nor pulpit, and only modestly the street corner, fostered any free speech movement in theory and practice—the sometimes violent speeches in the *Acta Alexandrinorum* constituting the only exception. Despite the tumultuous, riotous character of the people, neither students nor teachers made any attempt to throw off the Ptolemaic or Roman saddle for the momentary excitement of running hard, if only to exercise the mind. We find no romantic vision of what Alexandria and the Empire might become under different circumstances. Rather, speech education and practice had fallen into that dangerous trap shared by many institutions: idealizing itself, content to hear its own spokesmen in a secure, predicable atmosphere, but not sufficiently concerned or alert to push into areas of human affairs. *Pax Romana* strangled controversial speaking in a city which itself was filled with controversy and argument, so that Alexandria lacked the bracing adventurous air Athens had known in an earlier era.

To pronounce a plague on both houses—rules and rhetoric—without suggesting specifically what they might have done would be devious. It seems never to have occurred to teachers or political authorities that education could have been more exciting, transforming, and enduring if pointed and relevant controversy had found its rightful place. They preferred the more-attractive-for-the-moment procedures of reliving the past—the remote past—rather than facing the present. They could easily and discreetly have dealt with the governmental side and condemned either Christianity or upheld the Greek side of anti-semitism. The fact that the teachers and pupils, lacking the necessary bifocal vision, did not do so strongly suggests a pusillanimous spirit—typical of impetuous, excitable people—and a deep-seated suspicion that formal oral discourse, as conceived by the theorists and teachers, was irrelevant to many of the crucial needs of man. They were more comfortable looking backward than forward or even around them. An optimistic view of student speeches and the realization of the ultimate worth of debate—as their forefathers had known in Athens—would have proved more rewarding for Alexandrian youth, and certainly for the cause of truth and progress of man in the future. We hear nothing of the ultimate nature of man, of his relationship to his Creator, the rise of Christianity, of the intrinsic value of the gymnasium, or of the Greek way of life—all of which could have been "safely" treated. These topics escaped the young students and their mentors either because of educational myopia or because of the political climate. Values and philosophic inquiry seemed as remote to the Alexandrian forensic classroom as did self-control on the streets, and the absence of both are likely related, since each requires reflection and discipline.

Despite negative criticisms of the rhetorical theory and practice one finds at Alexandria, what positive contributions did it make? Several should be noted. First, the gymnasium and the schools preserved the literary papyri we now have, though in the nature of things we must usually look elsewhere in Egypt rather than to Alexandria proper for the particulars of that papyri. Had not the teachers insisted that the students must peruse and copy the classical texts and rhetorical theories of the past, or portions of them, we should have little inclination of what was taught in Alexandria's schools. The hundreds of papyri of rhetorical works provide us with broad outlines and some details of what went on in this academic world. In a land where the papyrus grew abundantly, copying manuscripts became easy and cheap, proliferating the many texts.

Second, scribal duplication of speeches of ancient orators, particularly the Attic Ten, provide some particulars in textual criticism not otherwise known, though normally points of minor significance. True, papyri have not been able to restore lacunae such as exist in the Roman Tacitus' *Dialogus* (35 ff) or in certain ambassadorial Greek speeches before the emperor, but the scholarly quality of the textual criticism rivals anything found in the twentieth century.

Third, Egyptian papyri have brought to light lost speeches of Hyperides and Lysias which we have known heretofore only vaguely from Harpocration or Pollux. Had it not been for discoveries of Hyperides' speeches we should have little firsthand evidence for his orations, for he is entirely the product of Egyptian discoveries. These and related findings suggest that the Greek community, with a huge collection of manuscripts housed at the Library, had a corpus of speeches of the great orators of the past as full as did their Athenian cousins. These books allowed scholars the opportunity for research at least at the Museum which could measureably aid students in their pursuit of learning. Training in the classical orators doubtless excelled what we find today in most Western undergraduate curricula, as few students of the last third of the twentieth century could meaningfully react to the names of Hyperides, Lysias, or Lycurgus, while Alexandrian youths had read and copied their speeches, even though the men had been dead hundreds of years.

Finally, papyri have enabled us to draw rather strong parallels with rhetorical instruction farther to the west. We know now that progymnasma, writing exercises, declamation, and itinerant sophists operated pretty much as they did in Athens and Rome; they preserved an ancient heritage long since past. Heretofore we had surmised as much, but now we can be more confident of our statements. As

Francis Bacon once said, half knowledge leads to unbelief; whole knowledge to belief.

Athens by means of popular discourse fought, argued, and radically handled domestic and international affairs, while Alexandria—scholarly and conservative—was entombed with its own generation. Yet both the radicalism and conservatism of the Mediterranean world help us today to reconstruct the ancient port city. Such reconstruction shows that in the broad sweep of time both reflection and activism play their proper roles in the chronicle of history and the lives of people.

Sic transit gloria
Graeci mundi Alexandriae

INDEX

Acta Alexandrinorum 68, 120, 160
Actium, Battle of 3
Acts of the Apostles 74(6-9)
Aelius Aristides, P. 39, 39(9), 147
Aelius Sabinus, prefect 30f
Aelius Theon 18, 51, 114, 137(82),
138f, 142, 156
 Progymnasmata 133ff, 139, 147,
 153, 159
 high view of rhetoric 134
 his purpose in writing 135
 the best rhetorical theorist in the
 Delta 136
 rhetorical works 137
Aeschines 14, 114, 124f, 128, 135, 148
Agatharchides, teacher 149
Alexander of Seleucia, sophist 15, 131
Alexander the Great 1ff, 114, 119
 and Jewish courts 53(47)
Alexandria
 founding 1
 rise and fall 3
 a well-planned city 4
 an independent city, not capital of
 Egypt 5
 citizenship *ibid.*
 economic problems 6ff, & *passim*
 scholarly center 8, 9(34)
 textual criticism 18(78)
 social, political tension 20ff
 Jews at (See also *Jews*) 22(5)
 little historical consciousness 23

 unruly, superficial, populace 24ff
 24(13), 29(26), 30(28), 130
 persecution and violence 28ff
 impact on theological thought 32
 free speech *ibid.*
 boule (See also *Boule*) 42ff
 political oratory 42(16) & *passim*
 influence of rhetorical theory 59
 church councils at 99(83)
 Aristotle's *Rhetoric* known at 136
 rhetoric's demise 155ff
 no history of eloquence 158
Alexandrian Canon of Ten Orators
 12, 13ff, 14(59), 122f
Ammianus Marcellinus 23, 153
Anaximenes (*Rhetorica ad Herennium*)
 24, 132, 135f
Andocides 14, 127
Antioch (Syria) 47, 78, 131f
Antiphon 14, 123ff
Antoninus Pius, emperor 39
Aphthonius 119
Apion, teacher, ambassador 50(46),
 52, 57(55)
Apollonius, book compiler 11(51)
Apollonius of Rhodes, librarian 11
 (51), 13
Apollos, preacher 75, 141
Aristarchus, librarian 11(51), 13, 13
 (56)
Aristophanes of Byzantium, librarian
 11(51), 13, 41